Microsoft®
365 Word

2nd Edition

by Dan Gookin

for
dummies®
A Wiley Brand

Microsoft® 365 Word For Dummies®, 2nd Edition

Published by: **John Wiley & Sons, Inc.,** 111 River Street, Hoboken, NJ 07030-5774, www.wiley.com

Table of Contents

Introduction

The only thing standing between you and your writing is your word processor. Yes, it tries to be helpful, but computers can do only so much. As a smart person, you desire more help than the computer is capable of giving, which I'm guessing is why you opened this book.

Welcome to *Word For Dummies,* which removes the pain from using Microsoft's greatest and most bewildering word processing software ever! This book is your friendly, informative, and entertaining guide to getting the most from Word.

Be warned: I'm not trying to force you to love Word. This book won't make you enjoy the program. Use it, yes. Tolerate it, of course. The only promise I'm offering is to ease the pain that most people feel from using Microsoft Word. If you get in a good laugh at Word's expense along the way, all the better.

About This Book

Please don't read this book from cover to cover. It's not a novel, and if it were, it would be a political space opera with an unlikely antihero and a plucky princess fighting corrupt elected officials who are in cahoots with an evil intergalactic urban renewal development corporation. The ending would be extremely satisfying.

This book is a reference. Each chapter covers a specific topic or task that Word otherwise pretends is easy. Within each chapter, you find self-contained sections, each of which describes how to perform a specific task or get something done. Here are some sample topics you encounter in this book:

>> Moving a block

>> Check your spelling

>> Save your stuff!

>> Text formatting techniques

>> Working with tables in Word

- » Plopping down a picture
- » Mail merge, ho!
- » Drafting with Copilot

I give you no codes to memorize, no secret incantations, and no tricks. Nothing is assumed, and everything is cross-referenced. Technical terms and topics, when they come up, are neatly shoved aside, where you can easily avoid reading them. The idea here isn't for you to master anything. This book's philosophy is to help you look it up, figure it out, and get back to writing that novel, grocery list, or secret plan to invade Liechtenstein.

How to Use This Book

You hold in your hands an active book. The topics between this book's yellow-and-black covers are all geared toward getting things done in Word. All you need to do is find the topic that interests you and then read.

Word uses the mouse and keyboard to get things done, but mostly the keyboard.

I use the word *click* to describe the action of clicking the mouse's main (left) button.

This is a keyboard shortcut: Ctrl+P. Press and hold down the Ctrl (Control) key and type the letter *P*, just as you would press Shift+P to create a capital *P*.

Sometimes, you must press more than two keys at the same time, such as Ctrl+Shift+T. Press Ctrl and Shift together and then press the T key. Release all three keys.

Commands in Word exist as *command buttons* on the ribbon interface. I refer to the tab, the command group, and then the button itself to help you locate a specific command button.

Menu commands are listed like this: Table ⇨ Insert Table. This direction tells you to click the Table command button and then choose the Insert Table item from the menu that appears.

 Some of Word's key commands dwell on the File screen. To access this screen, click the File tab on the ribbon. To return to the document, click the Back button, found in the upper left corner of the File screen and shown in the margin. Or you can press the Esc key.

When I describe a message or some text you see onscreen, it looks like this:

```
Why should I bother to love you, Evelyn, when my
female robot makes better tacos?
```

If you need further help with operating your computer, I can recommend my book *PCs For Dummies* (Wiley). It contains lots of useful information to supplement what you find in this book.

Foolish Assumptions

This book was written with a few assumptions. Foremost, I assume that you're a human being, though you might also be a pod person, but, heck, they need to write, too.

Another foolish assumption I make is that you use Windows as the computer's operating system. Both Windows 10 and Windows 11 are current, though which version you're using makes no difference to this book. This book doesn't cover Windows.

This book focuses on the Microsoft 365 subscription version of Microsoft Word. It also applies to the standalone version, as well as Microsoft Word online. Most recent versions of Word forward are similar, so you should be covered here. This book also mentions the Copilot artificial intelligence feature, which is an extra subscription service beyond Microsoft 365.

This book does not cover the macOS version of Word that runs on a Macintosh computer. This version of Word is different from what's covered in this book. Very little of the text here applies to the macOS version of Word. Sorry.

Icons Used in This Book

This icon flags useful, helpful tips or shortcuts.

TIP

This icon marks a friendly reminder to do something.

REMEMBER

WARNING

This icon marks a friendly reminder *not* to do something.

TECHNICAL STUFF

This icon alerts you to overly nerdy information and technical discussions of the topic at hand. The information is optional reading, but it may enhance your reputation at cocktail parties if you repeat it.

Where to Go from Here

Start reading! Behold the table of contents and find something that interests you. Or look up your puzzle in the index.

Read! Write! Let your brilliance shine!

My email address is dgookin@wambooli.com. Yes, this is my real address. I reply to all email I receive, and you get a quick reply if you keep your question short and specific to this book or to Word itself. Although I enjoy saying hi, I cannot answer technical support questions or help you troubleshoot your computer. Thanks for understanding.

You can also visit my web page for more information or as a diversion: www.wambooli.com.

My YouTube channel contains hundreds of videos about Word, including tips, tricks, and tutorials. Check it out at youtube.com/dangookin.

To find this book's online Cheat Sheet, simply go to www.dummies.com and search for *Word For Dummies Cheat Sheet* in the Search box.

Enjoy this book. And enjoy Word. Or at least tolerate it.

1

I'll Take Word for $100

See how to start Word and decipher the Word screen.

Explore differences between Word the program and Word online.

Get to know the computer keyboard and the touchscreen.

Learn how to read the status bar and discover special symbols representing secret characters in your text.

Chapter **1**

Word Origins

Before you get too far into word processing, keep in mind that the pencil is truly the ultimate writing tool. Its application is obvious. It's easy to use, it's wireless, and it features an eraser — the original Undo command. This information is presented in the seminal book *Pencils For Dummies*, which weighs in at a hefty six-and-a-half pages.

This book is far longer than *Pencils For Dummies*. The reason is that Microsoft Word is a far more powerful and sophisticated tool than your typical Ticonderoga #2. Though, as a bit of trivia, when Microsoft Word made its debut in 1983, one of the more popular word processing programs at the time was called Electric Pencil.

Word of the Day

Today's word is *Start.* Yesterday's word was *Run.* Tomorrow's word is *Launch.*

These terms all describe how to begin your word processing day with Microsoft Word. Even so, the method by which you coax Word into existence depends upon what you want to do with the program.

>> Obviously, you can't use Word unless your computer is on and toasty.

>> Please don't put toast into your computer.

>> Word can be obtained as its own program, which is part of the Microsoft Office suite of programs, or as a subscription to the Microsoft 365 service.

>> The computer version of Word dwells on your PC's mass storage device, where it labors as a program, like so many others.

>> The online version of Word abides ethereally on the Internet. Yes, the Internet must be available for you to access this version, though you can do so from a mobile device as well as from a computer.

>> Ensure that you sport a proper posture as you write. Your wrists should be even with your elbows. Your head should tilt down only slightly, though it's best to look straight ahead. Keep your shoulders back and relaxed. Uncross your toes.

Starting Word, the program

As a program on your computer, Word is nothing special. It's started like any other program, even those not used by great writers such as Tolstoy, Stein, and Faulkner. Follow these same steps as those authors writing their immortal texts:

1. **Tap the Windows key on the keyboard.**

   The Windows key sits squat between the left Ctrl and Alt keys on the keyboard. The key may be adorned with the Windows logo icon or the keyboard manufacturer's icon.

   Upon success, the Start menu pops up.

2. **Type** word.

   As you type, programs matching *word* appear on the Start menu. The program you desire is titled Word, with the subtitle App. Yes, App is the program's last name.

3. **Choose the Word app to start the program.**

Watch in amazement as the program unfurls upon the screen.

Starting Word, the online version

The web-based version of Word works best when you're already familiar with the program version. This pale version of the program is available at this address:

```
office.com/launch/word
```

TIP

POKING A PIN IN THE WORD PROGRAM

I use Word every dang doodle day. To make its initiation easy when inspiration strikes, I pin the Word program's icon to the taskbar (in Windows 10) or the Start menu (in Windows 11). This *pin* draws no blood, but instead permanently affixes the program's icon in a handy location from whence it can be started quickly.

To pin Word, follow Steps 1 and 2 in the earlier section "Starting Word, the program." Below the Open item that appears, you find two other actions: Pin to Start and Pin to Taskbar. (If you don't see these items in Windows 10, click the chevron to expand the list of actions.)

When you pin the Word icon to the Start menu, it's readily accessible each time you pop up the Start menu.

Pinning the icon to the taskbar means the icon always appears on the taskbar, at the bottom of the screen.

Clicking the Word icon from its pinned location starts the program instantly, which gets you writing more quickly, before those lingering thoughts escape from your head.

If you aren't already signed into your Microsoft account, you'll be pestered to do so. After identifying yourself to the digital warden, you see the online version of the Word Start screen. See the later section "Working the Word Start screen."

REMEMBER

>> The online version of Word is limited from the full power of the Word program. Differences are ridiculed throughout this book.

>> You need a Microsoft 365 account to use the online version of Word.

>> Word online grants you access to the documents saved to your OneDrive folder. *OneDrive* is Microsoft's cloud application, providing access to your files over the Internet. Microsoft badly wants you to use OneDrive and will pester you about it endlessly.

Opening a document to start Word

Word spawns documents like hens spawn eggs. Open an egg and you see breakfast. Open a Word document and you see the Word program with the document presented inside, ready for action — no cooking required.

To open a document and start Word, obey these steps:

1. **Locate the document icon.**

   Use your Windows *kung fu* to open the proper folders and hunt down a Word document icon, as shown in the margin.

   Online, browse your OneDrive folder for Word document icons, though the icon image is often replaced with a thumbnail image showing the document's teeny-tiny contents.

2. **Double-click the icon.**

   On OneDrive, a single click is all you need.

The document is opened and presented on the screen, ready to sate your writing whims.

>> You use Word to create documents. These are saved to storage on your computer or on the cloud. Details are offered in Chapter 8.

>> Documents you create on the cloud stay there — unless you have the cloud app (such as OneDrive) installed on your computer. In this configuration, the cloud files are also available on your computer. Likewise, files you save to the cloud storage folder (or one of its subfolders) on your computer are also available on the cloud, and you can use the online version of Word to abuse them.

>> The document's name is assigned when it's first saved. Use this name to determine the document's contents — providing that it was properly named when first saved.

TECHNICAL
STUFF

>> Documents are files. They exist separately from the Word program, saved individually on the computer's storage media. As such, they are managed by Windows. To organize, manage, and find lost documents, you use Windows, not Word.

Your First Word

As a program, Word presents itself on the screen in a window adorned with various gadgets and goobers designed to assist or thwart you in the writing process. If you've been victimized by computers for some time, this presentation should be familiar to you, though some items may be new or odd. After all, if every program worked the same, people would be far happier using computers, and such a notion chills me.

Working the Word Start screen

Word begins its existence by thrusting forward a Start screen, illustrated in Figure 1-1.

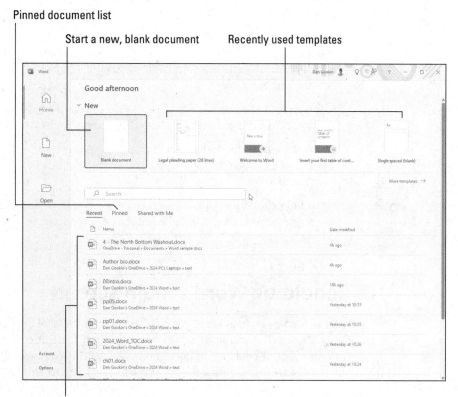

Pinned document list

Start a new, blank document

Recently used templates

FIGURE 1-1:
The Word
Start screen.

Recently opened documents

The advantage of the Start screen is that it shows recently opened documents. If you want to pick up working where you left off, choose a document from the items listed (refer to Figure 1-1).

To start a new document — that foreboding fresh sheet of digital paper — click the Blank Document button.

Recently used templates also appear in the list, allowing you to start a new document with styles, text, and stuff ready for you to work.

After making your choice, all excuses are gone. Time to start writing.

>> A *template* is a document that contains preset elements, such as formatting, styles, text, and possibly graphics. Use a template to help you start a common type of document, such as a résumé, a report, or an angry letter to the editor. See Chapter 16.

>> *Pinned* documents are those you want to keep in the list shown on the Start screen, such as a recipe you're working on to make it more digestible. Choose the Pinned tab (refer to Figure 1-1) to see the list. Chapter 8 coughs up details on pinning a document.

>> The Word Start screen doesn't appear when you open a document to start Word, as foretold in the earlier section "Opening a document to start Word."

>> You can disable the Start screen so that Word always opens with a blank document. Chapter 33 discloses the secret. The Start screen cannot be disabled in Word's web version.

REMEMBER

>> The Word Start screen appears only when you first start the Word program. It doesn't appear every dang time you start a new document while using the program.

Beholding Word's main screen

Writing is scary enough when you first see that ominous blank page. With a computer, the level of terror increases because Word festoons its program window with all kinds of controls, options, and doodads. I recommend that you refer to Figure 1-2 to recognize what these items are called. Ignore this jargon at your peril.

The details of how all these gizmos work, and the terms to describe them, are covered throughout this book. The good news is that the basic task of typing text is straightforward. See Chapter 2 to get started.

TIP

>> The view buttons (Read Mode, Print Layout, and Web Layout in the lower right corner in Figure 1-2) are absent from the online version of Word.

>> To get the most from Word's window, adjust its size: Use the mouse to drag the window's edges outward. You can also click the window's Maximize button (refer to Figure 1-2) to have the window fill the screen.

>> The largest portion of Word's screen is used for composing text. It looks like a fresh sheet of paper, but it doesn't smell the same. If you choose to use a template to start a new document, this area may contain some preset text.

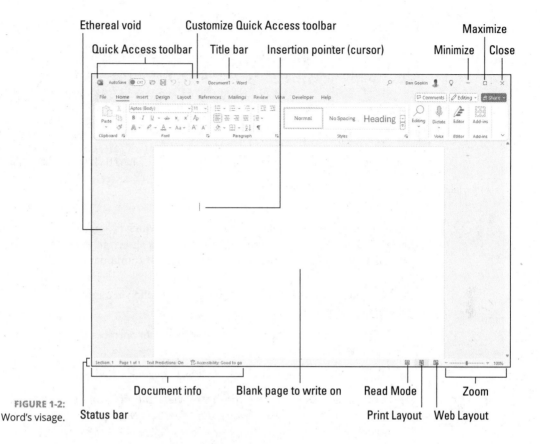

Ethereal void   Customize Quick Access toolbar   Maximize

Quick Access toolbar   Title bar   Insertion pointer (cursor)   Minimize   Close

Document info   Blank page to write on   Read Mode   Zoom

FIGURE 1-2:   Status bar   Print Layout   Web Layout
Word's visage.

Navigating the ribbon

An important part of Word's interface is the *ribbon.* This festive name refers to a location where the majority of Word's commands dwell and where settings are made. These items appear as buttons, input boxes, and menus. Alas, you find no bows on the ribbon.

The ribbon is divided into tabs, as illustrated in Figure 1-3. Each tab holds separate groups. Within the groups, you find the command buttons and doodads that carry out various word processing duties.

To use the ribbon, first click a tab and then choose a command from a group. For example, to set the right paragraph alignment, click the Home tab and then look in the Paragraph group for the Align Right button. Click the button to activate the command.

Some buttons feature a menu, which pops up automatically or when you click the down-pointing chevron next to the button.

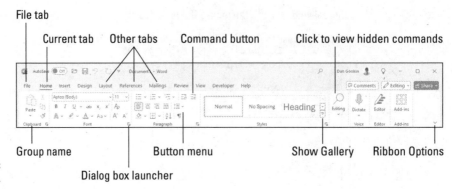

File tab

Current tab Other tabs Command button Click to view hidden commands

Group name Button menu Show Gallery Ribbon Options

Dialog box launcher

FIGURE 1-3:
The ribbon.

Various tabs on the ribbon may feature a gallery, which is a palette of buttons that preview information, such as the paragraph styles shown in Figure 1-3. Click the Show Gallery button to display the entire gallery of thumbnails.

>> This book describes finding commands on the ribbon in this manner: tab, group, command button.

>> The online version of Word features a different ribbon, more abbreviated than the full Word program.

>> Some items on the ribbon let you input text or values.

>> Use the Dialog Box Launcher icon in the lower right corner of a group to open a dialog box that's relevant to the group's function. Not every group features a dialog box launcher.

>> The amazingly frustrating thing about the ribbon is that it can change. Some tabs appear and disappear, depending on what you're doing in Word. Groups and icons (buttons) come and go, depending on the width of Word's program window.

TIP

>> To ensure that you always see all command buttons on the ribbon, adjust the program's window as wide as is practical.

>> Clicking the File tab replaces the contents of the Word window with a screen full of commands and other information. To return to the Word window, click the Back button (shown in the margin) or press the keyboard's Esc key.

Showing and hiding the ribbon

Yes, some users desire the ribbon to go away and be replaced by the familiar old menu system. Alas, this change will never happen. But, to ensure that you hold a continued level of frustration, Microsoft believes that showing and hiding the ribbon is a feature. Don't be surprised when the ribbon disappears altogether, though you can control its fate.

To resolve ribbon frustrations, use the Ribbon Options menu, located at the far right end of the ribbon, shown in Figure 1-3. Choose an item to determine how to display the ribbon. These are your choices:

Full Screen Mode: The most annoying choice; the Word program engulfs the entire screen, and the ribbon disappears. Click the top part of the screen to show the ribbon. With the ribbon again visible, choose another option from the Ribbon Options menu to revive the ribbon.

Show Tabs Only: With this choice, only the ribbon's tabs appear. Click a tab to reveal the bulk of the ribbon, which disappears again after you choose a command.

Always Show Ribbon: This option shows the entire ribbon — tabs and commands — as illustrated in Figures 1-2 and 1-3. This is probably the choice you want.

There's no truth to the rumor that the ribbon was originally going to be called *the enchilada*. Microsoft programmers joked that you could show "the whole enchilada" when using Word, though upper management lacked a sense of humor on the matter.

TECHNICAL
STUFF

Word 2007 was the first version of the program to introduce the ribbon interface. Before then, Word used a messy array of menus and toolbars to hold its commands.

Using Word on a touchscreen

Word processing is a typing thing, so my guess is that most of the time you work the Word program, you're using a keyboard and mouse. For laptops, tablets, and desktop PCs with a touchscreen, you can activate the ribbon's Touch mode. This mode adjusts the spacing between buttons on the ribbon, making it easier for you to stab various buttons by using your stubby fingers.

Follow these steps to enable Touch mode for Word's ribbon:

1. **Click or touch the Customize Quick Access Toolbar button.**

   The button appears to the right of the Quick Access toolbar (refer to Figure 1-2).

2. **Choose Touch/Mouse Mode.**

The Touch Mode button appears on the Quick Access toolbar, shown in the margin.

The Touch/Mouse Mode button doesn't activate the Touch Mode feature. No, that would make too much sense. Instead, tap the button to choose between Mouse mode and Touch mode for the ribbon's presentation.

In Mouse mode, the buttons on the ribbon appear closer together.

In Touch mode, more space is added between the buttons, which makes it easier for you to tap the proper command on the touchscreen.

Deactivating Touch mode doesn't remove any fingerprints or smudges from the monitor.

Changing the document view

You never had to worry about a sheet of paper changing its size or text when using a typewriter. The Microsoft Word program is far more fickle when it comes to presenting a document in its window: The blank area where you write can be altered to present information in different ways. Why would you want to do that? You don't! But it helps to know about the different ways the view can change so that you can change it back.

Here are your view choices:

Print Layout: This view is the standard way to view a document. Print Layout is the view shown in this book, and it's how Word typically presents a document. A virtual page appears on the screen, with four sides, like a sheet of paper with text in the middle. What you see on the screen is pretty much what you'll see in the results, whether printed or published as an electronic document.

Read Mode: Use this view to read a document like an eBook. The ribbon, and pretty much the rest of Word, is hidden while in Read Mode.

Web Layout: This view presents a document as a web page. It's available should you use Word's dubious potential as a web page editor.

Focus: It's the briefest of presentations. Only the document and your text appear — no controls or other whatnot.

Immersive Reader: This funky presentation allows Word to read your document to you.

Outline: This mode helps you organize your thoughts, as covered in Chapter 25.

Draft: Draft view presents only basic text, not all the formatting and fancy features, such as graphics.

To switch between Read Mode, Print Layout, and Web Layout views, click the related icon found in the lower right corner of the Word program window (refer to Figure 1-2). These buttons are absent in the online version of Word.

To get to Outline and Draft views, as well as to see all View modes in one location, click the View tab and choose the appropriate command button from the Views group. The Focus and Immersive Reader options appear in the Immersive group.

TIP

>> Not all views are available in the online version of Word.

>> When your document looks weird, switch back to Print Layout view. Click the Print Layout button on the status bar, or click the View tab and choose Print Layout in the Views group.

Viewing a document vertically or side-to-side

Since the first teletype machine, documents presented on a computer scroll vertically. Word documents inherit this vertical scrollability — unless you prefer a side-by-side presentation, like a book.

To make the switch, click the View tab and gander at the Page Movement group. Click the Vertical button to view a document vertically; click the Side to Side button to page through your document from left to right.

TIP

>> The side-to-side option works best on a large monitor when the Word program window is maximized. Otherwise, the text becomes too small to work with.

>> Word also lets you view two different documents side-by-side or even the same document in two windows. See Chapter 24 for details.

Making the document appear larger or smaller

Word's digital equivalent of a magnifying glass is the Zoom command. It enlarges or reduces a document's presentation, making it easier to see without altering the text size (font size).

Several methods are available to zoom in or out of a document in Word. The most obvious is to use the Zoom control, found in the lower right corner of the Word window on the status bar, illustrated earlier, in Figure 1-2. Adjust the slider right or left to make the text larger or smaller, respectively.

To set specific zoom sizes, click the 100% button on the status bar. Use the Zoom dialog box to set a size based on percentage, page width, or even multiple pages.

REMEMBER

>> Zooming doesn't affect how a document prints — only how it looks on the screen.

>> For more specific zoom control, click the View tab and use the commands found in the Zoom group.

TIP

>> If the computer's mouse has a wheel button, you can zoom by holding the Ctrl key on the keyboard and rolling the mouse wheel up or down. Rolling up zooms in; rolling down zooms out.

Last Word

It's the pinnacle of etiquette to know when to leave, or even whether to leave. Typically, I leave a party when the host returns to the room wearing his pajamas or when I realize that he's already in bed. Sadly, the Word program doesn't wear pajamas, so you're left with three options for bidding adieu: Quit the program outright, close a document, or put Word aside like that fresh cup of tea you forgot about in the kitchen three hours ago.

Quitting Word

When you've finished word processing and you aren't expecting to return to it anytime soon, quit the Word program: Click the X button in the upper right corner of the Word program window, as illustrated earlier, in Figure 1-2.

The catch? You must close every dang doodle Word document window that's open before you can proclaim that you've completely quit Word.

The other catch? Word won't quit during that shameful circumstance when you've neglected to save a document. If so, you're prompted to save, as shown in Figure 1-4. My advice is to click the Save button to save your work; see Chapter 8 for specific document-saving directions.

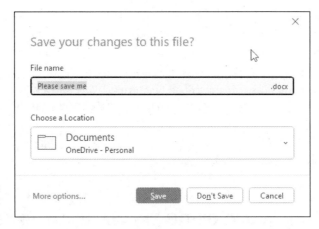

FIGURE 1-4:
Better click that
Save button.

When you click the Don't Save button, your work isn't saved and Word quits anyway, not thinking any less of you.

To continue working on the document, click the Cancel button.

REMEMBER

You don't have to quit Word just to start editing another document. Refer to the next couple of sections for helpful, time-saving information.

Closing a document without quitting Word

To finish one document and start on another, you close the first document. You don't need to quit Word to do so, which is a time-saver. Heed these directions:

1. **Click the File tab.**

   The File screen appears. Various commands litter the left side of the screen.

2. **Choose the Close command.**

   The Close command for the online version of Word doesn't close the document. Only the Close command for the Word program closes the open document.

3. **Save the document, if you're prompted to do so.**

   The shame! Always save before closing.

After the document has closed, you return to the main Word window. You don't see a document in the window, and many of the ribbon's command buttons are dimmed (unavailable). At this point, you can create a new document or open a previously saved document. These options are available from the File tab.

REMEMBER

>> There's no urgency to close a document. I keep mine open all day as I flit in and out of my office, pretending to do work — but save often. To return to the document-in-progress, click the Word button on the Windows taskbar.

>> The keyboard shortcut for the Close command is Ctrl+W. The letter *W* may seem weird, as I can think of no synonym for *Close* with a *W* in it, but it's a standard keyboard shortcut, used to close documents in many programs on several planets.

TIP

>> To swiftly start a new, blank document in Word, press the Ctrl+N keyboard shortcut. Yes, N stands for *new*.

Setting Word aside

Don't quit Word when you know that you'll use it again soon. In fact, I've been known to keep Word open and running on my computer for *weeks* at a time. The secret is to use the Minimize button, found in the upper right corner of the screen (refer to Figure 1-2).

Click the Minimize button to shrink the Word window to a button on the taskbar. With the Word window out of the way, you can do other things with your computer: shop, play games, argue on social media, and so on. Then when the boss shows up, click the Word button on the taskbar to restore the full, glorious Word window to the desktop.

Chapter **2**

The Typing Chapter

Long before all the fancy graphics, the mouse, and computer programs became popular, typing was how you processed words. I remember learning to type in junior high school, all 30 students clacking along at their manual typewriters in sync to *The Blue Danube*. Things move faster today, but typing is still a necessity.

You must know how to type to gain the most benefit from Word. But using a keyboard involves more than the old hunt-and-peck. Keyboard commands and shortcuts can tie your fingers into knots. Get to know how typing works on a word processor and your life will be easier — although I do miss that reassuring "ding!" when the typewriter reached the end of a line.

The New Hunt-and-Peck

When you process words, you use your fingers and one thumb to manipulate the computer keyboard. Typing is an important part of getting text on a page, but also important is the mouse. No, you don't type with the mouse, but you do some pointing and clicking in addition to clickity-clack-clacking.

Using the PC keyboard

When you're presented with a toaster, a forklift, and a computer keyboard, I'm guessing that you can successfully pick out the computer keyboard most of the time. But what do you know about the details? After all, the thing has over 100 keys. I know because I counted them. To avoid confusion (or to help promote it), the computer keyboard is organized into different areas, as illustrated in Figure 2-1.

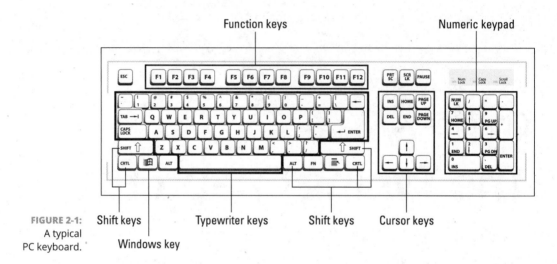

FIGURE 2-1:
A typical
PC keyboard.

Out of the 100-plus keys, a few play important roles in the word processing task:

Enter: Marked with the word *Enter* and sometimes a cryptic, bent-arrow thing, this key ends a paragraph of text. See the later section "Pressing the Enter key."

Spacebar: Not the place where Captain Kirk orders his drinks, this wide key inserts a space between words and sentences. Yes, just one space. See the section "Whacking the spacebar."

Tab: This key inserts the Tab character, which shoves the next text you type over to the next tab stop, as described in Chapter 12. The Tab key is also used to complete a predictive text suggestion; see the section "Using text predictions."

Backspace and Delete: Use these keys to back up and erase text. Read more about these keys in Chapter 4.

Each character key you press on the typewriter-keys area of the keyboard produces a character in your Word document, on the blank part where you write. Typing those character keys over and over is how you create text in a word processor. That's how Shakespeare did it.

>> A laptop keyboard's layout is different from the desktop keyboard layout, shown earlier, in Figure 2-1. For example, most laptop keyboards lack a numeric keypad. The cursor keys are clustered tightly around the typewriter keys in unusual and creative patterns. The function keys might be accessed by pressing special key combinations.

>> Keys on the numeric keypad can be number keys or cursor keys. The split personality is evident on each key cap, which displays two symbols. When the Num Lock key's lamp is on, the keys generate numbers. When the lamp is off, the keys serve as duplicate cursor keys.

>> Cursor keys control the cursor, which is officially known as the *insertion pointer* in Microsoft Word. The cursor keys include the four arrow keys (up, down, left, right) plus the keys Home, End, PgUp (or Page Up), PgDn (or Page Down), Insert, and Delete.

>> Ctrl is pronounced "control." It's the Control key.

>> The Delete key may also be labeled Del on the keyboard.

>> The *modifier* keys — Shift, Ctrl, and Alt — work in combination with other keys.

>> Yes, your keyboard may look different from what's shown in Figure 2-1. You may find bonus keys, knobs to adjust the computer's speaker volume, media keys, monkeys, and donkeys. These bonus keys have nothing to do with word processing.

Working the touch keyboard

Two-in-one laptops, tablets, and other touchscreen devices sport an onscreen keyboard called the touch keyboard. You can use this keyboard when a real keyboard is unavailable to type text in Word. In fact, in Windows, you can summon the onscreen keyboard regardless of whether the computer has a touchscreen: Press the Win+Ctrl+O (letter O) keyboard shortcut. The onscreen keyboard appears, as shown in Figure 2-2.

TIP

For email or short missives, the onscreen keyboard is tolerable. And though you look so high-tech using it, for true word processing, use a real keyboard instead. Don't torture yourself.

>> The onscreen keyboard's operation works basically the same as a physical keyboard: You type text using your fingers, albeit probably not as fast as on a physical keyboard.

>> Accessing some of the specialized keys (function keys, cursor keys, and others) is problematic. Sometimes they're available by choosing a different touchscreen keyboard layout, but often they're unavailable.

FIGURE 2-2:
The touch
keyboard.

Tap to view function keys   Onscreen keyboard settings

>> Using the Ctrl key on the onscreen keyboard is a two-step process: Tap the
Ctrl key and then touch another key — for example, Ctrl and then the S key,
for Ctrl+S.

>> Not all Ctrl-key combinations in Word can be replicated by using the
onscreen keyboard.

>> Refer to Chapter 1 for information on activating Touch mode, which makes it
easier to use Word on a tablet.

Understanding the mouse pointer

Though word processing is a keyboardy task, you inevitably lift your hand from
the keyboard to fondle the computer mouse. Use the mouse to choose commands,
to select text, and to scurry around the document. Specific information on these
tasks is concealed throughout this book. For now, it helps to understand how the
mouse pointer changes its appearance as you work in Word:

For editing text, the mouse pointer becomes the *I-beam.*

For choosing items, the standard 11 o'clock mouse pointer is used.

For selecting lines of text, a 1 o'clock mouse pointer is used.

The mouse pointer changes its appearance when the *click-and-type* feature is
active: Teensy lines appear below and to the left and right of the I-beam mouse
pointer. Refer to Chapter 32 to learn why no one uses click-and-type.

TIP

When you point the mouse at a command button or any icon on the Word screen, you see a pop-up information bubble. The text in the bubble describes the command and perhaps offers a hint on how the command is used. Do not try to pop the bubble.

Keyboard Do's and Don'ts

You don't need to be a 70-words-per-minute touch typist to use a word processor. And, if you don't know how to type, see the nearby sidebar, "Do I need to learn to type?" — although I can tell you that the answer is, "Yes, you need to learn to type." It also helps to know a few typing do's and don'ts that are specific to word processing.

Following the insertion pointer

Text you compose in Word appears at the *insertion pointer*'s location. The insertion pointer looks like a flashing vertical bar:

|

Open and close your eyes as you look at this insertion pointer on this page to form an idea of how it appears on the screen.

"DO I NEED TO LEARN TO TYPE?"

No one needs to learn to type to use any computer program, though knowing how to type is a huge plus. My advice is to find a computer program that teaches you to type. I can recommend the *Mavis Beacon Teaches Typing* program, even though I receive no money from her and none of her children resemble me. I just like the name Mavis, I suppose.

I'm forced to mention the program *Typing Instructor Platinum*, though none of these words pleases me.

No matter which software you choose for typing training, knowing how to type makes the word processing chore a tad more enjoyable.

Characters you type appear *before* the insertion pointer, one at a time. After a character appears, the insertion pointer hops to the right, making room for more text.

TECHNICAL STUFF

>> The insertion pointer moves as you type, but its location can be set to any position in the document's text. Chapter 3 covers moving the insertion pointer.

>> Some documentation refers to the insertion pointer as the cursor. The mouse pointer might also be referred to as the cursor. For clarity, this book refers to the insertion pointer and mouse pointer without using the term *cursor*.

Whacking the spacebar

Pressing the spacebar inserts a *space character* into the text. Spaces are important between words and sentences. Withoutthemreadingwouldbedifficult.

REMEMBER

The most important thing to remember about the spacebar is that you need to whack it only once when word processing. Only *one* space appears between words and after punctuation. That's it!

>> I'm serious! Back in the dark ages, typing instructors directed students to add two spaces between sentences. This extra space was necessary for readability because typewriters used monospaced characters. On a computer, however, the second space adds little to the text and potentially leads to formatting woes down the road.

>> Word flags two spaces between words as a grammatical error. See Chapter 7.

>> Anytime you feel like you need two or more spaces in a document, use a tab instead. Tabs are best for indenting text as well as for lining up text in columns. See Chapter 12 for details.

Backing up and erasing

Two keys are used to obliterate text: Backspace and Delete.

The Backspace key gobbles up the character to the left of the insertion pointer. This key may be labeled with a left-pointing arrow symbol, as shown in the margin.

The Delete key devours the character to the right of the insertion pointer. This key is labeled DEL or DELETE on the keyboard.

See Chapter 4 for more information on gobbling and devouring text.

Pressing the Enter key

In word processing, you press the Enter key only when you reach the end of a paragraph. Do not press the Enter key at the end of a line unless that line is a paragraph.

When your typed text wanders precariously close to the right margin, Word automatically moves the last word on the line down to the next line. This *word wrap* feature eliminates the need to press Enter at the end of each line of text.

» The Enter key may be labeled with the word *Enter* or marked with the arrow dingus shown in the margin.

» Don't use the Enter key to double-space your text. Double-spacing is a paragraph format in Word. See Chapter 11 for more information.

» Don't press the Enter key twice to add extra space between paragraphs. Space between paragraphs is added automatically, provided it's part of the paragraph format, also covered in Chapter 11.

Stuff That Happens While You Type

As you madly compose text, your fingers energetically jabbing the buttons on the keyboard, you may notice a few weird things happening on the screen. You might see spots. You might see lines and boxes. You may even see lightning! All these phenomena are side effects of typing in Word. They're normal, and they're presented to assist you.

Using text predictions

Relax: Your computer isn't possessed. Any phantom text that appears, accurately guessing what you're about to type next, is Word's *text prediction* feature in action. In Figure 2-3, the ghost in the machine guesses what I might type next. If the suggested text is what's desired, press the Tab key to insert it (refer to Figure 2-3). Otherwise, keep typing to foil the computer's feeble psychic capabilities.

» To disable text predictions, right-click the status bar and choose Text Predictions from the pop-up menu. Press Esc to dismiss the pop-up menu.

» Eventually, the Tab prompt, shown in Figure 2-3, no longer shows up. Word assumes you "get it" and know to press the Tab key to insert the predicted text.

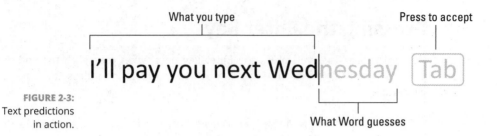

What you type

Press to accept

I'll pay you next Wednesday [Tab]

What Word guesses

FIGURE 2-3:
Text predictions
in action.

**TECHNICAL
STUFF**

>> Word learns the predictions as you type, which is how they seem uncanny at times. Be aware that these predictions are stored on your computer and are not shared on the Internet. If you use Word on multiple computers, each one keeps its own set of predictions.

Watching the status bar

At the bottom of Word's window dwells the status bar. The reason it's called the *status* bar is that it reveals the document's status, updating information as you type. A barrage of details appears, starting at the left end of the status bar and marching rightward. Some of these items are shown in Figure 2-4.

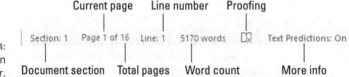

Current page   Line number   Proofing

Section: 1   Page 1 of 16   Line: 1   5170 words   [X]   Text Predictions: On

Document section   Total pages   Word count   More info

FIGURE 2-4:
Stuff that lurks on
the status bar.

The status bar can be a lively place — or not — depending on how it's configured. The details that appear — page, line, word count, and so on — are customizable. Chapter 29 explains how to control what appears on the status bar.

Observing page breaks

As your document gains length, Word shows you where one page ends and another page begins. This visual assistance helps you keep elements on the same page but also shows you how text flows between pages.

The visual clue for a new page is shown in Figure 2-5. In Print Layout view, the page break appears graphically. Text above the ethereal void is on one page, and text below the void is on the next page.

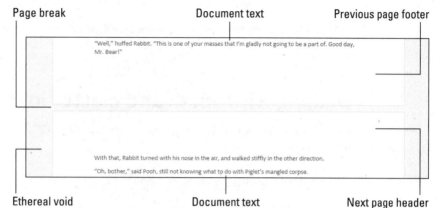

Page break   Document text   Previous page footer

"Well," huffed Rabbit. "This is one of your messes that I'm gladly not going to be a part of. Good day, Mr. Bear!"

With that, Rabbit turned with his nose in the air, and walked stiffly in the other direction.

"Oh, bother," said Pooh, still not knowing what to do with Piglet's mangled corpse.

Ethereal void   Document text   Next page header

FIGURE 2-5:
A page break in
Print Layout view.

In Draft view, the page break appears as a line of dots marching from left to right across the document. In other views, the page break may not show up, in which case you use the status bar to determine the page break. For example, when the page number indicator changes from 6 to 7, you've started a new page.

>> To control the gap between pages in Print Layout view, point the mouse at the gap. When the mouse pointer changes, as shown in the margin, double-click to either close or open the gap.

>> Never force a page break by pressing the Enter key a gazillion times! Instead, see Chapter 13 for information on inserting page breaks (new pages) in Word.

>> The space above and below your document's text on a page is where the page header and footer linger. See Chapter 14 for information on page headers and footers.

TECHNICAL STUFF

>> The topic of page breaks brings up the concept of widows and orphans, which is otherwise tremendously sad but not in this case. *Widow* and *orphan* refer to a single line of text at the page's top or bottom, respectively. Word automatically moves such text to the previous or next page to prevent widows and orphans from appearing. It's cruel but effective.

Working collapsible headers

You may see a tiny triangle to the left of various headings in your documents, as shown in the margin. This document doodad does not print. Instead, these triangles allow you to expand or collapse all text in the header's section. Click the icon once to collapse the text; click again to expand it.

>> The collapsible header icons appear in Print Layout view when the insertion pointer is hovering over the header's text.

>> See Chapter 25 for a longer and more scintillating discussion of collapsible headers, as well as information on Word's Outline view.

Dealing with spots and clutter in the text

There's no cause for alarm if you see spots — or dots — amid the text you type, such as

```
This•can•be•very•annoying.¶
```

What you're observing are *nonprinting* characters. Word uses various symbols to represent characters you normally don't see: spaces, tabs, the Enter key, and more. These jots and tittles appear when the Show/Hide feature is activated:

1. **Click the Home tab.**

2. **In the Paragraph group, click the Show/Hide command button.**

   The button features the Paragraph symbol as its icon, shown in the margin.

To hide the dots and clutter again, click the Show/Hide command button a second time.

>> Why bother with showing these goobers? Sometimes it's useful to check out what's up with formatting, to locate stray tabs visually, or to hunt down empty paragraphs, for example.

>> The keyboard shortcut for the Show/Hide command is Ctrl+Shift+8. Use the 8 on the typewriter area of the keyboard, not on the numeric keypad.

>> The Paragraph symbol is called the *pilcrow*.

TECHNICAL
STUFF

Understanding colorful underlines

When Word underlines your text without permission, it's drawing your attention to something amiss. These special underlines are not text formats. Here are a few of the underlines you may witness from time to time:

Red zigzag: Spelling errors in Word are underlined with red zigzags. See Chapter 7.

Blue double underline: Grammatical and word choice errors are flagged with a blue double underline, depending on the offense. Again, see Chapter 7.

Blue single underline: Word courteously highlights web page addresses by using a single blue underline. You can Ctrl+click the blue underlined text to visit the web page.

Red lines: You may see red lines in the margin, underneath text, or through text. If so, it means you're using Word's Track Changes feature. See Chapter 26.

Beyond these automatic underlines, you can apply the underline format to your text, choosing the type of underline and its color. See Chapter 10.

DICTATE THY PROSE

Some people desire to dictate to their computers rather than expend the energy to type. Straight out of science fiction, like Commander Adama in the original *Battlestar Galactica* or, more famously, Mr. Spock in *Star Trek*, this feature is called *dictation*. Word gives you this power.

On the Home tab, in the Voice group, you find the Dictate button. Clicking this button does not turn you into Julius Caesar. No, providing that your computer has a microphone attached, click this button and begin speaking. Word miraculously and often accurately translates your utterances into text. You can dictate some punctuation, such as "period," "comma," and "new line" to start a new paragraph.

Dictation is used to create text but comes up short for editing and formatting a document, which is this book's main topic. So blab away, but understand that dictating to Word to calculate *pi* to the last digit merely inserts this text into your document and does not drive evil spirits from the system.

Click the Dictate button again to deactivate this feature.

2

Your Basic Word

Discover how to use the scroll bars, move the insertion pointer, and get around with keyboard shortcuts.

Find out how to delete characters, lines, sentences, paragraphs, and pages. You're also introduced to the lifesaving Undo command.

Learn how to find and replace text in your documents.

Work with blocks of text and see how you can mark, select, copy, move, and paste blocks.

Customize the spell checker and AutoCorrect settings.

Become familiar with how to preview and print documents, both on paper and electronically.

Chapter **3**

Moving Around a Document

Perhaps your computer is blessed with a humongous monitor. Or maybe the system boasts multiple monitors, arrayed up the wall and higher than your head. I envy you. That's because it would be easy for you to scan your entire document in Word all at once. Yes, you may need a stepladder to work the program and craft your text, but you could easily avoid the tricks and suggestions offered in this chapter for moving around within a document.

Scroll the Document

It's ironic that the word *scroll* is used when referring to an electronic document. The scroll was the first form of portable recorded text, existing long before bound books. On a computer, *scrolling* is the process by which you view a little bit of a big document in a tiny window.

Working the vertical scroll bar

The document portion of the Word program window features a vertical scroll bar, illustrated in Figure 3-1. The scroll bar's operation works like the scroll bar in any

Windows program. For a review, the figure illustrates the mouse's effect on parts of the scroll bar.

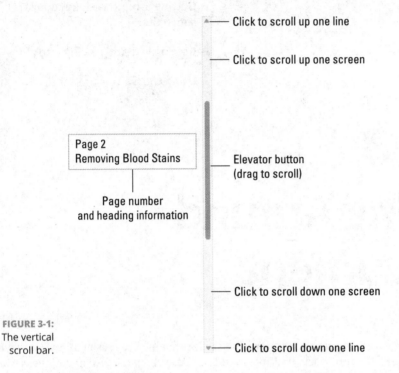

Click to scroll up one line

Click to scroll up one screen

Page 2
Removing Blood Stains

Page number
and heading information

Elevator button
(drag to scroll)

Click to scroll down one screen

FIGURE 3-1:
The vertical
scroll bar.

Click to scroll down one line

A key feature on the scroll bar is the elevator button (refer to Figure 3-1). Use the mouse to drag this button up or down to scroll the document.

>> As you drag the elevator button up or down, you see a page number displayed, as shown in Figure 3-1. When a document is formatted with heading styles, you also see the heading title below the page number, as shown in the figure.

>> The vertical scroll bar may disappear at times; move the mouse pointer over the text and it shows up again.

>> The elevator button's position on the scroll bar reflects the location of the text you see; its size represents how much of the total document is visible in the window. Due to this relationship, the button grows smaller as the document grows longer.

>> When the elevator button doesn't show up or is dimmed, the whole document appears in the window.

>> Using the scroll bar to scroll the document doesn't move the insertion pointer. If you start typing, don't be surprised when Word jumps back to where the insertion pointer lurks.

Using the horizontal scroll bar

When the document is wider than can be displayed in the window, a horizontal scroll bar appears. It shows up at the bottom of the document part of the window, just above the status bar. Use the horizontal scroll bar to shift the page back and forth, left and right.

>> Word automatically slides the document left and right as you type, but this movement can be jarring. Instead, try to adjust the horizontal scroll bar to display as much of the text as possible. You can also enlarge the document window to make it wider on the screen.

>> When the horizontal (left to right) shifting bugs you, consider using Word's Zoom tool to adjust the size of the document in the window. See Chapter 1.

Scrolling with the mouse wheel

The computer mouse's wheel button scrolls the Word document as it scrolls any other program window, such as on a web page. Roll the wheel to scroll up or down. The direction the document moves is set in Windows, so I can't for certain tell you whether rolling the wheel up scrolls the document up or down. Just try it to see how it works.

Some mice let you press the wheel button or tilt it from side to side. If so, press and hold down the wheel button and drag the mouse forward or backward to slowly scroll the document up or down. Tilt the wheel button from side to side to pan the document left and right.

>> Unlike using the scroll bars, when you use the mouse wheel to scroll the document, the insertion pointer moves with your view. Use the Shift+F5 keyboard shortcut to return the insertion pointer to the spot where you last edited text. See the later section "Return to the Previous Edit."

>> Be careful not to press the Ctrl key as you use the mouse wheel to scroll. The Ctrl+wheel trick zooms a document in and out.

Move the Insertion Pointer

Some writers work only at the end of their document. Other writers like to hop and skip around the document, working sporadically or wherever the mood hits them. The goal, of course, is to avoid finishing the document. Yet, no matter which approach you use, it helps to know how to move the insertion pointer to the exact spot you want.

» Knowing how to move the insertion pointer is important! Scientific studies have shown that merely looking at the computer screen does no good.

» New text appears only at the insertion pointer. Text is deleted at the insertion pointer's location. Text is pasted at the insertion pointer. Formatting commands affect text where the insertion pointer lies blinking.

Commanding the insertion pointer

The easiest way to put the insertion pointer exactly where you want it is to click the mouse at that specific spot in the text. Point. Click. The insertion pointer obeys.

If your computer or laptop features a touchscreen, tap the screen with your finger to relocate the insertion pointer. The tinier and sharper your finger is, the more accurate the results.

Moving the insertion pointer in small increments

For short hops, nothing beats using the keyboard's cursor keys to quickly relocate the insertion pointer. Pressing one of the four arrow keys moves the insertion pointer up, down, right, or left:

Press This Key	To Move the Insertion Pointer
↑	Up to the preceding line of text
↓	Down to the next line of text
→	Right to the next character
←	Left to the preceding character

If you press and hold down the Ctrl (Control) key and then press an arrow key, the insertion pointer gains superpowers and moves in larger increments. The invigorated insertion pointer leaps desperately in one of these four directions:

Press This Key Combo	To Move the Insertion Pointer
Ctrl+↑	Up to the start of the previous paragraph
Ctrl+↓	Down to the start of the next paragraph
Ctrl+→	Right to the start (first letter) of the next word
Ctrl+←	Left to the start (first letter) of the previous word

>> Moving the cursor doesn't erase characters. See Chapter 4 for information on deleting stuff.

REMEMBER

>> When you choose to use the arrow keys on the numeric keypad, ensure that the Num Lock light is off. (If it's on, press the Num Lock key.) If you forget, you see numbers in the text rather than the insertion pointer dancing all over — like444this.

Moving from start to end

The insertion pointer also bows to pressure from those cursor keys without arrows on them. The first couple consists of Home and End, which move the insertion pointer to the start or end of something, depending on how Home and End are used:

Press This Key or Combination	To Whisk the Insertion Pointer
Home	To the start of a line of text
End	To the end of a line of text
Ctrl+Home	To the tippy-top of the document
Ctrl+End	To the very bottom of the document

The remaining cursor keys are Page Up and Page Down, often abbreviated as PgUp and PgDn or even PU and PD. These keys do not move the insertion pointer based on a printed page, but rather the portion of the page you see in the Word document window. Here's the round-up:

Press This Key or Combination	To Whisk the Insertion Pointer
PgUp	Up one window full of text or to the tippy-top of the document if you're near there
PgDn	Down one window full of text or to the end of the document if you're near there
Ctrl+Alt+PgUp	To the top of the current window's text
Ctrl+Alt+PgDn	To the bottom of the current window's text

WHAT ABOUT CTRL+PGUP AND CTRL+PGDN?

Given the pattern of cursor keyboard shortcuts, you would think that the Ctrl+PgUp and Ctrl+PgDn key combinations would do something fun. Alas, no. These are shortcuts to the Browse Previous and Browse Next commands, respectively. Their function changes based on what you've recently done in Word.

For example, the Ctrl+PgDn keyboard shortcut may represent the Find Next command if you've recently used this command. It might also repeat the Go To command or any of a number of Word commands that move the insertion pointer.

Because of their changing behavior, I don't recommend using Ctrl+PgUp or Ctrl+PgDn as a consistent way to move the insertion pointer.

The key combinations to move to the top or bottom of the current window's text are Ctrl+Alt+PgUp and Ctrl+Alt+PgDn, respectively. That's Ctrl+Alt, not just the Ctrl key. And yes, few people know or use these commands.

Return to the Previous Edit

Considering all the various commands for moving the insertion pointer, it's quite possible to make a mistake and not know where you are in a document — or where you were. Yea, verily, the insertion pointer has boldly gone where no insertion pointer has gone before.

Rather than click your heels together three times, just remember this keyboard combination:

Shift+F5

Pressing the Shift+F5 keyboard shortcut forces Word to return you to the last spot where you edited text. You can use this keyboard shortcut three times before the cycle repeats. The first time should get you back to where you were before you got lost.

REMEMBER

Sadly, the Shift+F5 keyboard shortcut works only in Word; you can't use this command in real life.

Go to Wherever with the Go To Command

In Shakespeare's plays, the phrase "go to" means to "get thee the heck out of here." In Word, the Go To command banishes the insertion pointer in a similar manner, sending it on its merry way to a specific page or line or to the location of several interesting locations in a Word document.

To use the Go To command, follow these steps:

1. **Click the Home tab.**

2. **In the Editing group, click the Find button and choose Go To.**

    The Find and Replace dialog box appears with the Go To tab forward, as shown in Figure 3-2.

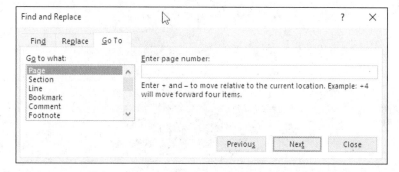

FIGURE 3-2:
Telling Word
to Go To
you-know-where.

And now, the shortcut: Press Ctrl+G to quickly summon the Find and Replace dialog box's Go To tab.

To zip the insertion pointer to a specific location, choose it from the Go to What list. For example, choose Page to visit a specific page. Type the page number in the Enter Page Number box, and then click the Go To button to go to that page in your document.

>> The Go To command is unavailable in the online version of Word.

TIP

>> The Enter Page Number box also accepts relative pages as input. For example, to go three pages forward, type +**3**. To go 12 pages backward, type –**12** in the box.

>> The Go To command's other keyboard shortcut? Press the F5 key. The only reason I remember this keyboard shortcut is that this book is in its 17th edition.

TECHNICAL STUFF

>> The last item you chose from the Go to What list affects the behavior of the Ctrl+PgUp and Ctrl+PgDn keyboard shortcuts. For example, if you choose Page and click the Go To button, the Ctrl+PgUp and Ctrl+PgDn keyboard shortcuts navigate through your document one page at a time.

Chapter **4**

Text Editing

t's said that the author Isaac Asimov wrote final drafts the first time. Yet most people I know can't even finish a document's first paragraph. That's because mortal humans labor through writing, deleting, and rewriting. This issue is no cause for concern because Word features an abundance of text editing tools, or commands you use to make your text look perfect — just like Dr. Asimov did the first time.

REMEMBER

One of the reasons budding writers get stuck is that they spend more time editing than writing. Therefore, my advice is to concentrate first on writing — then edit.

Remove Text You Don't Want

The genius who put the eraser on the end of the pencil made the keen observation that human beings are prone to make mistakes. The round, soft eraser counter-balances the sharp point of the pencil in many ways.

In Word, the keyboard both creates and destroys text. Most keys create text. Only two keys destroy: Backspace and Delete. These keys gain superpowers when used with other keys — and even the mouse — that help them eliminate vast swaths of text.

>> As text is deleted, the remaining text on the line, in the paragraph, or down the page scoots up to fill the void. Deleting text doesn't leave a hole in the document.

TECHNICAL STUFF

>> Document fields are not deleted like regular text. When you attempt to remove a field, Word highlights the field's text as a warning. To continue and remove the field, press either the Delete or Backspace key again. See Chapter 23 for more information on fields.

Plucking out single characters

The Backspace and Delete keys remove single characters:

>> Backspace deletes the character to the left of the insertion pointer.

>> Delete deletes the character to the right of the insertion pointer.

In the following example, the insertion pointer is flashing (okay, it *would* be flashing on a computer screen) between the *r* and the *p* in *superpowers.* Pressing the Backspace key deletes the *r*; pressing the Delete key deletes the *p*:

```
One of my super|powers is to buy a stock and watch the
price drop immediately.
```

You can press and hold down Backspace or Delete to rapid-fire delete characters. Release the key to halt such wanton destruction, though I recommend that you use other delete commands (covered in this chapter) rather than chew through your text one character at a time, like a hungry badger.

Deleting a word

To gobble up an entire word, use the Ctrl key with the Backspace or Delete key:

>> Ctrl+Backspace deletes the word to the left of the insertion pointer.

>> Ctrl+Delete deletes the word to the right of the insertion pointer.

These keyboard shortcuts work best when the insertion pointer is at the start or end of a word. When the pointer is in the middle of the word, these commands delete only from that middle point to the start or end of the word.

When you use Ctrl+Backspace to delete a word to the left, the insertion pointer sits at the end of the preceding word (or paragraph). When you use Ctrl+Delete to remove a word, the cursor sits at the start of the next word. This positioning is done to facilitate the rapid deletion of several words in a row.

No mere pencil eraser can match Ctrl+Delete or Ctrl+Backspace for sheer speed and terror!

Deleting more than a word

To remove chunks of text larger than a character or a word, the keyboard partners with the mouse. The process involves selecting a chunk of text and then deleting the chunk. See Chapter 6 for details on selecting text.

Delete a line of text

A line of text starts at one side of the page and moves to the other. It's not really a sentence or a paragraph, but the line can be removed easily:

1. **Move the mouse pointer into the left margin, next to the line of text.**

    You know you've found the sweet spot when the mouse pointer changes into a northeast-pointing arrow.

2. **Click the mouse.**

    The line of text is selected and appears highlighted on the screen.

3. **Press the Delete key to send the line into oblivion.**

Delete a sentence

A *sentence* is a grammatical thing. You know: Start with a capital letter and end with a period, a question mark, or an exclamation point. You probably mastered this grammatical concept in grammar school, which is why they call it grammar school anyway.

Making a sentence go bye–bye is cinchy:

1. **Position the insertion pointer in the offending sentence.**

2. **Press and hold down the Ctrl key and click the mouse.**

    The Ctrl and mouse-click combination (Ctrl+click) selects a sentence of text.

3. **Release the Ctrl key.**

4. **Press the Delete key.**

Delete a paragraph

A *paragraph* is one or more sentences, or a document heading, ending with a press of the Enter key. Here's the fastest way to delete a full paragraph:

1. **Click the mouse button thrice.**

   Thrice means "three times." The triple-click selects a complete paragraph of text.

2. **Press the Delete key.**

Another way to select a paragraph is to double-click the mouse in the left margin next to the paragraph.

Delete a page

A *page* of text includes everything on a page, top to bottom. This document-chunk isn't something Word directly addresses with specific keyboard commands. To remove a page full of text requires some legerdemain. Follow these steps:

1. **Press Ctrl+G.**

   The Find and Replace dialog box appears, with the Go To tab forward.

2. **From the Go to What list, click to select Page.**

3. **Type the number of the page you want to delete.**

   For example, type **2** to delete page 2.

4. **Click the Go To button and then click the Close button.**

   The insertion pointer is positioned at the top of the page.

5. **Press the F8 key.**

   Word enters Extended Selection mode. Now you must send the insertion pointer to the top of the next page.

6. **Press Ctrl+G to view the Find and Replace dialog box again.**

7. **Type the next page number.**

   For example, type **3** to delete page 2, which you entered in Step 3.

8. **Press the Delete key.**

All text is removed from the page.

> » If the page remains but it's blank, you might be dealing with a hard page break. See Chapter 13.

> » If you're trying to delete a blank page at the end of a document, see the sidebar in Chapter 9 about deleting the trailing blank page.

> » Chapter 3 offers more information on the Go To command.

> » The F8 key activates Extended Selection mode. If you chicken out after Step 5, press the Esc key to cancel this mode. See Chapter 6 for more F8 key tricks.

Delete an odd-size chunk of text

Word lets you delete any old odd-sized chunk of text anywhere in a document. The key is to select that text as a *block*. After the block is marked, press the Delete key to zap it to kingdom come. Refer to Chapter 6 for more information on selecting blocks of text — including selecting the entire document, should you want to erase everything and start over.

Paragraph Playtime

A paragraph is both an English grammatical entity and a Word formatting concept. In English, a paragraph is a basket of sentences that collectively express some thought, idea, or theme. In Word, a paragraph is a chunk of text that ends when you press the Enter key. While grammarians and software engineers duke it out over the different meanings, you can define a paragraph in a document by deftly applying the Enter key press.

Setting hard and soft returns

When you press the Enter key to end a paragraph, Word sets a hard return character. The paragraph ends and a new paragraph starts.

To end a line of text without terminating a paragraph, press Shift+Enter to set a soft return. This *soft return*, also known as a manual line break, ends the current line of text, but not the paragraph. The insertion pointer hops to the start of the next line. Keep typing at that point and, eventually, press Enter to end the paragraph.

The soft return is best used to split titles and headings. Using a soft return is also the secret behind typing an address. When you end each line with Shift+Enter, the text stays together as a single paragraph. For example:

```
The President
1600 Pennsylvania Ave.
Washington, DC 20500
```

Each line in this example ends with a soft return. The entire address is a paragraph in Word.

To help you identify hard returns and soft returns, use the Show/Hide command: Click the Home tab and, in the Paragraph group, click the Show/Hide command button, shown in the margin.

When the Show/Hide command is active, the soft return looks like this: ↵ The hard return looks like this: ¶ The address just shown appears as follows when the Show/Hide command is active:

```
The President↵
1600 Pennsylvania Ave.↵
Washington, DC 20500¶
```

» See Chapter 2 for more information on the Show/Hide command.

» Soft returns are affected by a paragraph's line spacing. See Chapter 11.

Splitting a paragraph

Goodness gracious! That paragraph contains *two* separate thoughts! To split it in twain, follow these steps:

1. **Click the mouse at the location where you want the new paragraph to begin.**

   Ideally, this location is at the start of a sentence.

2. **Press the Enter key.**

   Word inserts a hard return, splitting the paragraph in two. Text above the insertion pointer becomes its own paragraph, with the following text becoming the next paragraph.

Depending on how the paragraph was torn asunder, you may need to delete an extra space lingering at the end of the first paragraph or dawdling at the start of the next.

Joining two paragraphs

Behold! These two paragraphs contain the same thought! Better join them by following these steps:

1. **Set the insertion pointer at the start of the second paragraph.**

2. **Press the Backspace key.**

   The hard return from the preceding paragraph is ousted. The two paragraphs are now one.

Depending on how neatly the paragraphs were joined, you may need to add a space between the sentences at the spot where the paragraphs are thrust together.

Undo Mistakes with Undo Haste

That quaffing and drinking will undo you.
—RICHARD II, WILLIAM SHAKESPEARE

The Undo command undoes anything you do in Word, which includes formatting text, moving blocks, typing and deleting text — the whole enchilada. You have two handy ways to unleash the Undo command:

» Press Ctrl+Z.

» Click the Undo command button on the Quick Access toolbar.

I prefer using the Ctrl+Z key combination, but an advantage of the Undo command button is that it sports a drop-down menu that helps you review the past several actions you've taken, which can be undone.

» Regrettably, you cannot pick and choose from the Undo command button's drop-down menu; you can merely undo multiple actions with a single command.

» Word warns you should you attempt an action that cannot be undone. Proceed at your own peril.

>> The Undo command doesn't work when you have nothing to undo or when something simply cannot be undone. For example, you cannot undo a document save.

Undoing the Undo command with Redo

If you undo something and — whoops! — you didn't mean it, use the Redo command to set things back to the way they were. For example, you may type some text and then use Undo to "untype" the text. You can then use the Redo command to restore the typing. You have two choices:

>> Press Ctrl+Y.

 >> Click the Redo command button on the Quick Access toolbar.

The Redo command does exactly the opposite of whatever the Undo command does. So, if you type text, Undo untypes the text and Redo recovers the text. If you use Undo to recover deleted text, Redo deletes the text again.

Using the Repeat command

 When the Redo command has nothing left to redo, it changes functions and becomes the Repeat command. On the Quick Access toolbar, the command button changes as shown in the margin. The Repeat command's duty is to repeat the last thing you did in Word, whether it's typing text, applying a format, or carrying out a variety of other activities.

Lamentably, you can't use the Repeat command to ease your typing chores. That's because it repeats only the last single character you typed.

The keyboard shortcut for the Repeat command is Ctrl+Y, the same as the Redo command.

Chapter **5**

Search for This, Replace It with That

ittle Bo Peep has lost her sheep. Too bad she doesn't know about Word's Find and Replace commands — she could find the wayward ruminants in a matter of nanoseconds. Not only that, she could use search-and-replace to, say, replace all the sheep with Bitcoin. It's all cinchy after you understand and use the various Find and Replace command options. Sadly, only words are replaced. True, if Word could search-and-replace real things, there'd be fewer sheep in the world.

Text Happily Found

Finding text is one of the most basic and ancient tools available in a word processor. The only issue has been whether the command is called Find or Search. The terms Relentlessly Hunt Down and Fiendishly Locate were never considered.

>> In Word, finding duties are split between the traditional Find dialog box and the Navigation pane.

>> The online version of Word has only a single Find command, which is far more limited than the program version. Press the Ctrl+F key to activate it.

Finding a tidbit o' text

Don't bother with the ribbon! To find text in a document, press Ctrl+F, the memorable keyboard shortcut for the Find command. You see the Navigation pane, as shown in Figure 5-1.

Search text

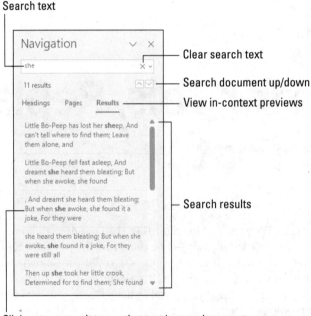

Clear search text

Search document up/down

View in-context previews

Search results

Click or tap a result to see that text in your document

In the Search Document box, type the text you want to locate. As you type, instances of matching text are highlighted in the document. Contextual chunks of text appear in the Navigation pane under the Results heading, as illustrated in Figure 5-1. To peruse found text, use the up and down arrows in the Navigation pane to hoppity-skip through the document, or click a text preview snippet to view that particular part of the document.

When text can't be found, the Navigation pane explains that "we" cannot find the text. Also, when too many tidbits of text are found, previews don't appear in the Navigation pane, which I find disappointing.

REMEMBER

>> To clear text from the Search Document box, click the X button found at the right end of the box.

>> Do not end the search text with a period unless you want to find the period, too. Word's Find command is persnickety.

>> Word finds text only in the current document (the one you see in the window). To find text in another document, switch to the other document's window and search again. Or, you can use the Search command in Windows, which is too messy to cover in this book.

Scouring your document with Advanced Find

The Navigation pane is a handy tool for locating text. In fact, I keep it open for all my documents. But when it comes to exercising some Find command muscles, you must turn to the more powerful Find and Replace dialog box. Its enlarged view is illustrated in Figure 5-2.

Reveal Search Options   Search-option superpowers

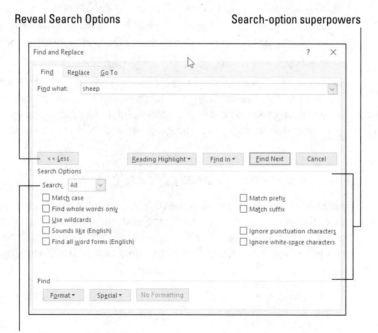

FIGURE 5-2:
The Find and Replace dialog box.

Set search direction

Follow these steps to conjure forth the Find and Replace dialog box, enlarged view:

1. **Click the Home tab.**

2. **In the Editing group, choose Find ⇨ Advanced Find.**

   The Find and Replace dialog box appears, with the Find tab forward. You use this dialog box to locate text in a document, but you want more power. So:

3. **Click the More button to reveal the dialog box's superpowers.**

   What you see now appears just like Figure 5-2.

4. **Type the search text into the Find What text box.**

5. **Use the dialog box's controls to make further adjustments.**

   Examples of using the various controls are found throughout this chapter.

6. **Click the Find Next button to locate the text.**

Once the text is found, you can edit it, change it, or click the Find Next button to continue looking for the same text.

After the Find command has scoured the entire document, you see an info box explaining that the search is finished. Click OK and then click the Cancel button to dismiss the Find and Replace dialog box.

REMEMBER

>> You can click outside the Find and Replace dialog box to edit found text or otherwise work in the document. Unlike other dialog boxes, this one is *nonmodal*, which means it shares the mouse and keyboard with the document window.

>> Though it's powerful, keep in mind that any options set in the Find and Replace dialog box remain set until deactivated. When you can't seem to locate text that you *know* is in a document, review this dialog box's settings. Disable the settings you no longer need, and then search again.

Find case-sensitive text

The Find command doesn't know the difference between *Pat* and *pat*: One is a noun; the other, a verb. To locate one and not the other, use the Advanced Find and Replace dialog box (refer to Figure 5-2). Select the Match Case option under Search Options. That way, *Pat* matches only words that start with an uppercase *P*.

Find a whole word

Word's Advanced Find command can locate *Pat* and not *pat*, but it might also flag the word *Pattern* at the start of a sentence. To avoid that situation, select the Find Whole Words Only option.

Find word variations

Two options in the Find and Replace dialog box assist you with finding words that may not be exactly what you're looking for:

>> **Sounds Like (English):** This option allows you to search for *homonyms,* or words that sound the same as the search word. These words include *their* and *there, deer* and *dear,* and *hear* and *here.* The command doesn't, however, locate rhyming words.

>> **Find All Word Forms (English):** This option expands the search to include different forms of the same word. With this option set, you can search for the word *hop,* and potential matches include *hops, hopped,* and *hopping.*

Search this way or that

The Find command searches from the insertion pointer's position to the end of a document and then back 'round the top again. To reverse its sense of direction, use the Search drop-down list (refer to Figure 5-2) to choose one of three direction options:

>> **Down:** The Find command searches from the insertion pointer's location to the end of the document.

>> **Up:** The Find command searches from the insertion pointer's location to the start of the document.

>> **All:** The Find command searches the entire document, from the insertion pointer's location down to the end of the document and back up to the beginning. Eventually, it stops at the point where the search began.

TIP

Two keyboard shortcuts are available to continue the search up or down. The Ctrl+PgDn key combination repeats the last search downward; the Ctrl+PgUp key combination repeats the most recent search upward. These keyboard shortcuts can change their function, so keep in mind that they only repeat a search immediately after you've used the Find command to initiate a search.

Finding stuff you can't type

The Find command is brilliant enough to locate non-typable items in your document, such as tab characters or red-colored text. The puzzle is how to input these details into the Find and Replace dialog box. The secret is to use the Format and Special buttons, lurking near the bottom of the Find and Replace dialog box (refer to Figure 5-2).

Find special characters

To hunt down special characters in a document, such as a tab or Enter key press, click the Special button in the Advanced Find dialog box. Up pops a list of 22 items that Word can search for but that you would have a dickens of a time typing.

From the menu's exhaustive list, here are the few items you may find handy:

>> **Any Character, Any Digit,** and **Any Letter** are options that represent, well, just about anything. These items can be used as wildcards for matching various word patterns.

>> **Paragraph Mark** (¶) is a special character that's the same as the Enter character — the one you press to end a paragraph.

>> **Tab Character** moves the insertion pointer to the next tab stop.

>> **White Space** is any number of blank characters: one or more spaces, tabs, empty lines, or a combination thereof.

>> **Caret Character** allows you to search for a caret (^) symbol, which may not seem like a big deal, but it is: Word uses the ^ symbol to find special text.

Choose an item from the list to search for the associated special character. When you do, a wildcard character is inserted into the Find What text box. This wildcard is prefixed with the ^ character followed by another character. For example, you see ^p to search for a paragraph (Enter key press), ^t to search for the tab character, ^w for whitespace, or even ^^ for the caret symbol.

Do not edit the wildcard (^) characters in the Find What box! They are the key to searching for the stuff you can't type.

Find formatting

In its most powerful superhero mode, the Find command can scour a document for text, paragraph, and other document formats. You can search for the formatting directly or as it's applied to specific text — which makes this feature kinda messy.

The secret to hunting down text formats is to use the Format button, found at the bottom of the Find and Replace dialog box, as shown earlier, in Figure 5-2. Click this button to view a menu full of formatting categories, such as Font, Paragraph, and Tabs. Choose a category to pluck out a specific format.

Suppose that you want to find the italicized text *red herring* in your document. Follow these steps:

1. **Click the Home tab.**

2. **In the Editing group, choose Find ⇨ Advanced Find.**

   The Find and Replace dialog box appears.

3. **Type the text you're searching for.**

   In this example, type *red herring*.

4. **Ensure that the dialog box details are displayed; click the More button, if necessary.**

5. **Click the No Formatting button to remove any previously applied formatting.**

   If the No Formatting button is disabled, you're good to go.

6. **Click the Format button and choose Font from the pop-up list.**

   The Find Font dialog box appears, which is identical to the Font dialog box, described in Chapter 10.

7. **Choose Italic as the font style.**

   You need not mess with any other options — only those that represent attributes to search.

8. **Click OK.**

   The Find Font dialog box goes away. Back in the Find and Replace dialog box, you see the text *Format: Font: Italic* appear below the Find What text box. These are the formatting attributes the Advanced Find command looks for.

9. **Click the Find Next button to locate the formatted text.**

If you want to search only for a format, leave the Find What text box blank (refer to Step 3). This way, you can search for formatting attributes without regard to text.

REMEMBER

The Find command retains any set formatting options! The next time you search text, ensure that you click the No Formatting button (refer to Step 5). Doing so removes any applied formatting attributes.

The Replace Part

Imagine Little Bo Peep's thrill as she uses Word's Find and Replace feature to help abandon her shepherdess career. Yes, she successfully replaced all those tailless sheep with lucrative Bitcoin. Granted, this change occurs only within a document, but she remains thrilled.

Replacing text

The same dialog box that finds text is also used for the find-and-replace operation. In fact, you can summon this dialog box in the same manner — just remember to click the Replace tab. Or, you can use the handy keyboard shortcut Ctrl+H, where the H means, "Hey! We ran out of logical keyboard shortcuts."

To globally change all instances of text throughout the document, follow these steps:

1. **Press the Ctrl+H keyboard shortcut.**

The Find and Replace dialog box appears with the Replace tab forward, shown in Figure 5-3.

FIGURE 5-3:
The Replace tab
in the Find and
Replace
dialog box.

2. **In the Find What box, type the text you want to replace.**

For example, *sheep*.

3. **In the Replace With box, type the replacement text.**

For example, *Bitcoin*.

4. **Click the Find Next button.**

At this step, the Replace command works like the Find command: Word scours your document for the text you typed in the Find What box. When the text is found, it's selected on the screen; proceed with Step 6.

When the text isn't found, start over again with Step 2 — or just abandon your efforts and close the dialog box.

5. **Click the Replace button.**

The found text (selected) is replaced.

6. **Repeat Steps 4 and 5 until all found text is replaced.**

Word reports the results when the original text can no longer be found.

If you're feeling rather confident, click the Replace All button in Step 5 to search-and-replace the text throughout the document in a single step.

>> If you goof up the replace operation, use the Undo command (Ctrl+Z) to restore a replaced word or the entire document, if necessary. See Chapter 4 for more information on Undo. Although:

>> For a large document, Word may inform you that it cannot undo a document-wide Replace All operation.

>> If you don't type anything in the Replace With box, Word replaces your text with *nothing!* It's wanton destruction!

>> You can use Replace to remove empty paragraphs, extra spaces, or tabs from a document: Search for two tabs (^t^t) and replace them with a single tab (^t), for example. Refer to the earlier section "Find special characters" for details on typing the non-typeable characters into the Find What and Replace With text boxes.

Replacing formatting

Just as you can search for specific text formats, you can use the Find and Replace dialog box to replace them. It's at this point that the Replace command becomes frighteningly powerful. For example, you can search for old, boring underlined text and replace it with italics. Here are my carefully crafted directions for using this lethal tool:

1. **Press the Ctrl+H keyboard shortcut to bring up the Find and Replace dialog box, Replace tab forward.**

2. **Ensure that both Find What and Replace With text boxes are empty.**

Truly you are a brave soul if you want to both find and replace text *and* formatting.

3. **Click the More button to expand the dialog box.**

When the dialog box looks as it does in Figure 5-2, you're good.

4. **Click the mouse in the Find What dialog box.**

Yes, even if the box is empty, this step is how you direct Word to search for formatting.

5. **Click the No Formatting button to remove any previously assigned formats.**

6. **Use the Format button to pluck a format category from the menu.**

For example, choose Font to display the Find Font dialog box. To replace the underline style, choose the solid underline from the Underline Style menu.

7. **Click OK to set the format to search for.**

8. **Click the mouse in the Replace With dialog box.**

9. **Click the No Formatting button to remove any preset formats.**

10. **Use the Format button to select a format category.**

For example, choose Font and select Italic from the Font Style list.

11. **Click OK when you're done setting the format.**

At this point, the dialog box should show the format to find and the format to replace it.

12. **Click the Find Next button.**

Proceed to review each formatting instance.

13. **Click the Replace button to confirm replacing the format.**

14. **Continue the process until the entire document has been scanned.**

If you're feeling confident, click the Replace All button at Steps 12 or 13.

TIP

The key to this operation is getting the format correct. Therefore, I recommend that you review the formatting options presented in Part 3 of this book. The more complex the format replacement, the more carefully you must apply the formats to the Find What and Replace With options, as described in this section.

Chapter **6**

Blocks o' Text

Writing is about blocks, from the moveable printing blocks used by the ancient Chinese to the universal writer's block. In word processing, the word *blocks* refers to selected chunks of text in a document, which I believe you'll find more useful to your productivity than the other types of blocks.

Meet Mr. Block

Mr. Block visits your document when you select text. He has a beginning and an end. He can be any size, from a single character to the entire document. Figure 6-1 shows a block of selected text in a document.

When a block of text is selected, certain actions affect only the text within the block. These actions include formatting, copying, moving, deleting, and more.

To help format a selected block of text, the Mini toolbar appears, illustrated in Figure 6-2. This pop-up thingy hosts popular commands found on the ribbon, allowing you to quickly format the block of text.

Selected block of text

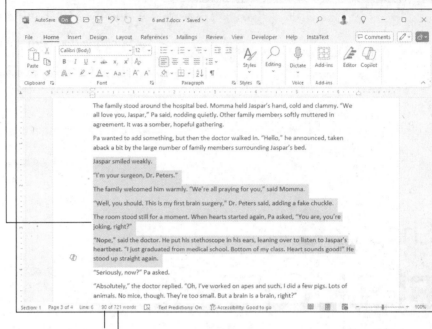

FIGURE 6-1:
A block of text
is selected.

Words in the block

Words in the document

Mini toolbar   Mini toolbar with right-click menu

FIGURE 6-2:
The Mini toolbar
and the block
pop-up menu.

Some people dislike the Mini toolbar. It can be disabled, which is a topic covered in Chapter 33. If you love the Mini toolbar, you can right-click in a document to pop it up at any time. When you do, a menu also appears below the toolbar, as shown on the right in Figure 6-2.

>> A block of text in Word includes both the text and its formatting.

>> Graphics and other non-text elements can also be selected as a block. In fact, you can select graphics along with text in the same block.

>> The status bar's word-count statistics reflect the number of words in a selected block of text (refer to Figure 6-1).

>> When a block is selected, the Find command locates text within the block. Refer to Chapter 5 for more information on the Find command.

>> Items on the Mini toolbar change depending on what's selected or right-clicked.

>> The Mini toolbar disappears after a few moments of neglect. Press the Esc key to hide it at once.

TECHNICAL STUFF

>> Selecting text also means selecting invisible characters such as the tab or the Enter character, which marks the end of a paragraph. When a block is selected, Word shows the Enter character as an extra blank space highlighted at the end of a paragraph. Selecting this blank selects the entire paragraph as a block. To avoid selecting the Enter character, don't select the blank space at the end of a paragraph.

Mark a Block of Text

You can use the keyboard to select text. You can use the mouse. You can use both at one time. Word comes with an abundance of options to confuse you: Pick a block-selection method as your favorite and feel free to ignore the rest.

Using the keyboard to select text

The secret to using the keyboard's cursor keys to select text is to press and hold the Shift key as you move the insertion pointer. While the Shift key is down, Word's standard cursor-key commands not only move the insertion pointer but also select chunks of text. Table 6-1 lists common key combinations.

TABLE 6-1   **Keyboard Selection Wizardry**

To Select This	Press This
A character at a time to the left of the insertion pointer	Shift+←
A character at a time to the right of the insertion pointer	Shift+→
A block of text from the insertion pointer to the beginning of the line	Shift+Home
A block of text from the insertion pointer to the end of the line	Shift+End
A block of text from the insertion pointer to a line above	Shift+↑
A block of text from the insertion pointer to a line below	Shift+↓

TIP

Though you can use any keyboard cursor-movement command, including some that move the insertion pointer a great distance, I recommend using this Shift-key technique for selecting only small chunks of text. Otherwise, you may end up tying your fingers into knots.

>> See Chapter 3 for the full list of Word's cursor-key commands.

>> Either Shift key works, although I prefer to use the left Shift key and then work the arrow keys on the right side of the keyboard.

Marking a block with the mouse

Mickey may rule a kingdom, but your computer's mouse rules over text selection in Word.

Drag over text to select it

Position the mouse pointer at the start of the text block, and then drag the mouse over the text you want to select. As you drag, the text becomes highlighted or selected.

TIP

>> This technique works best when you use the mouse to drag over only the text you can see in the document window. When you try to select text beyond this area, you must select and scroll, which can be unwieldy.

>> Using the mouse to select text in a table is funky. See Chapter 19.

>> Also see Chapter 33, which covers how to adjust Word so that you can use the mouse to select individual letters, as opposed to gobbling up entire words at a time.

Click the mouse to select text

A speedy way to select specific sizes of chunks of text is to match the power of the mouse with the dexterity of your button-clicking index finger. Table 6-2 explains some of these techniques.

TABLE 6-2   **Mouse Selection Arcana**

To Select This Chunk of Text	Click the Mouse Thusly
A single word	Double-click the word.
A line	Move the mouse pointer into the left margin beside the line you want to select. The mouse pointer changes to an arrow pointing northeastward. Click the mouse to select a line of text. Drag the mouse up or down to select several lines.
A sentence	Position the insertion pointer over the sentence and Ctrl+click (press the Ctrl key and click the mouse).
A paragraph	Point the mouse somewhere in the paragraph's midst and click thrice (triple-click).

Select text with the old poke-and-point

TIP

Here's the best way to select a chunk of text of any size, especially when that chunk of text is larger than what you can see in the document window:

1. **Click the mouse to set the insertion pointer wherever you want the block to start.**

   I call this location the *anchor point.*

2. **Scroll the document.**

   You must use the scroll bar or the mouse wheel to scroll the document. If you use the cursor movement keys, you reposition the insertion pointer, which isn't what you want.

3. **Hold down the Shift key and click the mouse where you want the block to end.**

   The text from the insertion pointer to wherever you clicked the mouse is selected as a block.

Using the F8 key to mark a block

TECHNICAL
STUFF

The seemingly random F8 key activates Word's Extend Selection command. Press this key to "drop anchor" at the insertion pointer's location. Then use either the mouse or the cursor keys to select text. In fact, you can't do anything but select text while Extend Selection mode is active.

To exit Extend Selection mode, you must either do something with the block of text or press the Esc key to cancel.

>> To help you with the F8 key and Extend Selection mode, right-click the status bar and choose the Selection Mode item. The text *Extend Selection* appears on the status bar whenever this mode is active.

>> Not only can you use the cursor keys while in Extend Selection mode — any of the character keys works as well. Text is selected from the anchor point to the character you type. Type an *N*, for example, and all text between the insertion pointer and the next letter *N* is selected.

>> You can also use the Find command to locate a specific bit of text in Extend Selection mode. Word highlights all text between the anchor and the text that the Find command locates.

>> Press the F8 key twice to select the current word.

>> Press the F8 key thrice (three times) to select the current sentence.

>> Press the F8 key four times to select the current paragraph as a block of text.

>> Press the F8 key five times to select the entire document, from top to bottom.

>> Be aware that no matter how many times you press F8, it always drops anchor. Whether you press F8 once or five times, Word is still in Extend Selection mode. Do something with the block or press Esc to cancel this mode.

Blocking the whole dang-doodle document

The biggest block you can mark is an entire document. Word has a specific command to do it. Follow these steps:

1. **Click the Home tab.**

2. **In the Editing group, choose Select ⇨ Select All.**

   The entire document is marked as a single block o' text.

And now, the keyboard shortcut: Press Ctrl+A to select an entire document as a block.

Deselecting a block

When you mark a block of text and change your mind, you must unmark, or *deselect*, the text. Here are a few handy ways to do it:

>> **Move the insertion pointer.** It doesn't matter how you move the insertion pointer, with the keyboard or with the mouse, but doing so deselects the block. (This trick doesn't work when you use the F8, Extend Selection, key to select text.)

>> **Press the Esc key and then the** ←**.** This method works to end Extend Selection mode.

>> **Press Shift+F5.** The Shift+F5 key combo (refer to Chapter 3) is the "go back" command, but it also deselects a block of text *and* returns you to the text you were editing before making the selection.

Block Manipulation

You can block punches, block hats, block and tackle, play with building blocks and engine blocks, take nerve blocks, suffer from mental blocks, jog for blocks, and, naturally, block text. But what can you do with these marked blocks of text?

Why, plenty of things! You can apply a format to all text in the block, copy a block, move a block, search for text in a block, proof a block, print a block, and even delete a block. This section focuses on the basics of copying and moving a block.

REMEMBER

>> Blocks must be selected before you can manipulate them. See the first half of this chapter.

>> When a block of text is marked, various Word commands affect only the text in that block.

>> To replace a block, type some text. The new text (specifically, the initial character) replaces the entire block.

>> To delete a block, press the Delete or Backspace key. *Thwoop!* The block is gone. (You must make the "thwoop" noise yourself.)

>> Formatting commands can be applied to any marked block of text — specifically, character and paragraph formatting. See Part 3 of this book.

>> Document proofing is covered in Chapter 7.

>> Also see Chapter 32 for information on Word's bizarre yet potentially useful Collect and Paste feature.

Copying a block

Selected blocks of text are easily duplicated and copied to another part of the document. The original block remains untouched by this operation. Follow these steps to copy a block of text:

1. **Mark the block.**

Detailed instructions for completing this task are offered in the first half of this chapter.

2. **Click the Home tab.**

3. **In the Clipboard group, click the Copy command button.**

You get no visual clue that the text has been copied; it remains selected.

4. **Click to set the insertion pointer at the position where you want to place the block's copy.**

Don't worry if it looks like the text won't fit! Word inserts the block into the text.

5. **Click the Paste command button.**

The block of text is inserted into your text just as though you had typed it there yourself.

Copy-and-paste is a common activity in Windows, so you probably know the common keyboard shortcuts: Ctrl+C to copy and Ctrl+V to paste. These shortcuts work in Steps 3 and 5 in the list, respectively.

TIP

>> See the later section "Setting the pasted text format" to discover various ways you can paste text into a document.

>> The Paste command continues to paste the copied text, over and over, until something else is copied (or cut). Pasting text again pastes down another copy of the block.

>> Because copy-and-paste is a common activity in Windows, you can paste the copied text into another document or even into another program window. Any program that accepts text input can have copied text pasted into it.

Moving a block

To move a block of text, you select the text and then *cut* and paste. This process is almost the same as copying a block, described in the preceding section, although in Step 3 you choose the Cut command button (shown in the margin) or press Ctrl+X on the keyboard. Otherwise, all steps are the same.

Don't be alarmed when the selected block of text vanishes! This result is cutting in action; the block of text is being *moved*, not copied. You see the block of text again when you paste it.

REMEMBER

>> Cut (and copied) text is stored in the Clipboard. See the later section "Viewing the Clipboard."

>> If you screw up, the Ctrl+Z Undo shortcut undoes a block move.

Setting the pasted text format

When you paste text in Word, you see the Paste Options icon appear, as shown in the margin. This button allows you to select formatting to apply to the pasted block. For example, you can choose to retain the formatting as pasted, choose to paste in the text plain and unformatted, or choose to have the pasted text match the style of the text around it.

To work the Paste Options button, click it with the mouse or press and release the Ctrl key on the keyboard. You see a menu of options, illustrated in Figure 6-3.

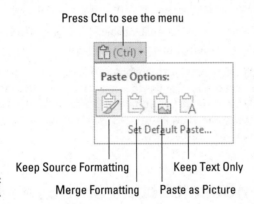

FIGURE 6-3:
Pasting options.

Table 6-3 summarizes some of the common paste options.

For example, to keep only text with a copied or cut block (no formatting), press the Ctrl key and then tap the T key after pasting. These are two separate, sequential key presses, not Ctrl+T.

Using the Paste Options icon is utterly optional. In fact, you can continue typing or working in Word and the icon bows out, fading away like some nebbish who boldly asked a power blonde to go out with him and she utterly failed to recognize his existence. Like that.

TABLE 6-3 **Paste Option Options**

Icon	Keyboard Shortcut	Name	Description
	K	Keep Source Formatting	The formatting is okay; don't do a thing.
	M	Merge Formatting	Reformat the pasted block so that it matches the text it's being pasted into.
	U	Paste as Picture	Paste in a graphical image of the text.
	T	Keep Text Only	Just paste in the text — no formatting.

>> Click the Set Default Paste text (refer to Figure 6-3) to direct Word to permanently deal with pasted text. It's a handy trick, especially when you find yourself repeatedly choosing the same Paste Options format.

>> The items on the Paste Options icon — and more — are also found on the Paste button menu, located on the Home tab in the Clipboard group.

>> If you find the Paste Options button annoying — for example, if it's blocking text you need to see — press the Esc key to banish it.

>> You can control whether the Paste Options icon appears after pasting text: Click the File tab and choose Options to summon the Word Options dialog box. Choose Advanced. In the Cut, Copy, and Paste area, add or remove the check mark by the option Show Paste Options Button When Content Is Pasted to show or hide the icon, respectively.

TECHNICAL STUFF

Using the mouse to copy or move a block

When you need to move a block only a short distance, you can use the mouse to drag-move or drag-copy the block.

 To move any selected block of text, hover the mouse pointer anywhere in the blocked text and then drag the block to its new location. As you drag the block, the mouse pointer changes, as shown in the margin. This mouse pointer modification means that you're moving a block of text.

To copy a block of text, point the mouse pointer at the block — just as though you were going to move the block — but press and hold down the Ctrl key as you drag. When you drag the block, the mouse pointer changes to resemble the icon shown in the margin. This change is your clue that the block is being copied and not just moved.

REMEMBER

The mouse move/copy trick works best when you're moving or copying a block to a location you can see in the document window. Otherwise, you're scrolling the document with the mouse while you're playing with blocks, which is like trying to grab an angry mongoose.

>> When you drag a block of text with the mouse, you're not copying or cutting it to the Clipboard. You cannot use the Paste (Ctrl+V) command to paste the dragged block again.

TECHNICAL STUFF

>> To create a *linked copy* of the block, drag the mouse and hold down *both* the Shift and Ctrl keys. When you release the mouse button, the copied block plops down into your document with a dark highlight. It's your clue that the copy is linked to the original; changes in the original are reflected in the copy and vice versa. If the linked copy doesn't update, right-click the text and choose the Update Link command.

Viewing the Clipboard

All text you copy or cut is stored in an ethereal location called the *Clipboard* — the standard cut-copy-paste holding bin for text in Windows. In Word, however, the Clipboard is more powerful than in other Windows programs. Specifically, you can use the Clipboard task pane to examine items cut or copied and then paste them again in your document in any order.

To copy a chunk of text from the task pane to a document, heed these steps:

1. **Place the insertion pointer in the document where you want the pasted text to appear.**

2. **Click the Home tab.**

3. **In the Clipboard group, click the dialog box launcher.**

   You see the Clipboard task pane, along with all text cut or copied since you've started the Word program, similar to what's shown in Figure 6-4.

4. **Click an item to paste its contents into the document.**

FIGURE 6-4:
The Clipboard
task pane.

Unlike using the Ctrl+V keyboard shortcut or the Paste button on the ribbon, you can paste text from the Clipboard in any order, and even summon text you copied or cut hours ago or text you copied or cut from other Microsoft Office programs.

Also see Chapter 32 for information on using the Collect and Paste feature, which takes advantage of the Clipboard task pane.

IN THIS CHAPTER

» **Dealing with typos and spelling errors**

» **Checking AutoCorrect settings**

» **Fixing grammatical boo-boos**

» **Adding or ignoring unknown words**

» **Correcting words automatically**

» **Reviewing your document**

» **Customizing proofing options**

Chapter **7**

Spell It Write

The reason that English is the most popular language on the planet has nothing to do with its sensible spelling and logical grammar. The quote attributed to Mark Twain goes, "I have no respect for a man who can spell a word only one way." Alas, Word has better ideas. It automatically corrects common English spelling errors and typos and offers suggestions (many of them accurate) for the embarrassing collection of exceptions commonly referred to as English grammar.

Check Your Spelling

Word's Spell Check feature works the second you start typing. Offending or unknown words are immediately underlined with the red zigzag of shame. Leave the word be, correct it, or add it to your personal spelling dictionary out of spite.

» Spell-checking works thanks to a digital dictionary stocked with zillions of words, all spelled correctly. Every time you type a word, it's checked against this dictionary. When the word isn't found, it's marked as suspect in the document.

TIP

>> Don't let the red zigzag of a failed elementary education perturb you. My advice is to keep typing. Focus on getting your thoughts on the page. Go back later to fix the inevitable typos.

>> The Spell Check feature also underlines repeated words in red. Your choice is to either delete the repeated word or just ignore it.

>> Word doesn't spell-check words with numbers in them or words written in all capitals.

>> Some misspelled words are corrected automatically without your seeing the red zigzag underline. See the later section "AutoCorrect in Action."

Fixing a misspelled word

To address that red zigzag of shame, heed these steps:

1. **Click the misspelled word.**

Up pops a shortcut menu, with the spelling issue highlighted and alternatives suggested, as shown in Figure 7-1.

2. **From the menu, choose the proper word.**

In Figure 7-1, the word *laughs* fits the bill.

If the word you intended to type isn't on the list, don't fret: Just take another stab at spelling the word phonetically and then correct it again. For extremely difficult spelling, type the word into a search engine on the web, which may also offer a correct spelling.

FIGURE 7-1:
Deal with
that typo.

Dealing with incorrectly flagged words

Occasionally, Word's spell checker bumps into a word it doesn't recognize, such as your last name or perhaps your city's name. Word dutifully casts doubt on the word by scribbling beneath it the notorious red zigzag. Yes, this is one of those cases where the computer is wrong.

To correct a falsely accused word, right-click it. Choose one of these two icons from the Spelling submenu, referenced earlier, in Figure 7-1:

 Click the **Ignore All icon** to direct Word to ignore the term and accept it as correctly spelled throughout the entire document — for example, Zagdazox, the chief bad guy in your alien invasion novel.

 Click the **Add to Dictionary icon** to set the word into your custom dictionary. The word is no longer flagged as misspelled in the current document or any other document — for example, Zagdazox, if that's your name.

If the word is intentionally misspelled and you don't want to ignore all instances or add it to the custom dictionary, just tolerate the angry red zigzag and leave it be.

>> See the section "Rechecking a document," later in this chapter, for information on reversing your decision to ignore a spelling error.

>> For information on viewing or editing the custom dictionary, see the later section "Editing the custom dictionary."

THE 25 MOST FREQUENTLY MISSPELLED WORDS

a lot	atheist	gauge	maneuver	ridiculous
accidentally	collectible	grammar	no one	separate
acquire	consensus	independent	occurrence	supersede
amateur	definite	kernel	realize	their
argument	embarrass	liaison	receive	weird

AutoCorrect in Action

Word quickly fixes hundreds of common typos and spelling errors on the fly, so you may never see the embarrassing red zigzag. The AutoCorrect feature is responsible — but you must be quick to see it.

For example, in Word you can't type the word *mispell* (with only one *s*). That's because AutoCorrect fixes that typo the split second you press the spacebar or use punctuation to end the word.

AutoCorrect also converts common text shortcuts into their proper single characters. For example, type **(C)** and AutoCorrect properly inserts the © copyright symbol. Ditto for typing **(TM)** for the trademark. Typing - - > is translated into an arrow, and **:)** becomes a happy face. ☺

Beyond spelling, AutoCorrect fixes common punctuation. It automatically capitalizes the first letter of a sentence. AutoCorrect capitalizes the letter *I* when you forget to, properly capitalizes the names of days, fixes the iNVERSE cAPS lOCK pROBLEM, plus other common typos.

Undoing an AutoCorrect correction

You can reverse AutoCorrect instant changes, but only when you're quick. The secret is to press Ctrl+Z (the Undo command) immediately after AutoCorrect makes its correction. The change is gone.

When you're not quick, you can peruse AutoCorrect's changes in a document. These are flagged by a weensy blue rectangle that appears under the first letter of the corrected text, as illustrated in Figure 7-2. Position the mouse pointer at the blue rectangle, and click to see various AutoCorrect options, also illustrated in Figure 7-2.

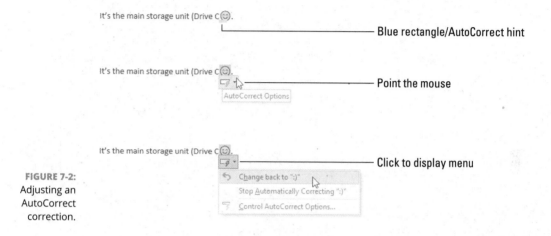

It's the main storage unit (Drive C☺).   — Blue rectangle/AutoCorrect hint

It's the main storage unit (Drive C☺). — Point the mouse
AutoCorrect Options

It's the main storage unit (Drive C☺). — Click to display menu
↺ Change back to ":)"
Stop Automatically Correcting ":)"
⌐ Control AutoCorrect Options...

FIGURE 7-2:
Adjusting an
AutoCorrect
correction.

To restore the text to how it was typed originally, choose the option Change Back to *whatever*, where *whatever* is the original text (shown as the :) in Figure 7-2).

To prevent AutoCorrect from ever making the change again, choose the option Stop Automatically Correcting *whatever*. Keep in mind that, although the text won't be automatically corrected, it may show up as a typo or a spelling error.

See the later section "Adjusting AutoCorrect settings" for information on the final option, Control AutoCorrect Options.

Creating a new AutoCorrect entry

It's possible, though not obvious, to create your own AutoCorrect entries. Heed these steps:

1. **Right-click a misspelled word that you want to add as an AutoCorrect entry.**

   The word must be flagged as misspelled, underlined by the red zigzag of shame.

2. **From the Spelling submenu, choose the menu to the right of the correctly spelled word.**

An example is shown in Figure 7-3.

Right-click the mangled word   Submenu by the correct spelling

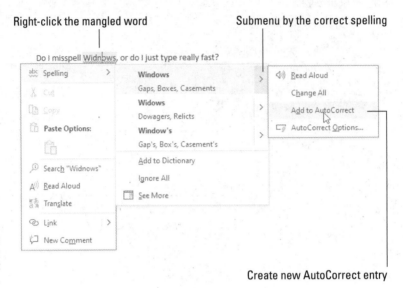

FIGURE 7-3:
Adding an
AutoCorrect
entry.

Create new AutoCorrect entry

3. **Choose Add to AutoCorrect.**

The spelling error is added to AutoCorrect's repertoire. It's automatically corrected for you from now on.

Words you accidentally add as AutoCorrect entries can be removed, should you make a mistake. See the next section.

Adjusting AutoCorrect settings

To control how AutoCorrect behaves, as well as manage the words it corrects, follow these steps:

1. **Click the File tab.**

2. **Choose Options.**

The Word Options dialog box appears.

3. **Choose the Proofing category on the left side of the window.**

4. **Click the AutoCorrect Options button.**

The AutoCorrect dialog box appears, with the AutoCorrect tab forward.

The AutoCorrect tab lists all of AutoCorrect's superpowers, such as capitalizing the first letter of a sentence. Use the Exceptions button to manage specific words where the rules need not apply, such as abbreviations.

More specific to your AutoCorrect purging desires is the list at the bottom of the dialog box showing those words automatically replaced as you type. There you may find items such as *teh,* which is autocorrected to *the.* You also find words you've added to the list. To remove an entry, click to select it and then click the Delete button.

To manually add an entry, use the Replace and With text boxes to set the incorrect word and its correction. Click the Add button to create the new entry.

Click the OK button when you're done adjusting, and then close the Word Options dialog box.

Also see Chapter 33 for information on disabling various AutoCorrect and Auto-Format features.

Grammar Be Good

Mark Twain once referred to English spelling as "drunken." If that's true, English grammar must be a hallucination. To help you detox, Word offers on-the-fly grammar checking. It works just like having your eighth grade English teacher inside your computer — only it's all the time and not just during third period.

Word's grammar checker works like the spell checker. In fact, both tools fall under the category of document proofing. With grammatical blunders, however, the offenses are flagged with a frigid blue double underline, as shown in Figure 7-4 (although the underline looks gray in this book). That's your hint of Word's sense of grammatical justice.

To address a grammar issue, click the blue-underlined text (refer to Figure 7-3). Use the pop-up menu to discover what's wrong and, optionally, choose an alternative. You can also choose to ignore the error, which I find myself doing quite often.

>> Most of Word's grammar suggestions can be cheerfully ignored. In fact, I know many English teachers who disagree with the grammar checker more than they disagree with each other.

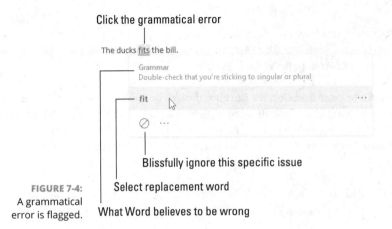

Click the grammatical error

The ducks fits the bill.

Grammar
Double-check that you're sticking to singular or plural

fit

⊘ …

Blissfully ignore this specific issue

FIGURE 7-4:
A grammatical
error is flagged.

Select replacement word

What Word believes to be wrong

>> The most common source of grammatical woe in English is *verb agreement,* or matching the subject quantity to the correct verb. In Figure 7-4, the subject *ducks* is plural, but the verb *fits* is third person singular.

>> The grammar checker is excellent at spotting two spaces between words when you need only one space. It's not so good at spotting fragments.

>> You may see false grammar errors when using Word's revision tracking feature with the No Markup setting enabled. Reveal all revision marks to see what's up. Refer to Chapter 26 for details.

>> To customize or turn off grammar checking, refer to the section "Disabling automatic proofing" later in this chapter.

All-at-Once Document Proofing

If you prefer to ignore the red zigzag underline of shame, or when this feature is disabled, you can perform a final document all-at-once proof. Word dutifully steps through each boo-boo in your document, explaining what it is and why you're a bad person for using it.

Reviewing all those errors

To perform all-at-once document proofing, top to bottom, follow these steps:

1. **Click the Home tab.**

2. **In the Editor group, click the Editor button.**

The Editor pane appears. Witness a rude judgment of your grammatical abilities, categorized into an ugly collection of spelling and grammar errors.

3. **Click the Spelling item.**

   This button is located below the Corrections heading.

4. **Review each spelling error and deal with the offense.**

   You can choose a suggested word, retype it, ignore it, or add it to the dictionary, for example.

5. **Click the forward chevron to page through the remaining spelling errors.**

After you're done checking the spelling, repeat the process by choosing Grammar at Step 3.

REMEMBER

>> You can easily enter a trancelike state while you're proofing and find yourself clicking the Ignore button too quickly. My advice: Use the Undo command, Ctrl+Z, to go back and change text that you may not have paid attention to.

WARNING

>> Word disables its on-the-fly proofing when your document grows larger than a certain size — say, 100 pages. You see a warning message when this change happens. At this point, you must perform an all-at-once document check, as described in this section.

>> Commands for document proofing are also found on the ribbon's Review tab.

Rechecking a document

When you're uncertain about proofing — for example, you feel you may have mistakenly clicked the Ignore or Ignore All options — you can direct Word to recheck the entire document. Obey these steps:

1. **Click the File tab.**

2. **Choose Options to display the Word Options dialog box.**

3. **Choose the Proofing category.**

4. **Click the Recheck Document button.**

   It's found beneath the heading When Correcting Spelling and Grammar in Word.

5. **Click the Yes button to confirm that you want to un-ignore items you've chosen to ignore.**

6. **Click the OK button to dismiss the Word Options dialog box.**

Word chews through your document afresh, flagging all those words and items you chose to ignore.

>> Rechecking a document doesn't undo any additions you've made to Word's custom dictionary. See the later section "Editing the custom dictionary."

>> If spelling and grammar errors fail to appear after rechecking, the option to hide them might be enabled, as described in the later section "Hiding all proofing errors in a document." Also see the section "Dealing with Word's refusal to spell-check."

Document Proofing Settings

Whether you adore or detest Word's capability to ridicule your language skills, you have the final say-so, with plenty of settings and options to control Word's document-proofing tools, turning them on or off at your whim.

Editing the custom dictionary

You build the custom dictionary by adding properly spelled words that are flagged as misspelled. You can also manually add words, remove words, or just browse the dictionary to see whether you're making old Noah Webster jealous. Follow these steps:

1. **Click the File tab.**

2. **Choose Options to display the Word Options dialog box.**

3. **Choose Proofing.**

4. **Click the Custom Dictionaries button.**

   The Custom Dictionaries dialog box appears.

   Word uses the file RoamingCustom.dic as its custom dictionary. You may see other files in the list, such as those for foreign languages (if installed). You might see custom dictionaries from older versions of Microsoft Word if you've upgraded.

5. **Select the item RoamingCustom.dic (Default).**

6. **Click the button labeled Edit Word List.**

   The custom dictionary's words appear in a scrolling list.

To add a word to the custom dictionary, type it in the Word(s) text box. Click the Add button.

To remove a word from the custom dictionary, select the word from the scrolling list. Click the Delete button.

Click the OK button when you're done with the custom dictionary. Then click the various OK buttons to close the open dialog boxes and return to the document.

Disabling automatic proofing

To banish those angry red and bitter blue underlines from a document, which effectively disables on-the-fly document proofing, follow these steps:

1. **Click the File tab and choose Options.**

   The Word Options dialog box appears.

2. **On the left side of the dialog box, choose Proofing.**

3. **Remove the check mark by the item Check Spelling as You Type.**

4. **While you're at it, remove the check mark by the item Mark Grammar Errors as You Type.**

5. **Click the OK button.**

If you'd rather just limit grammatical proofing, after Step 4, click the Settings button found in the section When Correcting Spelling and Grammar in Word. Use the Grammar Settings dialog box to uncheck those items you no longer desire Word to mark as offensive.

REMEMBER

You can train Word to ignore specific grammar incidents by clicking the option to ignore a rule when it's flagged in the document.

Hiding all proofing errors in a document

It's possible to direct Word to continue to spell-check yet hide the angry red zig-zag and chilly blue underlines. All-at-once document checking still works, and words are still flagged as misspelled, but they don't appear as such in the text. To hide the proofing marks, obey these steps:

1. **Summon the Proofing area in the Word Options dialog box.**

   Refer to Steps 1–3 in the preceding section.

2. At the bottom of the right side of the Word Options dialog box, place check marks by the options Hide Spelling Errors in This Document Only and Hide Grammar Errors in This Document Only.

3. Click OK.

The proofing flags disappear throughout the document.

When you open a document where proofing is disabled, a warning appears below the ribbon. Click the button to reactivate document proofing, or you can dismiss the warning.

Dealing with Word's refusal to spell-check

Word recognizes English spelling and grammar errors because one of the attributes applied to a document's text is a proofing language. If you know a word is misspelled (in English) and document proofing isn't disabled (refer to the preceding section), follow these steps:

1. Select the text that isn't being proofed.

2. Click the Review tab on the ribbon.

3. In the Language group, click the Language button and choose Set Proofing Language.

The Language dialog box appears. The selected option should be your native language, such as English (United States). If not, choose this language, lest Word employ its proofing skills in some foreign tongue.

4. Uncheck the box by the option Do Not Check Spelling or Grammar.

5. Click OK.

These steps should address the issue. Conversely, if you plan to use a foreign language in your text, you can apply the language attribute to the text so that Word performs proofing in that language as well. As they say in France, "*Cool.*"

Chapter **8**

Documents New, Saved, and Opened

I like the word *document.* It's elegant. It's much better than saying "a file" or "that thing I created with my word processor." A document can include everything from a quick shopping list to a vast cycle of medieval fantasy novels you keep reading despite knowing that the TV version didn't end so well.

Regardless of size or importance, a word processing file is called a *document.* It's the result of your efforts in Word. You create new documents, save them, open old documents, and close documents. This is the document cycle.

Some Terms to Get Out of the Way

TECHNICAL STUFF

To best understand the document concept, you must escape the confines of Word and wander into the larger dominion of computer storage. A basic understanding of files and storage is necessary if you're to get the most from your word processing efforts.

File: A Word document is a file. A *file* on a computer is information stored for the long term, which can be recalled again and shared with others. Windows manages files and their storage, backup, copying, moving, and renaming.

Folder: Files dwell in containers called folders. A *folder* stores files and other folders, which creates a hierarchical structure for data storage. This system is how folders play a role in file organization.

Local storage: Files are kept for the long term, saved to your computer's mass storage system. Because this hardware exists on your computer, it's referred to as *local* storage.

Cloud storage: Files can also be kept for long-term storage on the Internet. This storage is commonly referred to as *cloud* storage. For Word (and the rest of Microsoft Office), the preferred form of cloud storage is Microsoft OneDrive. Files saved to cloud storage are available to your computer as well, but the benefit is that you can access your cloud storage from any Internet-connected device.

Behold! A New Document

To conjure a new document when Word first starts, choose a template thumbnail as presented on the Word Start screen; the Blank thumbnail presents a fresh, empty document.

When Word is already up and running, press the Ctrl+N keyboard shortcut to summon a new, blank document. Or, if you desire to use a template for a new document, heed these directions:

1. **Click the File tab.**

   The File screen appears. A few recent templates appear atop the list, but you want more!

2. **Choose New from the left side of the window.**

   The New screen shows popular templates and recently opened documents.

3. **Choose a thumbnail to begin a new document using a template.**

   A new Word document window appears, ready for typing action.

HOW HUMONGOUS CAN A WORD DOCUMENT GET?

The quick answer is that no limit is assigned to the length of a Word document. If you like, your document can be thousands of pages long. Even so, I don't recommend putting this limit to the test.

The longer the document, the more apt Word is to mess up. You probably won't encounter any issues for typical-size documents, even those of 100 pages or more. For larger projects, however, I recommend splitting your work into chapter-size chunks. Organize those chapter documents in their own folder.

You can start as many new documents as are needed. Word lets you work with several documents at a time.

>> When the Backstage is disabled, Word opens with a new, blank document. See Chapter 33 for information on disabling the Backstage.

>> See Chapter 24 for details on how best to work with multiple document windows, all open at once.

>> Chapter 16 contains information on templates, which can greatly boost your performance by providing common document elements, including preset text and styles, for you automatically.

Save Your Stuff!

It doesn't matter whether you're writing the next Great American Novel or jotting down notes for tonight's meeting of the galactic rebel alliance's subcommittee for hairstylist selection, the most important thing you can do to a document is *save it*.

Save! Save! Save!

Saving creates a permanent copy of the document, encoding the text as a file. After saving, you can work on the document again, publish it electronically, or print it now or at any time in the future.

Saving a document for the first time

You don't have to complete a document before you save it. No! You should save immediately — right after you write "Once upon a time" or "Dear Editor." Follow these steps:

1. **Press Ctrl+S.**

You see the Save This File dialog box, shown in Figure 8-1. If it doesn't appear, the document has already been saved for the first time. See the later section "Saving or updating a document."

Filename

Filename extension
(set by Word)

FIGURE 8-1:
The Save This File
dialog box.

View the Save As backstage

See recent folders

Chosen folder to save the file

2. **Type a name for the document in the File Name box.**

Word automatically selects the first several words of the document as a filename and places this text in the File Name box. If what's chosen isn't okay, type a better name.

Be descriptive with the filename! The more concisely you name a document, the easier it is to recognize it by that name in the future.

REMEMBER

3. **Choose a location for the document.**

Word has already chosen a location for you, either the Documents folder in Windows or the Documents folder on OneDrive. Click the location button to choose another, recent folder. You can click More Locations to switch to the Save As screen, which isn't very helpful, but that's what happens.

4. **Click the Save button.**

   The file is safely stored.

The document window doesn't close after you save. You don't need to quit Word. You can keep working. As you do so, continue to save. See the later section "Saving or updating a document."

>> You can also save a document from the File tab: Choose the Save As or Save a Copy command. This part of Windows is known as the *Backstage*, and many users dislike it.

TECHNICAL STUFF

>> If you earned straight A's in high school algebra, use the F12 keyboard shortcut to save your files. This shortcut summons the familiar Save As dialog box from yesteryear.

>> If the computer's current folder-organization scheme isn't to your liking, use the New Folder button to create a new folder in the current folder. Word proceeds to save your document in the newly created folder.

>> For a folder you use frequently, such as a current project folder, point the mouse at the folder name and click the Pushpin icon, shown in the margin. Clicking the pushpin pins the folder to the top of the folder list or makes it available in the Pinned category on the Start screen. Use this technique to keep favorite folders handy when saving documents.

>> Your clue that the document is saved successfully is that its filename appears on the document's title bar, atop the Word window.

TIP

>> If you're saving a document to OneDrive, you can change the name after saving: Click the name at the top of the Word window and edit it at your pleasure. This trick works only when a document is saved to OneDrive.

>> The Save As command can also be used to save a document with a new name, to a different location, or in a different format. See Chapter 24.

WARNING

>> Do not save a document directly to removable media, such as a thumb drive or media card. Instead, save the document to the computer's primary storage device or to cloud storage. Then you can copy the file to the removable media.

TECHNICAL STUFF

>> You can change the file format by clicking on the filename extension (refer to Figure 8-1). See Chapter 9 for more information on file formats.

Dealing with document-save errors

Saving a document involves coordination between Word and Windows. This complexity doubles the chances of something going wrong, so it's high time for an error message. One such error message is

> The file *whatever* already exists

Here are your choices and my suggestions:

>> **Replace Existing File:** Nope.

>> **Save Changes with a Different Name:** Yep.

>> **Merge Changes into Existing File:** Nope.

Choose the middle option and click OK. Type a different filename as you repeat the initial save operation.

Another common problem occurs when a message that's displayed reads something like this:

> The filename is not valid

This message is Word's less-than-cheerful way of telling you that the filename contains a forbidden character, one of these: \ / : * ? " < > |. To be safe, use only letters, numbers, and spaces when naming a file.

Saving or updating a document

As you continue to work on your document, you should save as you work: Ctrl+S. When you frequently resave, any changes you've made since the last time you saved are retained. It never hurts to save a document multiple times.

>> I save my document whenever I pause to think, answer the phone, or fear that the computer is about to do something stupid.

 >> You can perform a quick save by clicking the Save button on the Quick Access toolbar.

Saving automatically on OneDrive

If you've saved a document to OneDrive and the AutoSave feature is active, you never really need to save again after the first time. Word automatically saves your document for you.

 To ensure that AutoSave is active, look for the AutoSave item on the Quick Access toolbar, as shown in the margin. If the switch is off, click it.

>> The AutoSave item is disabled when the document is saved to local storage or a location other than OneDrive.

 >> The Save icon on the Quick Access toolbar changes for documents saved to OneDrive. The updated icon appears in the margin. Click this button to force a save to the cloud.

>> If you don't see the AutoSave item, click the menu button on the far right end of the Quick Access toolbar. Choose Automatically Save from the menu.

>> The advantage of using OneDrive cloud storage is that the document is available to any device you use with Internet access. If you have a Microsoft 365 subscription, you can use Word on the web to edit the document. You can also employ Word's collaboration features to share and work with others on the same document. See Chapter 26.

TIP

Forgetting to save before you quit

When you close a document, or quit Word outright, and the document hasn't been saved before you do so, you see the Save Your Changes to This File? dialog box. Use it just as you do the original Save dialog box (refer to Figure 8-1) to save the document one last time.

Yes, it's possible not to save the document: Click the Don't Save button — and it's gone (almost) forever. See the later section "Recover a Draft" for information on "forever."

Click the Cancel button to return to the document for more editing and stuff.

 Documents opened from OneDrive cloud storage are saved automatically when you quit.

REMEMBER

Open a Document

Saving a document means nothing unless you have a way to retrieve that document later. As you might suspect, Word offers multiple ways to *open* a document.

TECHNICAL
STUFF

The original "open" command in Word was titled File, Transfer, Load. I think "open" sounds better.

Using the Open command

Open is the standard computer command used to fetch an existing document and plunge it into the middle of a program. Once you find and open the document, it appears in Word's window as though it's always been there.

To open a document in Word, follow these steps:

1. **Press the Ctrl+O keyboard shortcut.**

    If you have more time, you can click the File tab and choose the Open command. Either way, the Open screen materializes, as shown in Figure 8-2.

2. **Choose a recently opened file from the list.**

    TIP

    Refer to Figure 8-2. If you spy the desired document and click it, it opens at once. Congratulations — you're done.

3. **Choose a folder to start browsing for the document file.**

    If you don't see the folder you want, click the Browse button (refer to Figure 8-2). Use the traditional Open dialog box to hunt down the proper folder.

4. **Select a recent folder from the list.**

5. **Click a document to open it.**

After the document is open, you can edit it, look at it, print it, get frustrated and erase the entire thing to start over, or do whatever you want.

>> Word may highlight the last location where you were writing or editing, along with a "Welcome back" message. Click this message to pick up where you left off.

>> Documents not saved to OneDrive open with a banner urging you to back up the document on OneDrive. Click the X at the far right end of this banner to dismiss this notice.

Places to look for a document   Browse recent folders

Choose a recent document   Pinned documents appear here

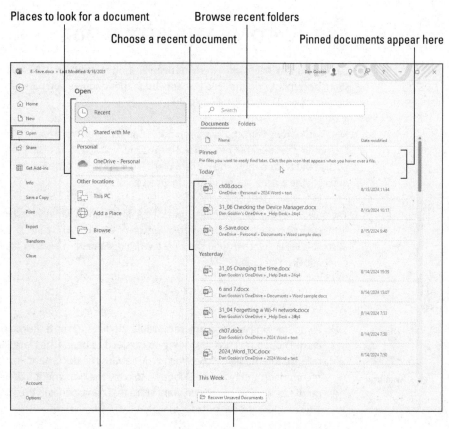

FIGURE 8-2:
The Open screen.

Access the traditional Open dialog box   Rescue a lost document

TIP

>> The keyboard shortcut to directly access the good ol' traditional Open dialog box is Ctrl+F12. I can't for the life of me remember this shortcut.

>> Opening a document doesn't erase it from storage. In fact, the file stays on the storage system until you use the Save command to save and update the document with any changes.

>> When you position the mouse pointer at a recently opened document or folder on the Open screen, the Pushpin icon appears, as shown in the margin. Click this icon to make a document or folder "stick" to the Open screen. This way, the document or folder is always available for quick access later.

>> To remove a document from the Recent list, right-click the document's entry. Choose the command Remove from List.

WARNING

>> Avoid opening a file on any removable media, such as a thumb drive or media card. Though it's possible, doing so can lead to headaches later, should you remove the media before Word is done with the document. Instead, I recommend that you use Windows to copy the document from the removable media to the computer's primary storage. Then open it in Word.

Opening one document inside another

Inserting the contents of one document into another is possible in Word, and no surgery or screaming is involved. For example, at the end of a paper, you can insert another document that may have a short bio — including your picture. To do so, follow these steps:

1. **Position the insertion pointer where you want the other document's contents to appear.**

   The text is inserted at this position.

2. **Click the Insert tab.**

3. **From the Text group, click the menu (downward-pointing chevron) by the Object button.**

   The Object button is shown in the margin.

4. **Choose the menu item Text from File.**

   The Insert File dialog box appears, which looks like the traditional Open dialog box.

5. **Locate and select the document you want to insert.**

   Browse the various folders to find the document icon. Click to select its icon.

6. **Click the Insert button.**

   The document's contents are inserted into the current document, just as though you had typed and formatted it yourself.

The resulting combined document retains the name of the first document. The document you inserted remains unchanged.

>> You can insert any number of documents into another document.

>> Inserting text from one document into another is often called *boilerplating*. For example, you can save a commonly used piece of text in a document and then insert it into other documents as necessary. This process is also the way that sleazy romance novels were written before AI came along.

>> If you find yourself inserting common bits of text into documents, consider instead creating a document template. See Chapter 16.

Recover a Draft

When you forget to save a document — or the computer crashed or the power went out — Word offers you a modicum of hope: You can recover some, but perhaps not all, of an unsaved document. Valiantly make this attempt:

1. **Press Ctrl+O to summon the Open screen.**

2. **Ensure that Recent is chosen as the file location.**

3. **Click the Recover Unsaved Documents button, found at the bottom of the list of recent files (refer to Figure 8-2).**

   The Open dialog box appears, listing the contents of a special folder reserved for unsaved files. It's Word's graveyard. Actually, it's more like a morgue in a county with a lousy EMS.

4. **Select a document to recover.**

    The document may have an unusual name, especially when it's never been saved. For example, it may be named AutoRecovery Save of Document 1. The name may also be similar to the original filename.

5. **Click the Open button to open and recover the document.**

If you picked the wrong document, try again and choose another document in Step 4.

Though this trick is a blessing, you may discover that the recovered document doesn't contain all the text you thought would be there. Remember that this feature is just Word being kind to you. Rather than be upset, just *remember to save everything* in the first place!

TECHNICAL STUFF

The recovery of drafts is possible because of Word's AutoRecover feature. Refer to Chapter 31 for more information on AutoRecover.

IN THIS CHAPTER

» Previewing a document before printing

» Printing a specific part of a document

» Printing multiple copies of a document

» Canceling a print job

» Making a document compatible for sharing

» Sending a document as an attachment

» Exporting a document as a PDF

Chapter **9**

Publish Your Document

The final step in document preparation is publishing. Don't get all excited: Publishing in Word isn't about seeing your book on *The New York Times* bestseller list, though it can still happen. No, publishing a document involves freeing it from the confines of your computer. Options are printing on paper and electronic document publishing. Only then, perhaps, can you be famous.

Your Document on Paper

The word processor is the best writing tool ever invented, much less noisy than chisels and stone tablets. It's also the first writing tool that avoids paper until your document is complete. Even then, you choose whether to generate a dead-tree version of the document, also called a *printout* or *hard copy*.

>> Configuring a computer's printer is done in Windows, not Word. Use the Settings app, though it's pretty much an automatic operation.

>> I assume that your computer has a printer available directly or on a network, and that everything is set up just peachy. Ensure that the printer is stocked with ink or toner and plenty of paper.

>> Printing works differently when using the online version of Word. Primarily, it's your web browser that does the printing, not Word, as described in this chapter.

Previewing before printing

TIP

Before you print, preview the final look of the document. Yes, even though Word is supposed to show your document the same on the screen as it does on paper, you may still find surprises: missing page numbers, blank pages, screwy headers, and other jaw-dropping blunders, for example.

Fortunately, a print preview of your document appears as part of the Print screen, which you see before printing. Follow these steps:

1. Save the document.

Saving before printing is a good idea.

2. Press Ctrl+P.

The Print screen appears, shown in Figure 9-1. This screen is also available from the File tab; choose the Print item.

3. Use the buttons at the bottom of the Print screen to page through your document.

Look at the margins. Examine footnotes, headers, or footers, to see how they lay out. The idea is to spot anything that's dreadfully wrong *before* you print. You can use the Zoom control (refer to Figure 9-1) to enlarge or reduce the image.

When you're ready, print the document. Details are offered in the next section, but when issues must be addressed, click the Back button or press the Esc key to return to your document.

Printing the entire dang doodle document

It's time to enshrine your document on paper. Heed these directions:

1. Make sure that the printer is on and ready to print.

Printing works fastest when the printer is on.

2. **Save the document.**

3. **Press Ctrl+P, or, if you're being paid by the hour, click the File tab and choose the Print item.**

   The Print screen appears (refer to Figure 9-1).

4. **Click the big Print button.**

   The Print screen closes and the document spews forth from the printer.

Back button/Return to document

Print document

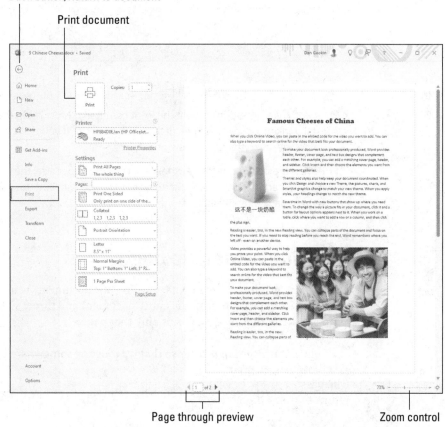

FIGURE 9-1:
The Print screen.

Page through preview

Zoom control

AI images generated using Microsoft Copilot.

Printing speed depends on the complexity of the document and how dumb the printer is. Fortunately, you can continue working while the document is printing.

DELETE THE TRAILING BLANK PAGE

TIP

One of the most annoying things you discover when printing a document is that an extra, blank page pops out of the printer. This mistake is easily caught if you use print preview, as described in this chapter. But because you're reading this sidebar, you probably want to know how to rid the document of the extra blank page.

To remove the blank page that follows your document like a phantom caboose, press Ctrl+End. With the insertion pointer at the very bottom of your document, press the Backspace key repeatedly until the extra page is gone. How can you tell? Keep an eye on the total page-count tally on the status bar. When the page count decreases by one, you can stop whacking the Backspace key.

WARNING

>> Obligatory Ctrl+P joke goes here.

>> If nothing prints, don't repeat the Print command! Most likely, the computer is still thinking or sending information to the printer. If you don't see an error message, everything prints eventually.

>> When the document format specifies a unique paper size, the printer urges you to load that paper size. Stand by to produce and load the proper paper when the printer prompts you.

Printing a specific page

Because the printer chewed up page 16 in your document, you must reprint that one page. Rather than reprint the entire document and throw away everything but page 16, follow these steps to print only that page:

1. **Move the insertion pointer so that it's roosting somewhere on the page you want to print.**

TIP

Double-check the page number on the status bar to ensure that you're on the correct page.

2. **Press Ctrl+P.**

3. **Click the Print Range button below the Settings heading.**

Refer to Figure 9-2 for the button's location. It typically says Print All Pages.

4. **Choose Print Current Page from the menu.**

The sole page to reprint appears in the preview.

5. **Click the Print button.**

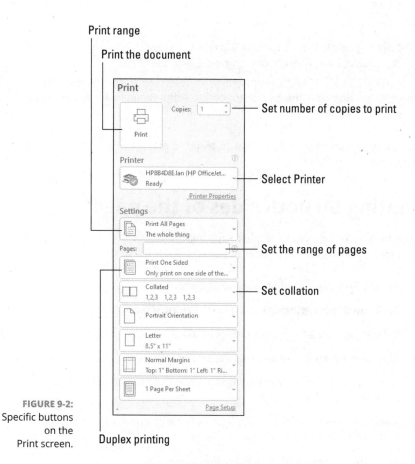

Print range

Print the document

Set number of copies to print

Select Printer

Set the range of pages

Set collation

Duplex printing

The single page prints with all the formatting you applied, including footnotes and page numbers and everything else, just as though you plucked that page from a complete printing of the entire document.

Printing a range of pages

Word enables you to print a range of pages, odd-numbered pages, even-numbered pages, or a hodgepodge combination of given pages from within a document. To print a range or group of pages, summon the Print screen: Press Ctrl+P.

On the Print screen, look for the Pages text box, illustrated earlier, in Figure 9-2. Here are some suggestions for what to type in that text box:

To print pages 3 through 5, type **3–5**.

To print pages 2, 6, and 10, type **2,6,10**.

To print page 3, pages 5 through 9, pages 15 through 17, and page 19 (boy, that coffee went everywhere, didn't it?), type **3, 5–9, 15–17, 19**.

Typing any value into the box changes the Print Range selection from Print All Pages to Custom Print.

Click the big Print button when you're ready to print. Only the pages you specify churn from the printer.

Printing on both sides of the page

If the printer is capable of duplex printing, you can direct Word to print your document on both sides of a sheet of paper. Follow these steps:

1. **Press Ctrl+P right after saving the document.**

2. **Click the Duplex Printing button on the Print screen.**

   Refer to Figure 9-2 for the button's location.

3. **Choose Print on Both Sides, Flip Pages on Long Edge.**

   Don't bother with the Short Edge option unless you plan to bind the document that way.

   If you don't see the Print on Both Sides options, you must manually print on both sides of the paper. See the next section.

4. **Click the big Print button to print the document.**

The document is sent to the printer with directions to print on both sides of a sheet of paper. It's the printer's job at this point to perform the magic. If not, read the next section.

Printing odd- and even-numbered pages

When your printer lacks duplex capability, you must perform the task manually: First, print all odd-numbered pages in the document. Flip the paper and reinsert it in the printer. Then print all even-numbered pages. The result is text printed on both sides of the page.

To print all odd-numbered pages or all even-numbered pages, follow these steps:

1. **Press Ctrl+P to summon the Print screen.**

2. **Click the Print Range button below the Settings heading.**

   Refer to Figure 9-2 for the button's location.

3. **Choose Only Print Odd Pages from the menu.**

4. **Click the Print button to print odd-numbered pages in the document.**

To print even pages, repeat these steps, but in Step 3 choose Only Print Even Pages.

TIP

I recommend printing only a single odd-and-even page first, to ensure that when you reinsert the paper, it's set in the proper orientation.

Printing a block

After you mark a block of text in your document, you can beg the Print command to print only that block. Here's how:

1. **Mark the block of text you want to print.**

   See Chapter 6 for all the block-marking instructions in the world.

2. **Press Ctrl+P to summon the Print screen.**

3. **Click the Print Range button below the Settings heading.**

4. **From the menu, choose the Print Selection item.**

   The Print Selection item is available only when a block is selected in the document.

5. **Click the Print button.**

The selected block prints at the same page position and with the same formatting (including headers and footers) as though you had printed the entire document.

Printing more than one copy of something

When it comes time to provide your report to all five members of the cult but the high priest's photocopier is broken, just print multiple copies. Here's how:

1. **Press Ctrl+P on the keyboard to summon the Print screen.**

2. **Enter the number of copies in the Copies text box.**

   To print five copies, for example, click the box and type **5**.

3. **Click the big Print button to print your copies.**

Under normal circumstances, Word prints each copy of the document, one after the other. This process is known as *collating*. However, if you're printing five copies of a document and you want Word to print five copies of page 1 and then five copies of page 2 (and so on), choose the Uncollated option from the Collated menu button, illustrated earlier, in Figure 9-2.

Choosing another printer

Your computer may have access to several printers, depending on how many are available directly or over the network. To choose a specific printer, such as that fancy color printer that's on the network but hidden in Ed's office, follow these steps:

1. **Press Ctrl+P to summon the Print screen.**

2. **Click the Select Printer button below the Printer heading.**

   The button shows the name of the currently selected printer, the one set by Windows as the default.

3. **Choose another printer from the list.**

   Unfortunately, not every printer features a clear and descriptive name. Also, not every printer listed is a physical printer. Some are digital printers, such as Microsoft Print to PDF, which is covered later in this chapter.

4. **Click the Print button to print the document on the selected printer.**

TECHNICAL STUFF

Adding and managing printers falls under the domain of Windows, not Word. To add printers, rename printers, or set the default printer, use Windows. Windows is also to blame if the default printer keeps changing.

Canceling a print job

The fastest, easiest way to cancel a print job is to rush up to the printer and set it on fire. Lamentably, this method is frequently met with frowns by local fire officials.

Check the printer's control panel for a Cancel button. Press this button to stop a print job run amok. Printing may not stop all at once, but the button cancels the rest of the document from printing.

You can also use Windows to check on the status of printing jobs. Obey these steps:

1. **Press the Win+I keyboard shortcut to summon the Settings app.**

2. **Choose Bluetooth & Devices.**

3. **Choose Printers & Scanners.**

4. **Select your printer from the list of printers.**

5. **Choose the item titled Open Print Queue.**

The Print Queue window lists any pending printing jobs. Click a job's three-dot menu button to pause, resume, or cancel. Sometimes, pausing and resuming a job does the trick. But keep in mind that the printer is really its own computer. Oftentimes, a printing problem is related directly to the printer and is not an issue with Word or Windows.

Electronically Publishing Your Document

Not every document needs to hit paper. For example, it's been years since I've printed a manuscript. Today, my books are submitted via email. eBooks need not be printed. Documents are sometimes more effectively distributed digitally than by paper. It's all part of electronically publishing your document.

Preparing a document for publishing

Lots of interesting things can find their way into your Word document, information that you may not want published. These items include comments, revision marks, hidden text, and other tidbits useful to you or your collaborators that would mess up a document you share with others. The solution is to use Word's Check for Issues tool, like this:

1. **Ensure that your document is finished, finalized, fabulous, and saved.**

2. **Click the File tab.**

3. **Choose Info from the list of items on the left side of the window.**

4. **Click the Check for Issues button.**

5. **Choose Inspect Document.**

   The Document Inspector window appears. All items relevant to your document are selected.

6. **Click the Inspect button.**

   After a few moments, the Document Inspector window summarizes any potential problems.

7. **Optionally, click the Remove All button next to any issues you want to clear up.**

   Or, now that you know what the issues are, you can click the Close button and return to your document to manually inspect the flagged issues.

8. **Click the Close button, or click Reinspect to give your document another once-over.**

After completing the inspection, you can go forward with publishing the document or continue working.

Making a PDF

The Word document file format is considered a standard. Therefore, it's perfectly acceptable to send one of your document files as an email attachment or make it available for sharing with others, such as on cloud storage.

It's also possible to save, or publish, your document in the Adobe Acrobat document format, also known as a PDF file. Obey these steps:

1. **Finish your document.**

   Yes, this step means saving it one last time.

2. **Press Ctrl+P to summon the Print screen.**

3. **Click the Printer button.**

   A list of available printers appears.

4. **Choose Microsoft Print to PDF.**

5. **Click the Print button.**

   Nothing is printed on paper, but the document is "printed" to a new PDF file. This step requires the use of the special Save Print Output As dialog box.

6. **Work the dialog box controls.**

   Locate a proper folder in which to save the file, and specify a filename.

7. **Click the Save button.**

The PDF file is created. The original document remains in the Word window, unchanged by the print-to-PDF operation.

>> PDF stands for Portable Document Format.

>> You can use the Open command to open and edit PDF files in Word. In the traditional Open dialog box, choose the item PDF Files (*.pdf) from the File Type menu. Only PDF documents appear in the folder window. Choose one. Click OK to confirm that the process may take time. Once complete, the PDF file is open for editing as a Word document.

>> You need a copy of the Adobe Acrobat Reader program to view PDF files. Don't worry: It's free. Go to get.adobe.com/reader.

Exporting your document

Beyond the Word document format and PDF, you can export your document into other, common file formats. These formats allow for easy document sharing, though they're not as common as they once were.

To export your document into another file format, follow these steps:

1. **Click the File tab.**

2. **Choose Export from the items on the left side of the screen.**

3. **Choose Change File Type.**

   A list of available file types appears on the right side of the screen. These types include Word formats and other file types such as Plain Text, Rich Text Format (RTF), and Web Page (HTML).

4. **Select a file type.**

5. **Click the Save As button.**

   You may have to scroll down the list to find the Save As icon.

   The Save As dialog box appears. It's the same Save As dialog box as covered in Chapter 8, though the Save As Type menu lists the file type you selected in Step 3.

6. **Work the dialog box to set a folder or another location for the file, or to change its name.**

7. **Click the Save button to export the document into the alien file type.**

WARNING

   It may look like the document hasn't changed, but it has! The title bar now specifies that you're working on the exported document, not the original Word document.

8. **Close the document.**

   Press Ctrl+W or otherwise dismiss the document.

By closing the document, you ensure that any changes you make aren't made to the exported copy. To continue working on the original document, open it again in Word.

TECHNICAL
STUFF

The file format is indicated by the filename extension, which is often hidden in Windows. The Word document file format is .docx (the leading dot identifies the extension.) Use Word's Save As or similar dialog boxes to set this extension; do not type it in yourself, because Word would just add the extra text to the filename without changing its format or extension.

3

Fun with Formatting

Choose a font, size, and color for your document's text.

Apply paragraph formats, including indenting, line spacing, and space before and after.

Get to know the ruler and all the ways you can use tabs to align the text.

Find out how to change page size, orientation, and margins.

Become familiar with adding headers, footers, and cover pages.

Learn all you need to know about creating and applying styles and using templates.

Chapter **10**

Character Formatting

Uncle Oscar is quite the character. How he sticks corncobs in his ears and imitates President McKinley will always be the high point of our Thanksgiving dinners. But unlike text in a Word document, Uncle Oscar can't be formatted. Letters, numbers, and non-human characters can be bold, underlined, italicized, small or large, in different fonts or colors, and with all sorts of pretty and distracting attributes. Word gives you this level of control over the appearance of your text, but people like Uncle Oscar are forever free to be themselves.

Text Formatting Techniques

You can format text in a document in one of two ways:

» Use text formatting commands as you type, turning them on or off.

» Type the text first. Go back and select the text to format. Apply the format.

Either method works, though I recommend that you concentrate on your writing first and return to formatting later.

Suppose that you want to write and format the following sentence:

His big toe looked *comically* like President McKinley.

The first way to format is to type the sentence until you reach the word *comically*. Press Ctrl+I to apply the italic format. Type the word. Press Ctrl+I again to turn off the format. Continue typing.

The way I formatted the sentence was to type the entire thing first. Then I double-clicked the word *comically* to select it. Finally, I pressed Ctrl+I to apply the italic format.

Refer to Chapter 6 for more information on marking blocks of text.

Basic Text Formats

Word stores the most common text-formatting commands on the Home tab, in the Font group, as illustrated in Figure 10-1.

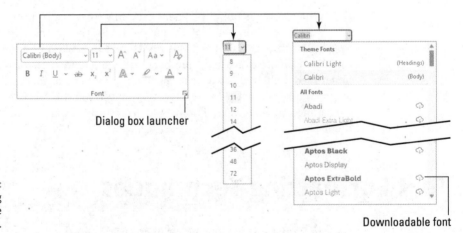

FIGURE 10-1:
Text formatting commands in the Font group.

The Font group's gizmos not only control the text format but also describe the format for the selected text: In Figure 10-1, the text format uses the Calibri font, and the text size is 11 points.

In addition to the Home tab's Font group, text formatting commands are available on the Mini toolbar. It appears whenever text is selected, as described in Chapter 6.

Setting a font

The base attribute of text is its typeface, or font. The *font* sets the way the text looks and its overall style. Choosing the best font can be agonizing (and, indeed, many graphic artists are barely paid to choose just the right font), but the process isn't too difficult. It goes like this:

1. **Click the Home tab.**

2. **In the Font group, click the down arrow by the Font item.**

   A list of fonts appears, shown on the right in Figure 10-1.

3. **Select a font.**

   As you point the mouse pointer at a font, any selected text in the document changes to preview the font. Click to choose the font.

The Font menu is organized to help you locate the desired font. The top part of the menu lists fonts associated with the document theme. The next section contains fonts you've chosen recently (not shown in Figure 10-1), which is handy for reusing fonts. The rest of the long list shows all fonts available to Word, including fonts you can download by selecting them. The fonts appear in alphabetical order and appear in the list as they do in the document.

TIP

>> To quickly scroll to a specific part of the Font menu, type the first letter of the font you need. For example, type T to find Times New Roman.

>> When a font name doesn't appear in the Font text box (it's blank), it means that multiple fonts are selected in the document.

>> Refer to Chapter 16 for more information on document themes.

>> Fonts available and installed fall under the control of Windows. Bazillions of fonts are available online, many at no cost.

TECHNICAL
STUFF

>> Graphic designers prefer to use two fonts in a document: one for the text and one for titles. Word is configured this way as well. The Body font is set for text. The Heading font is set for titles. These two fonts are set as part of the document theme.

Applying character formats

On the lower left side of the Font group, you find some of the most common character attributes. These formats enhance the selected font or typeface.

B To make text bold, press Ctrl+B or click the Bold command button.

Use **bold** to make text stand out on a page — for titles and captions or when you're uncontrollably angry.

I To make text italic, press Ctrl+I or click the Italic command button.

Italic has replaced underlining as the preferred text emphasis format. Italicized text is light, wispy, poetic, and often lacking undergarments.

U Underline text by pressing Ctrl+U or clicking the Underline command button. You can click the down arrow next to the Underline command button to choose from a variety of underline styles or set an underline color.

The double-underline format is available from the Underline command button's menu, but it does have a keyboard shortcut: Ctrl+Shift+D.

Also available is word underlining format. Word underlining looks <u>like this</u>. The keyboard shortcut is Ctrl+Shift+W.

~~ab~~ Strike through text by clicking the Strikethrough command button. (The keyboard shortcut was removed during legal proceedings.)

I don't know whom the Strikethrough command bribed to make it into the Font group. If I were the king of Microsoft, I would have put small caps up there instead. But who am I? Strikethrough is commonly used in legal documents, when you mean to say something but then ~~change your mind~~ and think of something better to say.

X_2 Click the Subscript command button to make text subscript. The keyboard shortcut is Ctrl+= (equal sign).

Subscript text appears below the baseline, such as the 2 in H_2O.

X^2 To make text superscript, click the Superscript command button. The keyboard shortcut is Ctrl+Shift+= (equal sign), which is the shifted version of the subscript keyboard shortcut.

Superscript text appears above the line, such as the 10 in 2^{10}.

Another popular format, but apparently not popular enough to sport a command button in the Fonts group, is small caps. The small caps keyboard shortcut is Ctrl+Shift+K.

Small caps formatting is ideal for headings. I use it for character names when I write a script or play:

BILL: That's a clever way to smuggle a live grenade into prison.

The all caps text format sets the text to uppercase letters only. As with small caps, this format doesn't feature a command button, though it has a shortcut key: Ctrl+Shift+A.

To find all these text formats and more, open the Font dialog box. Refer to the section "Behold the Font Dialog Box," later in this chapter.

>> More than one character format at a time can be applied to any text. For example, use Ctrl+B and then Ctrl+I to apply the bold and italic formats.

TIP

>> The best way to use superscript or subscript is to write text first and then apply the superscript or subscript format to selected text: Write 42 and then format it as 4^2. Write CnH2n+1OH and then format it as $C_nH_{2n}+_1OH$. If you apply superscript or subscript as you type, the text can become difficult to edit.

TECHNICAL STUFF

>> When will the Underline text attribute die? I'm baffled. Honestly, I think we're waiting for the last typewriter-clutching librarian from the 1950s to pass on before underlining officially disappears as a text attribute. And please don't fall prey to the old rule about underlining book titles. It's *Crime and Punishment*, not <u>Crime and Punishment</u>.

Text Transcending Teensy to Titanic

Text size is set in a document based on the ancient typesetter's measurement known as *points*. One point is equal to $\frac{1}{72}$ of an inch. Although this value is mysterious and fun, don't bother committing it to memory. Instead, here are some point pointers:

>> The bigger the point size, the larger the text.

>> Most printed text is either 10 or 12 points tall.

>> Headings are typically 14 to 24 points tall.

- >> In Word, fonts can be sized from 1 point to 1,638 points. Point sizes smaller than 6 are too small for mortals to read.

- >> A 1-inch-high letter is roughly 72 points.

TECHNICAL STUFF

- >> The point size of text is a measure from the bottom of the descender to the typeface's cap height, which is often above the ascender — for example, from the bottom of the lowercase *p* to the top of the capital *E*. Because of this measurement, the typical letter in a font is smaller than its given point size. In fact, depending on the font design, text formatted at the same size but with different fonts (typefaces) doesn't appear to be the same size. It's just one of those typesetting oddities that causes regular computer users to start binge-drinking.

Setting the text size

To set the size of text you're about to type, or text in a selected block, heed these steps:

1. **Click the Home tab.**

2. **In the Font group, click the down arrow next to the Font Size box.**

   A menu of font sizes appears, as shown in the center in Figure 10-1.

3. **Choose a font size.**

   As you point the mouse pointer at various values, selected text in the document changes to reflect the size. Click to set the size.

The Size menu lists only common text sizes. To set the text size to a specific value, type the value in the box. For example, to set the font size to 11.5, click in the Size box and type **11.5**.

TIP

The keyboard shortcut to set text size is Ctrl+Shift+P. Think P for points.

Nudging text size

Rare is the student who hasn't fudged the length of a term paper by inching up the font size a notch or two. To accommodate those students, or anyone else trying to set the text size visually, Word offers two command buttons in the Home tab's Font group.

To increase the font size, click the Increase Font Size command button. The keyboard shortcut is Ctrl+Shift+>.

The Increase Font Size command nudges the font size up to the next value listed on the Size menu (refer to Figure 10-1). So, if the text is 12 points, the command increases its size to 14 points.

To decrease the font size, click the Decrease Font Size command button. Its keyboard shortcut is Ctrl+Shift+<.

The Decrease Font Size command works in the opposite direction of the Increase Font Size command: It reduces text size to the next-lower value displayed on the Size menu (refer to Figure 10-1).

TIP

To remember the text-size keyboard shortcuts, think of the less-than and greater-than symbols. To make the text size greater than the current size, use the Ctrl+Shift+> shortcut. To make the text size less than its current size, use Ctrl+Shift+<.

To increase or decrease the font size by point-sized increments, use these shortcut keys:

Ctrl+]	Makes text one point size larger
Ctrl+[	Makes text one point size smaller

More Colorful Text

Adding color to your text doesn't make your writing more colorful. All it does is make you wish that you had more color ink when it's time to print the document. Regardless, you can splash color on your text, without the need to place a drop cloth below the computer.

Coloring the text

To change the color of text in a document, follow these steps:

1. **Click the Home tab.**

2. **In the Font group, click the Font Color command button.**

   The current word, any selected text, or any new text you type is assigned the button's color.

The Font Color button shows which color it assigns to text. To change the color, click the menu triangle to the button's right and choose a new color from the palette that's displayed.

>> To restore the font color, choose Automatic from the Font Color menu. The Automatic color is set according to the text style. See Chapter 15 for details on styles.

>> Theme colors are associated with the document theme. Refer to Chapter 16.

>> To craft your own, custom colors, select the More Colors item from the Font Color menu to display the fun Colors dialog box.

REMEMBER

>> The printer companies would love it if you'd use more colored text in your documents. Colored text works only on a color printer, so buy more ink!

>> Avoid using faint colors for a font, which can make text extremely difficult to read.

WARNING

>> Don't confuse the Font Color command button with the Text Highlight Color command button, to its left. Text highlighting is used for document markup, as described in Chapter 26.

Shading the background

To set the text background color, use the Shading command. It's really a paragraph formatting command, but I'm sneaking it into this chapter. Follow these steps:

1. Click the Home tab.

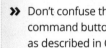

2. In the Paragraph group, click the Shading command button.

The color shown on the button shades the current word or selected block or sets the background color for new text you type.

To switch colors, click the menu button to the right of the Shading command button. Select a color from the list or choose More Colors to create a custom color.

TIP

>> If you want to remove the background color, choose No Color from the Shading command's menu.

>> The Shading command is used also to shade other objects on the page, such as cells in a table. This is the reason it dwells in the Paragraph group.

>> To create white-on-black text, first select the text. Change the text color to white, and then change the background (shading) to black.

>> If you need to apply a background color to an entire page, use the Page Color command. See Chapter 13.

Change Text Case

When you forget to type text the proper way in the first place, or when the Auto-Correct and AutoFormat features forget to do their jobs, the Change Case command is available. Follow these steps:

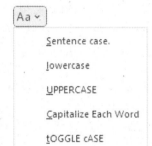

1. **Click the Home tab.**

2. **In the Font group, click the Change Case command button.**

3. **Choose the proper case from the menu.**

   The list of menu items reflects how the case is changed, as shown in Figure 10-2.

Aa ⌄

Ṣentence case.

ḻowercase

ỤPPERCASE

Ḉapitalize Each Word

ṭOGGLE ċASE

FIGURE 10-2:
Options for
changing the
text case.

The Change Case command isn't really a formatting command; its application doesn't stick with the text you type.

» The keyboard shortcut for the Change Case command is Shift+F3. Press this key combination to cycle between three case options: ALL CAPS, lowercase, and Capitalize Each Word.

» Back in the days of mechanical type, a font came in a case, like a briefcase. The upper part of the case held the capital or majuscule letters. The lower part held the miniscule letters. This is where the terms *uppercase* and *lowercase* originated.

**TECHNICAL
STUFF**

Clear Character Formatting

So many Word formatting commands are available that it's possible for your text to look more like a pile of runes than a modern document. Word understands this problem, so it offers the Clear Formatting command. Use it to peel away all formats from the text, just like peeling a banana. Follow these steps:

1. **Click the Home tab.**

2. **In the Font group, click the Clear Formatting command button.**

   Text formats are removed from selected text or from all new text you type.

The formatting isn't removed as much as it's restored: After you issue the Clear Formatting command, text reflects the currently applied style. This style includes font, size, and other attributes.

>> The keyboard shortcut for the Clear Formatting command is Ctrl+spacebar.

>> The Clear Formatting command removes the ALL CAPS text format, but doesn't otherwise change the text case.

>> You cannot use the Clear Formatting command to remove text highlighting, which is covered in Chapter 26.

>> See Chapter 15 for more information on styles.

Behold the Font Dialog Box

Word features a single location where all your font formatting dreams can come true. It's the Font dialog box, shown in Figure 10-3.

To summon the Font dialog box, obey these steps:

1. **Click the Home tab.**

2. **In the Fonts group, click the Dialog Box Launcher button-thing.**

   The button-thing is found in the lower right corner of the Font group (refer to Figure 10-1).

The Font dialog box hosts *all* the commands for formatting text, including quite a few that didn't find their way into the Font group on the ribbon. As with all text formatting, the commands you choose in the Font dialog box affect any new text you type or any selected text in your document.

When you've finished setting up your font stuff, click the OK button. Or click Cancel if you're just visiting.

FIGURE 10-3:
The neatly
organized Font
dialog box.

TIP

>> Use the Ctrl+D keyboard shortcut to quickly summon the Font dialog box.

>> The best benefit of the Font dialog box is its Preview window, at the bottom. This window shows you exactly how your choices affect text in the document.

>> The font names +Body and +Heading refer to the fonts set by the current document theme. These names allow you to use Word's theme commands to quickly change body and heading fonts for an entire document all at one time.

>> Click the Font dialog box's Text Effects button to access interesting text attributes, such as Shadow, Outline, Emboss, and Engrave. See Chapter 17 for information about these wacky features.

>> The Font dialog box's Advanced tab hosts options for changing the size and position of text on a line — typesetter stuff.

WARNING

>> The Set As Default button in the Font dialog box changes the font that Word uses for new documents. If you prefer to use a specific font for all your documents, choose the font (plus other text attributes) in the Font dialog box, and then click the Set as Default button. In the dialog box that appears, choose the option All Documents Based On the Normal Template. Click the OK button. Afterward, all documents start with the font options you selected, which is probably not what you want, so don't mess with this option until you understand Word's templates. See Chapter 16.

Chapter **11**

Paragraph Formatting

G rammatically, a paragraph is supposed to express a single thought. But what if you're scatterbrained and a single thought is effectively the entire document? Truly, is it up to the grammarians to define our thought patterns? And what about 5G! Are the Lizard People following me to Walmart?

Regardless of where you stand on thought patterns or the capability of the Illuminati to read your mind, formatting a paragraph in Word can be a daunting experience. The commands are vast — though, happily, the adjustments you make appear instantly. The goal is to customize and present text just the way you like, even if the government already knows what you're going to write before you type it.

Paragraph Formatting Rules and Regulations

Grammatical conventions aside, to Word, a *paragraph* is any chunk of text that appears before you press the Enter key. A paragraph can be a single character, a word, a sentence, or a document full of sentences. Once you've stabbed the Enter key, you've created a paragraph, according to Word.

Formatting a paragraph

You can format a paragraph in one of several ways:

Change an existing paragraph. With the insertion pointer in a paragraph, use a paragraph formatting command. Only the current paragraph format is affected.

Change a block of paragraphs. Select one or more paragraphs and then use the formatting command to affect the lot.

Just start typing. Choose a paragraph formatting command, and then type a paragraph. The chosen format is applied to the new text.

TIP

>> To format every dang doodle paragraph in a document, press Ctrl+A to select all text and then apply the format.

>> If your desire is to apply the same format to multiple paragraphs in the document, consider creating a style. See Chapter 15.

TIP

SHOWING THE PARAGRAPH MARKS

Secretly, the hidden Paragraph symbol (¶) appears in a document to mark the end of a paragraph. To direct Word to display it for you, click the File tab and choose the Options command. In the Word Options dialog box, choose Display. Place a check mark by the Paragraph Marks item, and then click OK.

Now, every time you press the Enter key, the ¶ symbol (called a *pilcrow*) appears, marking the end of a paragraph.

Also see Chapter 2 for information on the Show/Hide command, which displays paragraph symbols — as well as other, secret text — in a document.

Locating the paragraph formatting commands

In a vain effort to confuse you, Word uses not one but *two* locations on the ribbon to house its paragraph formatting commands. The first Paragraph group is found on the Home tab. The second is located on the Layout tab. Both groups are illustrated in Figure 11-1.

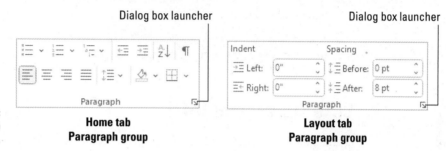

FIGURE 11-1:
Paragraph
groups.

**Home tab
Paragraph group**

**Layout tab
Paragraph group**

But wait! There's more.

To conjure the Paragraph dialog box, shown in Figure 11-2, click the Dialog Box Launcher button in either of the Paragraph groups (refer to Figure 11-1). In it, you find controls and settings not offered by the command buttons on the ribbon.

REMEMBER

A smattering of paragraph formatting commands are also found on the Mini toolbar, which appears after you select text. See Chapter 6.

FIGURE 11-2:
The Paragraph
dialog box.

Justification and Alignment

Paragraph alignment has nothing to do with politics, and justification has little to do with the reasons behind putting text in a paragraph. Instead, both terms refer to how the left and right edges of the paragraph look on a page. The four options are Left, Center, Right, and Fully Justified, each covered in this section.

>> All alignment-formatting command buttons are found on the Home tab, in the Paragraph group.

>> The left and right indents of a paragraph are measured from the page margin, not from the edge of the page. See Chapter 13 for information on page margins.

Line up on the left!

Left alignment is considered standard, probably thanks to the mechanical typewriter and, before that, generations of grammar school teachers who preferred text lined up on the left side of a piece of paper. Writing English from left to right might also have something to do with this standard.

To left-align a paragraph, press Ctrl+L or click the Align Left command button, found in the Home tab's Paragraph group.

>> This type of alignment is also known as *ragged right.*

>> Left-aligning a paragraph is how you undo the other types of paragraph alignment.

TIP

Everyone center!

Centering a paragraph places each line in that paragraph in the center of the page, with an equal amount of space to the line's right and left.

To center a paragraph, press Ctrl+E or use the Center command button, found in the Home tab's Paragraph group.

>> Centering is ideal for titles and single lines of text. It's ugly for longer paragraphs and makes reading the text more difficult — unless you're a poet, in which case you'll ignore me anyway.

>> Use a center tab stop to center a single word in the middle of a line. See Chapter 12.

>> See Chapter 17 for information on centering text on a page, top to bottom.

Line up on the right!

The mirror image of left alignment is *right alignment:* The right edge of the paragraph is aligned, and the left margin is not. When do you use this type of formatting? I have no idea, but it sure feels funky typing a right-aligned paragraph.

 To flush text along the right side of the page, press Ctrl+R or click the Align Right command button.

>> This type of alignment is also known as *ragged left* or *flush right.*

>> Dates can be right-aligned in their own paragraph at the top of a letter.

>> To right-justify text on a single line, use a right tab stop. See Chapter 12 for more info.

Line up on both sides!

Lining up both sides of a paragraph is *full justification:* Both the left and right sides of a paragraph are neat and tidy, flush with the margins.

 To apply full justification, press Ctrl+J or click the Justify command button, located, as you might guess, in the Home tab's Paragraph group.

>> Fully justified paragraph formatting is often used in newspapers and magazines, which makes the narrow columns of text easier to read.

>> Full justification is preferred when using multiple columns of text on a page.

TECHNICAL STUFF

>> Word makes each side of the paragraph line up by inserting tiny slivers of extra space between words in a paragraph. The extra space is recycled from government computers that are designed to look impressive but merely create extra space.

Make Room Before, After, or Inside Paragraphs

Sentences in a paragraph can stack as tightly as a palette of plywood. Alternatively, you can choose to keep paragraphs all light and airy, like a soft, fluffy cake. Space can cushion above or below the paragraph. These paragraph air settings are illustrated in Figure 11-3.

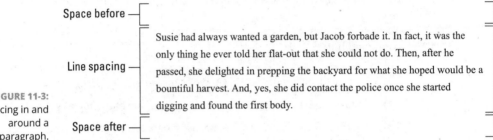

FIGURE 11-3: Spacing in and around a paragraph.

Commands to control paragraph spacing include the traditional line spacing commands as well as the Space Before and Space After commands. These commands are found in the Paragraph groups on both the Home and Layout tabs.

TIP

Use a document theme to affect overall spacing within, above, and below a paragraph. See Chapter 16.

Setting the line spacing

To set the space between lines in a paragraph, follow these steps:

1. **Click the Home tab.**

2. **In the Paragraph group, click the Line Spacing command button.**

   A menu appears.

3. **Choose a new line spacing value.**

Word adds the extra space below each line of text in the current or selected paragraphs.

Four keyboard shortcuts are available for common line-spacing values:

Ctrl+0: Choose 1.15 line space — don't ask me to explain this value.

Ctrl+1: Apply single-spacing.

Ctrl+2: Apply double-spacing.

Ctrl+5: Apply 1½ line spacing.

When you need text to stack up one line atop another line, such as when typing a return address, use the *soft return* at the end of a line: Press Shift+Enter. Refer to Chapter 4.

Making space between paragraphs

To help separate one paragraph from another, you add space either before or after the paragraph (refer to Figure 11-3). What you don't do is press Enter twice to end a paragraph. Doing so is extremely unprofessional, potentially causing rooms full of educated people to scowl at you.

PERSNICKETY LINE SPACING OPTIONS

For seriously precise line spacing, turn to the Paragraph dialog box: Click the Home tab, and in the lower right corner of the Paragraph group, click the Dialog Box Launcher icon.

In the Paragraph dialog box, the Line Spacing drop-down list features some specific items: At Least, Exactly, and Multiple. These items are used with the At box to indicate line spacing as follows:

At least: The line spacing is set to a minimum value. Word disobeys this value to add more space whenever necessary to make room for larger type, different fonts, or graphics on the same line of text.

Exactly: Word uses the specified line spacing and doesn't adjust the spacing to accommodate larger text or graphics.

Multiple: Use this option to enter line spacing values other than those specified in the Line Spacing drop-down list. For example, to set the line spacing to 4, choose Multiple from the Line Spacing drop-down list and type **4** in the At box.

Click the OK button to confirm these settings and close the Paragraph dialog box.

To add space before or after a paragraph, follow these steps:

1. **Click the Layout tab.**

2. **In the Paragraph group, use the Before gizmo to add space before a paragraph of text, or use the After gizmo to add space after the paragraph.**

   Measurements are made in points, the same measurement used for font size.

To create the effect of pressing the Enter key twice to end a paragraph, set the After value to a point size about two-thirds the size of the current font. As an example, for a 12-point font, an After value of 8 looks good.

TIP

>> Most of the time, space is added after a paragraph. You can add space before a paragraph — for example, to further separate text from a document heading or subhead.

>> The space you add before or after a paragraph becomes part of the paragraph format. Like other formats, it sticks with subsequent paragraphs you type or can be applied to a block of paragraphs.

TECHNICAL STUFF

>> Graphics designers prefer to insert more space between paragraphs when the first line of a paragraph isn't indented, as in this book. When you indent the first line, it's okay to have less or no spacing between paragraphs. See the next section.

Paragraph Indentation Madness

Paragraphs fill the page's margin from side to side, as dictated by the alignment, or *justification*. Exceptions to this rule can be made. A paragraph's first line can be indented, the rest of the lines can be indented, and the left and right sides can be indented. It's paragraph indentation madness!

>> Adjusting a paragraph's indentation doesn't affect its alignment.

>> Paragraphs are indented relative to the page's margins. Refer to Chapter 13 for information on page margins.

Indenting the first line of a paragraph

Back in the old days, writers would press the Tab key to start each new paragraph. The tab indents the first line, helping the reader identify the new paragraph. Word can save you some tab-typing energy by automatically formatting each paragraph with an indent on the first line. Here's how:

1. **Click the Home tab.**

2. **In the Paragraph group, click the dialog box launcher.**

   The Paragraph dialog box appears.

3. **Click the Special drop-down list and choose First Line.**

4. **Confirm that the By box lists the value 0.5".**

   The By box shows half an inch, which is the standard tab stop and a goodly distance to indent the first line of text.

5. **Click OK.**

   The first line of the current paragraph or all selected paragraphs is indented per the amount specified in the By box.

To remove the first-line indent from a paragraph, repeat these steps but select (none) from the drop-down list in Step 3.

 Word's AutoCorrect feature automatically indents the first line of a paragraph, which is handy but also annoying. What AutoCorrect does is convert the tab character into the First Line Indent paragraph format, which may not be what you want. If so, click the AutoCorrect icon (shown in the margin), and choose the Convert Back to Tab command. I recommend using the steps in this section and not AutoCorrect to format first-line indents.

 If you choose to indent the first line, you don't need to add space after the paragraph. Refer to the earlier section "Making space between paragraphs."

REMEMBER

Making a hanging indent (an outdent)

A *hanging indent* isn't in imminent peril. No, it's a paragraph in which the first line breaks the left margin or, from another perspective, in which all lines but the first are indented. Here's an example:

```
Capt. Parker: I admit it. I did it! I know my sense of duty, but
    after nine months in space, we couldn't help ourselves. The
    aliens just smelled ... delicious! We went through the
    protocols. We followed diplomatic procedures. But our senses
    were overwhelmed. So, yes, we ate them.
```

The simple way to create such a beast is to press Ctrl+T, the Hanging Indent keyboard shortcut. The command affects the current paragraph or all selected paragraphs.

The not-so-simple way to hang an indent is to use the Paragraph dialog box: In the Indentation area, click the Special menu and choose Hanging. Use the By text box to set the indent depth.

TIP

>> Every time you press Ctrl+T, the paragraph is indented by another half-inch.

>> To undo a hanging indent, press Ctrl+Shift+T. This keyboard combination is the Unhang shortcut, the chiropractor that puts the paragraph's neck back in shape.

Indenting a whole paragraph

To draw attention to a paragraph, its left side can be drawn in a notch. This presentation is often used for quoted material in a longer expanse of text.

To indent a paragraph, heed these steps:

1. **Click the Home tab.**

2. **In the Paragraph group, click the Increase Indent command button.**

   The paragraph's left edge hops over one tab stop (half an inch).

To unindent an indented paragraph, click the Decrease Indent command button in Step 2. This command also pops a paragraph's left edge out into the margin.

When you want to get specific with indents, as well as indent the paragraph's right side, click the Layout tab and use the Indent Left and Indent Right controls to set specific indentation values. Set both controls to the same value to set off a block quote or a nested paragraph.

>> The keyboard shortcut to indent a paragraph is Ctrl+M. The shortcut to unindent a paragraph is Ctrl+Shift+M.

>> To undo any paragraph indenting, click the Layout tab, and in the Paragraph group, set both Left and Right indent values to 0.

>> Indent only one paragraph or a small group of paragraphs. This format isn't intended for long stretches of text.

WARNING

>> Don't try to mix left and right indenting with a first-line indent or a hanging indent while drowsy or when operating heavy equipment.

Using the ruler to adjust indents

The most visual way to adjust a paragraph's indents is to use the ruler. This tip is helpful only when the ruler is visible, which it normally isn't in Word. To unhide the ruler, follow these steps:

1. **Click the View tab.**

2. **In the Show area, ensure that the Ruler option is active.**

   Click to place a check mark by the Ruler option if it isn't active.

The ruler appears above the document text. In Print Layout view, a vertical ruler also appears on the left side of the document.

On the ruler, you see the page margins left and right, and to the far left is something I call the *tab gizmo* (covered in Chapter 12). Figure 11-4 illustrates the parts of the ruler that are important for paragraph formatting.

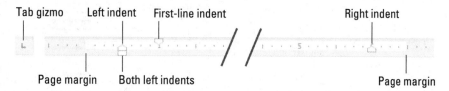

Tab gizmo   Left indent   First-line indent   Right indent

FIGURE 11-4:
The ruler.

Page margin   Both left indents   Page margin

Four doojobbies on the ruler reflect the current paragraph indents. Use these controls to adjust the paragraph indents in a visual manner.

Drag the Left Indent control left or right to adjust a paragraph's left margin. Moving this gizmo doesn't affect the first-line indent.

Drag the First Line Indent control left or right to set the first-line indent independently of the left margin.

Drag the Both control to adjust both the left indent and first-line indent together.

Drag the Right Indent control right or left to adjust the paragraph's right margin.

As you drag controls on the ruler, a vertical guide drops down into the document. Use this guide to visually adjust indents for the current paragraph or any selected paragraphs.

>> The ruler measures from the page's left *margin,* not from the left edge of the page. The page's left margin is set when you format a page of text. See Chapter 13.

PARAGRAPH FORMATTING SURVIVAL GUIDE

This table contains all the paragraph formatting commands you can summon by holding down the Ctrl key and pressing a letter or number. By no means should you memorize this list.

TIP

>> For more precise setting of indents, use the Paragraph dialog box instead of the gizmos on the ruler.

Format	Key Combination	Command Button
Center	Ctrl+E	
Fully justify	Ctrl+J	
Left-align (flush left)	Ctrl+L	
Right-align (flush right)	Ctrl+R	
Indent	Ctrl+M	
Unindent	Ctrl+Shift+M	
Hanging indent	Ctrl+T	n/a
Unhanging indent	Ctrl+Shift+T	n/a
Line spacing	Alt+H, K	n/a
Single-spaced lines	Ctrl+1	n/a
1.15 line spacing	Ctrl+0	n/a
Double-spaced lines	Ctrl+2	n/a
1.5-spaced lines	Ctrl+5	n/a

Chapter **12**

Tab Formatting

tab is like a big space, which is how it works in Word and how it worked on ancient typewriters. Called the Tab or Tabulator or a similar name, the name comes from the same root as *table*, from the Latin word *tabula*, meaning "list." In Word, you use tabs to make lists, to indent text, or to become super frustrated because tabs are one of the most complex formatting topics.

Once Upon a Tab

As with other keys on the keyboard, pressing the Tab key inserts a tab *character* into a document. This character works like a huge space character. Its width depends upon predefined locations, marked across a page, called *tab stops*.

It's the tab stop that makes the tab character work: Press the Tab key, and the insertion pointer hops over to the next tab stop position. You use tabs and tab stops to precisely align text on multiple lines. This approach is more effective than whacking the spacebar multiple times to line up text.

REMEMBER

» Word presets tab stops at every half-inch position across the page. And, of course, you can create your own tab stops.

» Whenever you press the space bar more than once, you *need* a tab. Believe me, your documents will look prettier, and you'll be happier after you understand and use tabs instead of multiple spaces to line up text.

» What happens to text after you type the tab character is determined by the type of tab stop. In Word, multiple tab-stop types are used to format a line of text in many ways.

» As with any other character, you press either the Backspace or Delete key to remove a tab character.

» Tabs work best on a single line of text or for only the first line of a paragraph. For more complex formatting, use Word's Table command. See Chapter 19.

TECHNICAL STUFF

» The diet beverage Tab was named for people who like to "keep a tab on" how much they consume.

Viewing the invisible tab characters

Tab characters are normally hidden in a document. They look like blank spaces, which is probably why too many Word users use spaces instead of tabs.

It's not necessary to see tab characters to use them, although if you're having trouble setting tab stops and using tabs, viewing the tab characters is helpful.

Use the Show/Hide command to quickly view tabs in a document: Click the Home tab and, in the Paragraph group, click the Show/Hide command button, which looks like the Paragraph symbol (¶).

When Show/Hide is active, tab characters appear in the text as right-pointing arrows, similar to the one shown in the margin.

To direct Word to always show tab characters regardless of the Show/Hide command setting, follow these steps:

1. **Click the File tab.**

2. **Choose Options.**

   The Word Options dialog box appears.

3. **Choose Display from the left side of the window.**

4. **Put a check mark by the Tab Characters option.**

5. **Click OK.**

With the Tab Characters option set, tabs always appear in a document. The teensy arrow characters don't print, but by viewing them in the text, you can solve some formatting puzzles.

Viewing the invisible tab character is a good way to spot formatting weirdness in a document. Just as you don't need multiple spaces in a row, two or more tabs in a row indicate misplaced tab stops.

Seeing tab stops on the ruler

Tab stops don't appear in a document, but they affect the text that's typed after you press the Tab key. The best way to view the tab stop locations and types, as well as to set new ones, is to summon the ruler. Follow these steps:

1. **Click the View tab.**

2. **In the Show area, ensure that the check box by the Ruler item has a check mark in it.**

   If not, click to set the check mark.

The ruler appears just above the document. Figure 12-1 illustrates how the ruler might look with various tab stops set. It also shows the location of the tab well, which is a handy gizmo used to access different tab stop types.

Tab well

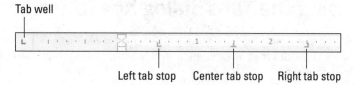

FIGURE 12-1:
Tab stops on the ruler.

Left tab stop   Center tab stop   Right tab stop

If tab stops aren't visible on the ruler, Word is using its default setting of one tab stop every half-inch. The default tab stops don't appear on the ruler.

>> When several paragraphs are selected, you may spot a light gray, or *phantom*, tab stop on the ruler. This ghostly appearance indicates that a tab stop is set in one paragraph but not in all. To apply the tab stop to all selected paragraphs, click the phantom tab stop.

>> See the later section "Tab Stop, Begone!" for information on using the ruler to remove, or unset, a tab stop.

Using the ruler to set tab stops

The visual and quick way to set a tab stop is to use the ruler. Assuming that the ruler is visible (see the preceding section), the process involves these two steps:

1. **Click the tab well until the desired tab stop type appears.**

   Later sections in this chapter discuss what each of the five types of tab stops does.

   The tab well also shows paragraph-indent controls, which are covered in Chapter 11. These items don't relate to setting tabs.

2. **Click the ruler at the exact spot where you want the tab stop set.**

   For example, click the number 2 to set a tab stop 2 inches from the page's left margin. The Tab Stop icon appears on the ruler, marking the paragraph's tab stop position.

You drag the Tab Stop icon left or right to further adjust it. When a tab character already sits in the current paragraph, its format updates the text as you drag the tab stop hither and thither.

REMEMBER

>> The ruler can be sensitive when it comes to setting tab stops. To remove them, see the section "Tab Stop, Begone!" later in this chapter.

>> A tab stop is a paragraph-level format. It's applied to the current paragraph, selected paragraphs, and any further paragraphs you type. Refer to Chapter 6 for details on selected text.

Using the Tabs dialog box to set tabs

For precisely setting tabs, summon the Tabs dialog box. It's also the only way to access special types of tabs, such as dot leader tabs, which are covered elsewhere in this chapter.

Keep in mind that the Tabs dialog box doesn't work like a typical Word dialog box: You choose the tab stop's position and type first, and then click the Set button. Click the OK button only when you're done setting tabs. The process works like this:

1. **Click the Home tab.**

2. **In the lower right corner of the Paragraph group, click the dialog box launcher.**

   The Paragraph dialog box appears. Tab stops are, after all, a paragraph-level format.

3. **Click the Tabs button.**

The Tabs dialog box appears, as shown in Figure 12-2.

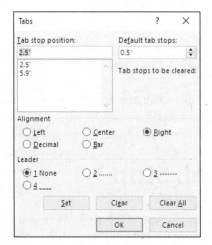

4. **Enter the tab stop position in the Tab Stop Position box.**

You can be precise, if you like, such as 3.11 inches.

5. **Choose the type of tab stop from the Alignment area.**

Word's tab stop types are covered elsewhere in this chapter.

6. **Click the Set button.**

The tab stop is added to the Tab Stop Position list.

RESET WORD'S DEFAULT TAB STOPS

Word presets left-aligned tab stops, marching them across the page at half-inch intervals. These default tab stops provide somewhere for the tab character to go when you press the Tab key.

Any default tab stops are removed when you set your own tab stop. For example, setting a tab stop at the 3-inch position erases all default tab stops to the left of this location.

You can't eliminate the default tab stops, but you can change their spacing. In the Tabs dialog box, type a new interval value in the Default Tab Stops box (refer to Figure 12-2). For example, to set default tab stops to 1-inch intervals, type **1** in the box and then click the OK button.

7. **Continue setting tab stops.**

   Repeat Steps 2–6 for as many tab stops as you need to set.

8. **Click OK.**

   Now you can click OK.

You must click the Set button to set a tab stop! I don't know how many times I click OK instead, thinking that the tab stop is set when it isn't.

When the ruler is visible, double-click any existing tab stop to quickly summon the Tabs dialog box.

The Standard Left Tab Stop

The left tab stop is the traditional type of tab stop. When you press the Tab key, the insertion pointer hops over to the left tab stop position, where you continue to type text. This type of tab stop works best for typing lists, organizing information in single-line paragraphs, and indenting the first line of a multiline paragraph.

Creating a basic tabbed list

A common use for the left tab stop is to create a simple 2-column list, as shown in Figure 12-3.

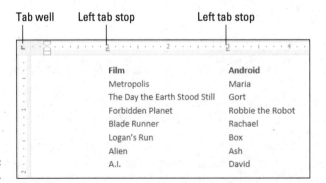

FIGURE 12-3:
Two-column list.

Follow these steps to create this type of list:

REMEMBER

1. **On a new line, press Tab.**

   Write first, set the tab stops later.

2. **Type the item for the first column.**

   This item should be short — two or three words, max.

3. **Press Tab again.**

4. **Type the item for the second column.**

   Again, make it short.

5. **Press Enter to start a new line.**

6. **Repeat Steps 2–5 for each line in the list.**

   After the list is finished, you use the ruler to help visually set the tab stops.

7. **Select all lines of text that you want to organize in a 2-column tabbed list.**

8. **Choose a left tab stop from the tab well on the ruler.**

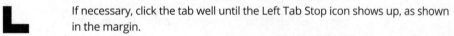

   If necessary, click the tab well until the Left Tab Stop icon shows up, as shown in the margin.

9. **Click and drag on the ruler to set and position the first tab stop.**

   If the text doesn't line up right, drag the tab stop left or right to adjust.

10. **Click to set the second tab stop.**

    Drag the tab stop left or right, if necessary, to line up text.

You could add a third column to the list, but then the text starts to get crowded. In fact, anytime you need this type of complex list, consider instead cobbling together a table. See Chapter 19.

REMEMBER

You need only one tab between items in a column list. That's because the tab *stop*, not the tab character, lines up the text.

Creating a 2-tab paragraph-thing

You can use the power of tabs coupled with a paragraph's hanging-indent format to create a tab-tab-paragraph list, similar to the one shown in Figure 12-4.

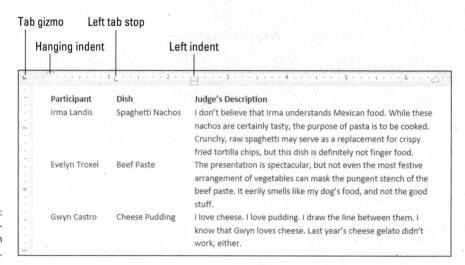

Tab gizmo   Left tab stop

Hanging indent   Left indent

Participant	Dish	Judge's Description
Irma Landis	Spaghetti Nachos	I don't believe that Irma understands Mexican food. While these nachos are certainly tasty, the purpose of pasta is to be cooked. Crunchy, raw spaghetti may serve as a replacement for crispy fried tortilla chips, but this dish is definitely not finger food.
Evelyn Troxel	Beef Paste	The presentation is spectacular, but not even the most festive arrangement of vegetables can mask the pungent stench of the beef paste. It eerily smells like my dog's food, and not the good stuff.
Gwyn Castro	Cheese Pudding	I love cheese. I love pudding. I draw the line between them. I know that Gwyn loves cheese. Last year's cheese gelato didn't work, either.

FIGURE 12-4:
Tab-tab-
paragraph
format for text.

This format looks horrendously complex, but it's easy to construct when you follow these steps:

1. **On a new line, type the first item.**

   The shorter, the better. This item sits at the left margin, so don't type a tab to start the line.

2. **Press Tab.**

3. **Type the second item and press Tab.**

4. **Type the paragraph text.**

   You're free to type more text here. This final paragraph column-wraps, as shown in Figure 12-4, so it can be longer than the first two items. Don't let the lack of formatting bother you at this point.

5. **Press Enter to start the next line.**

6. **Repeat Steps 1–5 for each item in the tab-tab-paragraph list-thing.**

7. **Select all the lines of text you want to organize into a tab-tab-paragraph list.**

8. **Ensure that the left tab stop is chosen on the tab well.**

   If you don't see the Left Tab Stop icon (shown in the margin), click the tab well until it shows up.

9. **Set a left tab stop on the ruler to mark the second item in the list.**

   The first item is set at the start of the line. After you set the left tab stop for the second item in the list, the second column snaps into place.

10. **Slide the paragraph's left indent to the start of the text item.**

The Left Indent (shown in the margin and in Figure 12-4) sets the left margin for all text in a paragraph, except for the first line. (See Chapter 11 for details.) Slide the triangle rightward on the ruler until its location passes items in the second column. Use Figure 12-4 as your guide.

You can continue to fiddle with the tab stops and indent on the ruler to set things just right. Or, if you find this formatting frustrating, it's perfectly okay to give up and stick this type of text into a table. See Chapter 19.

The Center Tab Stop

The *center tab* is a unique critter with a special purpose: Unlike centering an entire paragraph, only text typed after the tab character is centered on a line. This tab stop is best used for centering text in a header or footer, which is about the only time you need a center tab stop.

Figure 12-5 shows an example of a center tab in a page header. The text on the left is left-justified at the start of the line. The tab character hops to the text over to the center tab stop, where any text typed is centered on the same line. Follow these steps to create such a beast:

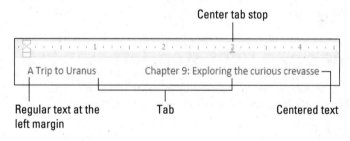

FIGURE 12-5: Center tab stop in action.

1. **Start a new paragraph, one containing a line of text that you want to center.**

Center tabs thrive in single-line paragraphs.

2. **Click the tab well on the ruler until the center tab stop shows up.**

The Center Tab Stop icon is shown in the margin.

3. **Click the ruler to set the center tab stop's position.**

Most often, the center tab stop dwells in the center of the line.

4. **Optionally, type text to start the line.**

    In Figure 12-5, the text *A Trip To Uranus* appears at the start of the line.

5. **Press the Tab key.**

    The insertion pointer hops over to the center tab stop.

6. **Type the text you want centered.**

    The text is magically centered as you type. Don't type too much text; the center tab is a single-line thing.

7. **Press Enter to end the line of text.**

TIP

To center text on a line without any text before it (see Figure 12-5), use the center paragraph format instead of a center tab stop. See Chapter 11.

See Chapter 14 for information on headers and footers.

The Right Tab Stop

The right tab stop's effect is to right-align the text you type after pressing the Tab key. As with the center tab stop, the right tab stop is used in headers and footers or when a paragraph contains only a single line of text. Otherwise, use the Right Justification paragraph formatting command to right-align text, as described in Chapter 11.

Making a right-stop, left-stop list

A clever way to format a 2-column list is to employ both right and left tab stops. The list lines up on a centerline, as shown in Figure 12-6.

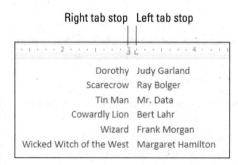

FIGURE 12-6: Right tab stops are used to center-align this list.

To build such a list, follow these steps:

1. **Start out on a blank line, the line you want to format.**

2. **Click the tab well until the right tab stop shows up.**

The Right Tab Stop icon appears in the margin.

3. **Click near the center of the ruler to set the right tab stop.**

4. **Click the tab well until the left tab stop appears.**

Click, click, click until you see the Left Tab Stop icon, as shown in the margin.

5. **Click to place the left tab stop just to the right side of the right tab stop on the ruler.**

Use Figure 12-6 as your guide.

With the tab stops set, you can type the text.

6. **Press the Tab key.**

The insertion pointer hops over to the right tab stop's position.

7. **Type text for the first, right-justified column.**

The text aligns on the right as you type.

8. **Press the Tab key.**

9. **Type some text for the second, left-justified column.**

This text aligns on the left.

10. **Press Enter to end the line of text.**

11. **Repeat Steps 6–10 to complete the list.**

If further adjustments are required after you've finished, select all lines and use the mouse to adjust the tab stops' positions on the ruler.

Building a 2-column right-stop list

The right tab stop can be used on the second column of a 2-column list. The presentation appears commonly in theatrical programs, as shown in Figure 12-7.

Here's how to concoct such a thing:

1. **Start on a blank line of text.**

2. **Click the tab well until the right tab stop appears.**

The Right Tab Stop icon is shown in the margin.

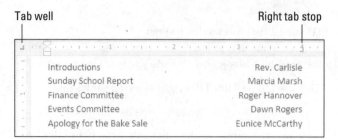

FIGURE 12-7:
Right tab stops right-align the second column of this list.

Introductions	Rev. Carlisle
Sunday School Report	Marcia Marsh
Finance Committee	Roger Hannover
Events Committee	Dawn Rogers
Apology for the Bake Sale	Eunice McCarthy

3. **Place the right tab stop on the far right end of the ruler.**

The position is just a guess at this point.

4. **Type the first-column text.**

The text is left-justified, as it is normally.

5. **Press the Tab key.**

The insertion pointer hops to the right tab stop.

6. **Type the second-column text.**

The text you type is right-justified, pushing to the left as you type.

7. **Press Enter to end the line of text.**

8. **Repeat Steps 4–7 for each line in the list.**

Afterward, you can adjust the list's appearance: Select all text as a block, and then drag the right tab stop back and forth on the ruler.

The Decimal Tab

Use the decimal tab to line up columns of numbers. You could set the right tab stop for this job, but the decimal tab is a better choice. Rather than right-align text, as the right tab does (see the preceding section), the decimal tab aligns numbers by their decimal — the period in the number, as shown in Figure 12-8. Follow these steps:

1. **Start a blank line of text.**

2. **On the ruler, click the tab well until the decimal tab stop appears.**

The Decimal Tab Stop icon is shown in the margin.

3. **Click the ruler to set the decimal tab stop.**

You can adjust the position later.

Tab well   Decimal tab stop

Baggage check (per bag)	$25.00
Window / aisle seat	$15.00
Realistic leg room	$35.00
Early boarding	$25.00
Reserved overhead bin space	$20.00
Unlimited lavatory use	Free!

4. **Type the first-column text.**

   This step is optional, though in Figure 12-8 you see the first column as a list of items.

5. **Press the Tab key.**

6. **Type the number.**

   The number is right-justified until you press the Period key. After that, the rest of the number is left-justified.

7. **Press Enter to end the line of text.**

8. **Repeat Steps 4–7 for each line in the list.**

You can adjust the list once it's complete: Select all lines, and then drag the decimal tab stop left or right.

TIP

When a line doesn't feature a period, text typed at a decimal tab stop is right-justified, as shown by the word *Free* in Figure 12-8. You can always reformat such a line to set a left tab stop, which may look better on the page.

The Bar Tab

Aside from being a most excellent pun, the bar tab isn't a true tab stop in Word; it has no effect on the tab character. Instead, the bar tab is considered a text decoration.

Setting a bar tab inserts a vertical bar in a line of text, as shown in Figure 12-9. Using a bar tab is much better than using the pipe (|) character on the keyboard to create a vertical line in a multicolumn list. Unlike with the pipe character, you can adjust all the bar tab characters, just as you can adjust any tab stop.

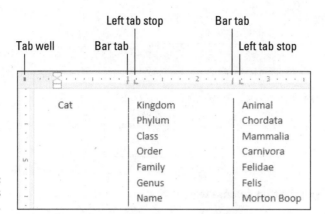

FIGURE 12-9:
The mysterious
bar tab.

To set a bar tab stop, follow these steps:

1. **Click the tab well until the bar tab stop appears.**

   The Bar Tab Stop icon is shown in the margin.

2. **Click the ruler to set the bar tab stop.**

   At each position, a vertical bar appears in the text. The bar appears even when the current line contains no tab characters.

To best use the bar tab stop, mix in a few other tab stops. For example, in Figure 12-9, left tab stops are set to the side of each bar tab stop. The effect is that text is organized into columns, but the bar tab serves only to decorate the text. It has no effect otherwise.

Fearless Leader Tabs

Press the Tab key, and the insertion pointer hops over to the next tab stop. The space occupied by the tab character is empty, but it doesn't have to be. Word lets you apply different styles to the empty tab space, which helps to create something called a leader tab.

A *leader tab* shows a series of dots or other characters where the tab character appears on the page. Three styles are available: dot, dash, and underline, as illustrated in Figure 12-10.

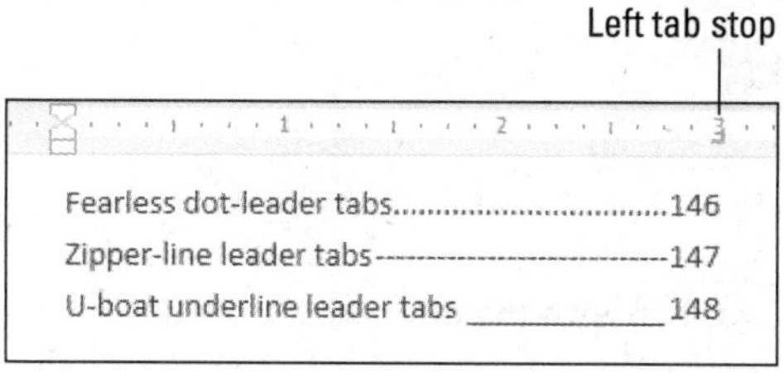

Left tab stop

FIGURE 12-10:
Leader tab
styles.

You can apply a leader to any tab stop in Word other than the bar tab. To do so, follow these steps:

1. **Create the tab-formatted list.**

   Refer to sections elsewhere in this chapter for information on creating a list of items.

2. **Select the text as a block.**

3. **Bring forth the Tabs dialog box.**

   The quick shortcut is to double-click a tab on the ruler. Also see the earlier section "Using the Tabs dialog box to set tabs."

4. **Select the tab stop from the Tab Stop Position list.**

5. **In the Leader area, choose the leader style.**

6. **Click the Set button.**

   Don't click OK before you set the tab stop to add the leader. This step is the one you forget most often.

REMEMBER

7. **Click OK.**

   The leader is applied.

TIP

Use the underline leader tab to create fill-in-the-blank forms. In the Tabs dialog box, set a left tab stop at the far-right margin (usually, 6.0 inches). Choose the underline leader style (number 4). Click Set and then click OK. Back in the document, type a tab to create a fill-in-the-blank line, such as this one:

```
Your name: _____
```

This format is far better than typing a zillion underlines.

Tab Stop, Begone!

To unset or clear a tab stop, follow these steps:

1. **Select the paragraph(s) with the offending tab stop.**

2. **Drag the tab stop from the ruler.**

   Drag downward. The tab stop is removed from the paragraph(s).

Removing the tab stop doesn't remove the tab character from the paragraph. Refer to the earlier section "Viewing the invisible tab characters," for help in hunting down rogue tabs.

REMEMBER

Word places default tab stops on every line of text. These cannot be removed.

For complex tab stop removal, such as when tab stops are close to each other or to the paragraph indent controls on the ruler, use the Tabs dialog box: Click to select the tab in the Tab Stop Position list and then click the Clear button. Click OK to exit the Tabs dialog box.

>> Clicking the Clear All button in the Tabs dialog box removes all tab stops from the current paragraph or selected paragraphs in one drastic sweep.

>> Tab characters are deleted like any other character: Press the Delete or Backspace keys.

Chapter **13**

Page Formatting

A *page* is the container for text. But unlike in the real world, where a page is a physical sheet of paper with readable ink marks, Word conjures new pages as needed, manifesting them from the electronic ether. This digital magic makes the concept of a page ethereal. To connect with reality, Word lets you define the paper format, which includes the page size, orientation, and margins as well as other format and attribute tidbits. The goal is to match the physical reality of a sheet of paper, even when that sheet may end up as a digital document.

Describe That Page

Sheets of paper come in various sizes, such as letter and legal in the US. But page size isn't limited to these common formats. For example, paperback novels have a specific page format, as does this book. The point is that the concept of the page varies. Word demands that you describe a page in specific terms. After all, the page is the canvas upon which you paint the document's text.

Setting page size

For a new, blank document, the page size is based upon Word's Normal template. In the US, it's defined as a standard sheet of letter paper, 8½ by 11 inches. In Europe, the A4 size is used. You're not stuck with this default, because the page size can be changed. Follow these steps:

1. **Click the Layout tab on the ribbon.**

2. **In the Page Setup group, click the Size button.**

   The Size icon is shown in the margin.

3. **Choose a page size from the list.**

   For example, if you want to print on that tall, legal-size paper, choose Legal from the list.

The entire document is updated to reflect the new page size, from first page to last.

>> To set a size not shown on the menu (refer to Step 3), choose the More Paper Sizes menu item. The Page Setup dialog box appears. Use the controls on the Paper tab to manually set the paper size.

>> Page size can be changed at any time, whether the document is empty or full of text. Obviously, page size affects layout, so this major change is probably something you don't want to do at the last minute.

>> A document can sport multiple page sizes. To do so, split the document into sections and apply a different page size to each section. See Chapter 14 for information on sections. Applying page formats one section at a time is done in the Page Setup dialog box, as described later in this chapter.

REMEMBER

>> Page size comes into play primarily when a document is printed. Despite your zeal to choose an oddball page size, unless the printer can handle that paper size, the document can't be printed. It can, however, be published electronically. That process is covered in Chapter 9.

>> See Chapter 15 for information on styles, which set the default text and paragraph formats. Chapter 16 covers templates.

Changing orientation (landscape or portrait)

An aspect of page size is whether the page is oriented vertically or horizontally. (I'm assuming it's no longer the fashion to print on square paper.) Page orientation can be set by adjusting the page size, but an easier way is available to change it. Follow these steps:

1. **Click the Layout tab.**

2. **Click the Orientation button.**

   The Orientation button is illustrated in the margin. It has two items on its menu: Portrait and Landscape.

3. **Choose Portrait to set the page vertically or Landscape to set the page horizontally.**

Word shifts the orientation for every page in the document. Text still prints from left to right across the page; only the paper's orientation has changed.

TIP

>> Make the decision to have your document in landscape orientation before you do any extensive formatting. This orientation affects paragraph formatting, which may require you to adjust the document's margins; see the next section.

>> Page orientation changes affect the entire document unless you split the document into sections; otherwise, the change applies to only the current section. Read Chapter 14 for details on sections, including directions on how to stick a single landscape page into a document that's otherwise portrait-oriented.

>> Scientists who study such things have determined that human reading speed slows drastically when people must scan a long line of text, which happens when you use landscape orientation. Reserve landscape orientation for printing lists, graphics, and tables for which portrait page orientation is too narrow.

TIP

>> Landscape printing is ideal for using multiple columns of text. See Chapter 20.

>> If you just want sideways text without turning the page, use a text box. See Chapter 23 for information on text boxes.

Setting the page margins

Margins create the area where text appears on a page, defining a rectangle with space left, right, above, and below. These margins provide room between the text and the page's edge, which keeps the text from leaking out of a document and spilling all over the computer.

Word automatically sets page margins at one inch from every page edge. Most English teachers and book editors want margins of this size because these people love to scribble in the margins. (They even write this way on blank paper.)

To adjust page margins in Word, obey these steps:

1. **Click the Layout tab.**

2. **Click the Margins button.**

   It's found in the Page Setup group and shown in the margin. You see a menu full of common margin settings.

3. **Pluck a proper margin setting from the menu.**

   Or choose More Margins to visit the Page Setup dialog box and set your own, custom page margins. Refer to the next section for more information.

The new margins affect all pages in the document — unless you split the document into sections, in which case the changes apply to only the current section. See Chapter 14 for information on sections.

>> The Layout tab's Margins button sets page margins. To set paragraph indents, also confusingly called margins, refer to Chapter 11.

>> Any orange stars appearing on the Margins menu's icons represent popular or recent margin choices you've made.

TECHNICAL STUFF

>> Many printers cannot print on the outside half-inch of a piece of paper, usually on one side — top, bottom, left, or right. This space is an *absolute* margin. You can direct Word to set a margin of zero inches, though text may not print there. Instead, use a minimum of 0.5 inches for all margins.

Using the Page Setup dialog box

When you want more control over page formatting, you must beckon the Page Setup dialog box, as shown in Figure 13-1. Specifically, you use the Margins tab in this dialog box (shown in the figure) to set specific margins on the page.

To use the Page Setup dialog box to specifically set page margins, obey these steps:

1. **Click the Layout tab.**

2. **Click the dialog box launcher in the lower right corner of the Page Setup group.**

   The Page Setup dialog box appears.

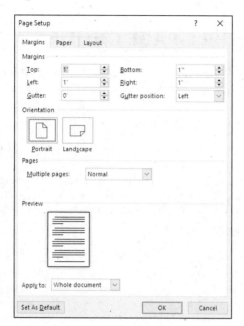

FIGURE 13-1:
The Margins tab
in the Page Setup
dialog box.

3. **Click the Margins tab.**

4. **Type the margin offsets in the Top, Bottom, Left, and Right boxes.**

   Or you can manipulate the spinner gizmo to set the values.

   Use the preview part of the dialog box to check the margins as they relate to page size.

TIP

5. **Ensure that Whole Document is chosen from the Apply To menu button.**

   You can reset margins for only a section or for selected text if you instead choose those options from the menu. See Chapter 14 for information on sections.

6. **Click the OK button to confirm the new settings and close the Page Setup dialog box.**

The Gutter settings help set margins when you need extra space on one edge of the page for binding. For example, if you plan to use a 3-hole punch on the left side of a page, choose Left from the Gutter Position menu. Then increase the Gutter margin to accommodate the three holes in the page without affecting the left margin setting.

Page Numbering

I remain puzzled by people who manually number their pages in Word. Such a thing is silly beyond belief. That's because

Your word processor numbers your pages for you!

Memorize it. Live it. Be it.

Adding an automatic page number

Word automatically numbers your pages. But wait! There's more: Word also lets you place the page number just about anywhere on the page and in a variety of fun and useful formats. Heed these directions:

1. **Click the Insert tab.**

2. **In the Header & Footer area, click the Page Number command button.**

   A menu drops down, showing various page number locations: Top of Page, Bottom of Page, Page Margins (the sides of the page), and so on.

3. **Choose from the submenu where to place the page numbers.**

   I want my page numbers on the bottom of the page, so I regularly choose the Bottom of Page submenu.

4. **Pluck a page numbering style from the list.**

   You see oodles of samples, so ensure that you check out the entire menu. You can even choose those famous *page X of Y* formats.

Dutifully, Word numbers each page in your document, starting with 1 on the first page, up to however many pages long the thing grows.

Here's the good part: If you delete a page, Word renumbers everything for you. Add a page? Word renumbers everything for you again, automatically: Insert the page number as described in this section, and Word handles everything.

>> To change the page number format, choose a different one from the Page Number menu.

>> To reference the current page number in your document's text, choose the Current Position item in Step 3. Word inserts the current page number at the insertion pointer's location. Also see Chapter 23.

>> The page numbers inserted atop or at the bottom of the document are placed in the document's header or footer. See Chapter 14 for information on headers and footers.

>> Page numbers are removed just as easily as they're added: See the section "Removing page numbers," later in this chapter.

TECHNICAL STUFF

>> The page number is inserted as a field, not as plain text. In Word, *fields* are updated and affected based on changing information.

>> When an inserted page number looks something like **{ PAGE * MERGEFORMAT }**, right-click that ugly thing and choose the Toggle Field Codes command. You can also click the mouse inside the hideous text (which is a field) and press Shift+F9.

Starting with a different page number

You and I know that the first page of a document is page 1, but Word doesn't care. It lets you start numbering your document at whichever value you want. If you want to start numbering your document at page 42, you can do so.

Assuming that page numbers are already set in your document, heed these instructions:

1. **Click the Insert tab.**

2. **In the Header & Footer area, choose Page Number ⇨ Format Page Numbers.**

   The Page Number Format dialog box materializes, as shown in Figure 13-2.

3. **Click the Start At button.**

4. **Type the starting page number in the box.**

5. **Click OK.**

FIGURE 13-2: Gain more control over page numbers.

Word starts numbering your document at the specified page number. So, if you enter 42 in Step 4, the first page of the document is now page 42, the next page is 43, and so on.

TIP

For more page number control, split the document into sections. Different page numbering styles or sequences can be set for individual sections. You can even suppress page numbers for a section, such as not numbering the first *(cover)* page of a document. See Chapter 14 for more information on sections.

Numbering with Roman numerals

When the urge hits you to regress a few centuries and use Roman numerals to tally a document's pages, Word is happy to oblige. *Sic facite:*

I. **Set the location for page numbers in the document.**

    Refer to the earlier section "Adding an automatic page number." After page numbers are established, you can set a different format.

II. **Click the Insert tab.**

III. **Click the Page Number command button and choose Format Page Numbers.**

    The Page Number Format dialog box appears.

IV. **Choose a style from the Number Format menu.**

    Two Roman numeral styles are available: lowercase and uppercase.

V. **Click OK.**

Veni. Vidi. Scrivii.

Removing page numbers

To banish automatic page numbers from above, below, or anywhere else amidst or around your text, follow these steps:

1. **Click the Insert tab.**

2. **Click the Page Number button to unfurl its menu.**

3. **Choose Remove Page Numbers.**

    And they're gone.

These steps remove only those page numbers set by using the Page Number command button, as described earlier in this chapter. Page numbers you've inserted in the text are unaffected, as are any page numbers you've manually added to a document's header or footer.

To remove a manually inserted page number, press the Backspace key twice because these page numbers are document fields, not regular text. See Chapter 23 for information on fields.

New Pages from Nowhere

With Word, you never have the excuse "I need more paper" when writing text. That's because Word adds new, blank pages as needed. These pages are appended to the end of the document, so even if you're typing in the midst of a chapter, the extra pages keep appearing so that no text is lost and nothing falls off the edge. This feature is refreshing, but it's not the end of Word's capability to thrust new pages into a document.

Starting text on a new page

You're writing a play and you've ended Act I. Sarah is seen holding up a bloody knife as Jacob bursts into the room. He says, "Oh my, Sarah! Where did you buy that dress?" Blackout. It's time to start writing Act II, which you want to begin at the top of the next page.

Your first choice is to keep whacking the Enter key until a new page shows up. This approach is horribly wrong. It works, but it leads to trouble later as you continue to craft your document.

The second, and preferred, choice is to insert a hard page break:

1. **Position the insertion pointer where you want one page to end and the next page to start.**

   I recommend splitting the page at the start of a new paragraph.

2. **Click the Insert tab.**

3. **In the Pages group, click the Page Break command button.**

   Text typed after the page break rests on the next page.

The hard page break stays with the text. No matter how you edit or add text before the break, the split between pages remains.

TIP

>> The keyboard shortcut to split pages is Ctrl+Enter.

>> To remove a hard page break, position the insertion pointer at the top of the page, just after the break. Press the Backspace key. If you goof up, press Ctrl+Z to undo.

>> Use the Show/Hide command to view the hard-page-break character. See Chapter 2 for information on the Show/Hide command.

>> The hard page break is easier to see in Draft view.

Inserting a blank page

Suddenly, you need a blank page in the middle of a document. Follow these steps:

1. **Click the Insert tab.**

2. **In the Pages group, click the Blank Page command button.**

   A new, blank page appears at the insertion pointer's position.

Any text before the insertion pointer appears before the blank page. Any text after the insertion pointer appears after the new page.

WARNING

>> The Blank Page command inserts *two* hard page breaks in the document.

>> Be mindful of the material you place on the new, blank page. Because two hard page breaks generated the new page, it's best suited for single-page items, such as graphics or a table. Any material longer than a page makes the rest of the document formatting look funky.

>> You don't need to use this command to add a new page at the end of your document. Just keep typing.

Page Background Froufrou

A page is also a canvas, a background upon which your document rests. This background sports a few formatting options of its own, items that dwell outside a document but remain part of the page formatting.

Coloring pages

The best way to print colored pages is to use color paper. When the price of printer ink isn't an option, however, you can direct Word to format each page in a document with a different background color. Follow these steps:

1. **Click the Design tab.**

2. **In the Page Background group, click the Page Color button.**

   You see a menu full of colors.

3. **Choose a color from the palette.**

   Or choose the More Colors menu item to mix your own page background color.

The color chosen in Step 3 is applied to the document's pages.

To remove the color, in Step 3 choose the No Color item.

>> The colors displayed on the Page Color menu are based on the document theme. See Chapter 16 for information on document themes.

>> Page color is independent of text foreground and background colors. See Chapter 10 for information on text colors.

>> Unlike page size, orientation, and numbering, page background color is unaffected by document sections. The color is applied to every page in the document. See Chapter 14 for more information on document sections.

>> Choose the Fill Effects menu item in Step 3 to view the Fill Effects dialog box. Click the Gradient tab to set *gradients,* or multiple colors, as the page background. Use the Picture tab to apply an image to each page's background.

Printing colored pages

Viewing a colored page on the screen is one thing. Seeing it printed is another. In Word, you must direct the printer to print the page background color by following these steps:

1. **Click the File tab and choose Options.**

   The Word Options dialog box appears.

2. **Choose Display from the left side of the Word Options dialog box.**

3. **In the Printing Options area, put a check mark by the item labeled Print Background Colors and Images.**

4. **Click OK.**

   The page background color now appears whenever the document is printed — well, assuming that you use a color printer.

TECHNICAL STUFF

Because Word's page color isn't part of the paper, it doesn't cover the entire printed page. The reason is that your printer cannot mechanically access the outside edge of a page, so a white border (or whatever other color the paper is) appears around the colored page. Yes, it's just easier to print on colored paper than to waste all that expensive printer ink or toner.

Adding a watermark

Word's watermark feature isn't like the watermark you see when you hold up a sheet of fine paper to the light. Nope, it's for slapping a quick background on the page to let people know it's a draft or sample, or to warn people not to copy the page. Yes, this watermark feature is utilitarian, which is why you see it used a lot in government.

To slap a watermark on every page in your document, follow these steps:

1. **Click the Design tab.**

2. **In the Page Background group, click the Watermark button.**

   A menu plops down with a host of predefined watermarks you can safely tuck behind the text on the document's pages.

3. **Choose a watermark from the menu.**

   The watermark is applied to every page in the document.

To rid the document's pages of the watermark, choose the Remove Watermark command in Step 3.

>> To customize the watermark, choose the Custom Watermark command from the Watermark menu. Use the Printed Watermark dialog box to create your own watermark text or to import an image, such as the company logo.

>> The watermark is unaffected by section breaks. See Chapter 14 for information on section breaks.

>> If the watermark doesn't show up in the printed document, you must enable the Print Background Colors and Images setting. Refer to the preceding section.

IN THIS CHAPTER

» Using sections

» Placing a cover page on your document

» Adding a header or footer

» Creating unique headers and footers

» Suppressing the header and footer on the first page

» Working with headers and footers in sections

» Deleting a header or footer

Chapter **14**

Section Formatting

A document is composed of text littering upon pages. Both the text and the pages have formats. For text, the formatting is confined to characters and paragraphs. For pages, formats apply to all pages in a document — unless you cleave the document in page formatting containers called sections.

I confess that when I first started using Word, I balked at the concept of a section. Then, for some silly reason, I wanted one page in my document to be oriented horizontally. The only way to create this effect — or to remove the page number from the first page in a document — is to use sections.

» Section formatting affects page size, margins, orientation, and columns, all of which are covered in Chapter 13.

» Sections also affect headers and footers, which are text tidbits that appear at the top or bottom of each page in a document.

TECHNICAL STUFF

» Section breaks are unavailable in the online version of Word.

A Document Sliced into Sections

A *section* is a page formatting container. All documents feature one section, which is why the various page formatting commands affect the entire document — they're applied to a single section. A document, however, can be sliced into multiple sections. Each section sports its own page format, independent of the other sections.

Figure 14-1 illustrates three examples of how sections can affect page formatting.

Example 1: Change the page number style

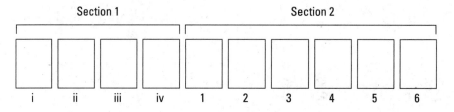

Example 2: No page number on the first page

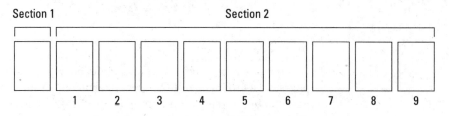

Example 3: Change the page orientation

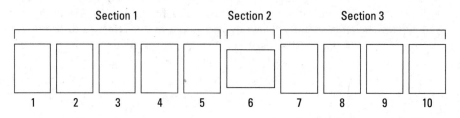

In Example 1, the document contains two sections. The first section uses Roman numeral page numbers. The second uses human numerals. Each section restarts page numbering.

The document in Example 2 contains a single-page section for its cover page. The second section — all remaining pages — uses page numbering.

In Example 3, the document has three sections. The first and third sections sport the same page formatting; the second section exists on page 6 so that it's presented in landscape orientation.

In all three examples, the document's text and paragraph formats remain unaffected by sections. Only page-level formatting is affected.

Reviewing section types

Word offers four different types of section breaks. Each one is applied in specific circumstances based on what you're doing with the page format. Here's the list as these items appear at the bottom of the Breaks menu on the ribbon's Layout tab:

Next Page: Start a new section and break the page, like a hard page break. (See Chapter 13.)

Continuous: Start a new section on a flexible boundary, depending on which page formatting command is used. A continuous section break may start anywhere on a page.

Even Page: This section break works like the Next Page break, but the new section starts on an even-numbered page, the left side of a bound manuscript.

Odd Page: This section break works like an Even Page section break, though a new page starts on the right side (odd page side) of a bound manuscript.

The most common section break is Next Page. A Continuous section break might be used in the middle of a page to reset page margins or to start a two-column text format. The Even Page and Odd Page section breaks help format documents such as eBooks, where you want a chapter to start on the odd page or a figure to appear on an even page.

Creating a new section

To create a section in a document, you insert a section break. Think of the section break like a hard page break (covered in Chapter 13), though it's also a boundary for page formatting. Follow these steps:

1. **Position the insertion pointer where you want the new section to start.**

   Click the mouse where you need to begin a new section, like creating a hard page break. For most section types, position the insertion pointer at the start of a paragraph.

2. **Click the Layout tab on the ribbon.**

3. **In the Page Setup area, click the Breaks button.**

   The last four items on the menu are various section breaks.

4. **Choose Next Page from the Breaks button menu.**

   A section break is inserted into the document, which starts the new section. This new section works like a hard page break.

Pages before the section break are in one document section, and pages after are in the next. Page formatting commands can be applied independently to either section.

Examples of when to use section breaks are available later in this chapter.

Using sections

You have two options to apply a page formatting command to a specific section within a document. In both instances, the insertion pointer must roost in the section you want to format.

To apply a page format to the current section, choose the page format item (margins, page number, orientation, and so on), as described in Chapter 13. In the Page Setup dialog box, however, use the Apply To drop-down menu to apply page formatting changes to the current document section, as illustrated in Figure 14-2.

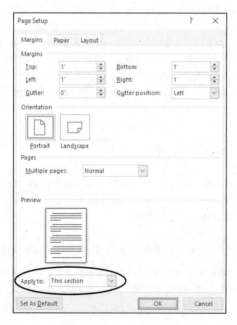

FIGURE 14-2:
Applying page formatting to one section only.

Each tab in the Page Setup dialog box features the Apply To drop-down menu, like the one shown in Figure 14-2. Use it to apply page formatting changes to the entire document or to only the current section.

When working with sections, I recommend activating the Section item on the status bar: Right-click the status bar and choose Section from the pop-up menu. The Section item shows the current section by number as you work through the document.

Removing a section break

Section breaks are invisible in Print Layout view, though you can see them in Draft view. To remove the section break, you delete it. Follow these steps, though you can start at Step 3 when using Draft view:

1. **Click the Home tab.**

2. **In the Paragraph group, click the Show/Hide command button.**

The Show/Hide button's icon is shown in the margin. After you click it, hidden codes and characters are revealed in the document.

3. **Position the insertion pointer to the start (left end) of the double-dashed lines that say Section Break.**

4. **Press the Delete key.**

The section break is gone.

5. **Click the Show/Hide command button again to hide the codes.**

After the section break vanishes, the page formatting from the deleted section adopts the format from the previous section. This update is to be expected, but it may alter things you can't see, such as page numbering and headers and footers.

That First Page

Even when you're blessed with a superior knowledge of paragraph formatting and you fully understand the magic of the section break, formatting that first page can be a bother. The kids at Microsoft are aware of your frustration, so they added some special first-page formatting features to Word.

Adding a cover page

The sneakiest way to slap down a cover page on a document is to use Word's Cover Page command. Here's how it works:

1. **Click the Insert tab.**

2. **In the Pages group, click the Cover Page button.**

    If you don't see the Pages group or Cover Page button, click the Pages button and then click the Cover Page icon.

    The Cover Page button displays a fat, fun menu full of various cover page layouts.

3. **Choose a cover page layout that titillates you.**

    The cover page is immediately inserted as the first page in the document.

Many preset cover pages feature replaceable text, such as [COMPANY NAME]. Click this text and type something appropriate, such as your actual company name, unless you actually work for the Company Name Corp. Do so for all bracketed text on the inserted cover page.

>> You can change a cover page at any time by choosing a new one from the Cover Page menu. The new cover page retains any replacement text you typed.

>> To remove a cover page, summon the Cover Page menu and choose the Remove Current Cover Page item.

>> The cover page that's added is followed by a hard page break. It's *not* a section break. Even so, it's treated differently from certain page formatting commands applied to the rest of the document. That means if you add page numbers or a header or footer to your document, the formatting applies to only the second page and later pages, not to the cover page.

Inserting a cover page manually

When you're dissatisfied with Word's cover page designs, you can craft your own cover page. All the formatting tools and document tricks presented in this book are at your disposal. You just need to insert the page at the start of the document.

Here are the general steps to take:

1. **Before writing the cover page, position the insertion pointer at the tippy-top of the document.**

    The keyboard shortcut is Ctrl+Home.

2. **Click the Layout tab.**

3. **Choose Breaks ⇨ Next Page.**

   A section break effectively inserts a new, first page into the document as its own section.

4. **Create the cover page.**

   On the new first page, add a title, additional text, graphics, and various document froufrou.

Because the first (cover) page is now its own section, the page formatting it sports is separated from the rest of the document. For example, you can apply page numbering to the second section, which keeps the cover page unnumbered (refer to Example 2 in Figure 14-1).

Headers and Footers

It's easy to confuse the concept of headers and footers with headings and footnotes. To help you understand the difference, consider these definitions:

» A *header* is text that appears atop every page in a document.

» A *heading* is a text style used to break up a long document, to introduce new concepts, and to help organize the text. See Chapter 15.

» A *footer* is text that appears at the bottom of every page in a document.

» A *footnote* is a tiny bit of text that appears at the bottom of a page, usually a reference to some text on that page. See Chapter 21.

» A *football* is a ball used in the game of football, which is also called football.

In Word, headers and footers dwell in exclusive areas outside the realm of regular text. These areas are found, top and bottom, on all pages in a document. Unless you place some text or other items inside these areas, they remain invisible.

Text that finds its way into a header or footer (or both) includes page numbers, your name, the document name, the date, and other information that's handy to have on every page.

Using a preset header or footer

Most documents use standard, noncreative headers and footers, placing common information into one or both locations. To accommodate your hurried desires, you can quickly shove one of these preset headers or footers into your document. Heed these steps:

1. **Click the Insert tab.**

2. **From the Header & Footer group, choose the Header button.**

   The Header menu shows a list of preformatted headers.

3. **Choose a header design.**

   The design's contents are added to the document, saved as part of the page format. Also, the Header & Footers Tools Design tab appears on the ribbon.

4. **Change any [Type here] text in the header.**

   Click the bracketed text and type to personalize your header.

5. **Use the commands on the Insert group of the Header & Footer Tools Design tab to add specific items in the header.**

   Examples are offered in the sections that follow.

6. **When you're done working on the header, click the Close Header and Footer button.**

   This button appears on the Header & Footer Tools Design tab. Alternatively, you can double-click in the main text body.

To add a footer, choose the Footer button in Step 2 and think of the word *footer* whenever you see the word *header* in the preceding steps.

After you exit from the header or footer, you see its text at the top or bottom of the document in Print Layout view. It appears ghostly, to let you know that it's there but not part of the document's text. To edit the header or footer, double-click this ghostly text.

Creating a custom header or footer

When one of the preset header/footer designs doesn't cut it, consider creating your own. The secret is to double-click the space at the top or bottom of the page in Print Layout view. This location is the header or footer area, respectively. When it becomes active, you can manually craft a header or footer to match your inner-most desires.

A header or footer can contain text, a graphical goober, a field, or any other item you can slap down into the main part of the document. Common and useful commands appear on the Header & Footer Tools Design tab, but you can use other tabs on the ribbon to create and customize a header or footer.

TIP

To switch between the header and footer while editing, click the Go to Footer or Go to Header button. These buttons are found on the Header & Footer Tools Design tab in the Navigation group.

Type text

Any text you type in a header or footer becomes part of the header or footer. It doesn't have to be fancy text — just whatever text you want appearing at the top or bottom of every page in the document.

Word's default format for lines in a header or footer includes two tab stops: a center tab stop in the middle of the page and a right tab stop aligned with the right margin. Use these tab stops, as illustrated in Figure 14-3, to create useful header text.

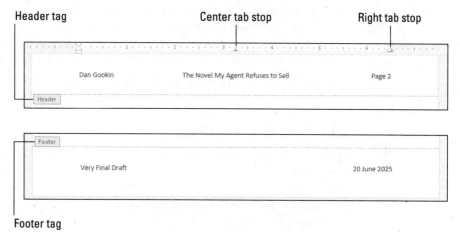

Header tag   Center tab stop   Right tab stop

Dan Gookin   The Novel My Agent Refuses to Sell   Page 2

Header

Footer

Very Final Draft   20 June 2025

FIGURE 14-3:
Text in a header and a footer.

Footer tag

Add a page number

It's tempting, and it seems like the obvious choice, but don't use the Page Number command on the Header & Footer Tools Design toolbar. If you need a page number in a header or footer, add a document page-number field. Follow these steps:

1. **Position the insertion pointer where you want the page number to appear in the header or footer.**

2. **On the Header & Footer Tools Design tab, in the Insert group, click the Document Info button and choose Field.**

   The Field dialog box appears. It's a busy place, covered in full detail in Chapter 23.

3. **From the Categories menu, choose Numbering.**

4. **In the Field Names list, select Page.**

5. **Choose a page number style from the Format list.**

   For example, choose the item 1, 2, 3, to use that numbering style.

6. **Click the OK button.**

   The Page field is inserted in the header. It reflects the current page number for every page printed in the document.

REMEMBER

>> You need not go to Page 1 to insert a page number in a header. Word is smart enough to place the proper number on the proper page, no matter where you're editing the header in the document.

TIP

>> If you want one of those *Page 3 of 45* indicators in a header or footer, you need two fields: the Page field, as described in this section, and the NumPages field. To add this field, repeat the steps in this section, but in Step 3 choose the Document Information category and in Step 4 choose the NumPages field name.

>> Refer to Chapter 12 for details on how the center and right tab stops work.

Add the date and time

To place the current date or time or an updating time field in a header or footer, follow these steps:

1. **Position the insertion pointer where you want the date or time to appear.**

2. **On the Header & Footer Tools Design tab, in the Insert group, click the Date & Time command button.**

   The Date and Time dialog box appears.

3. **Choose a format for the date or the time, or both.**

4. **To keep the date and time information current, place a check mark by the Update Automatically option.**

5. **Click OK.**

Also see Chapter 23 for information on the PrintDate field.

Working with multiple headers and footers

Headers and footers can change, depending on whether the page is odd or even. You can also alter the header or footer for a given document section, such as suspending the header and footer for a page or two, providing those pages dwell in their own section. Such agility requires knowing a few tricks, which I'm happy to share.

Odd and even headers and footers

See how this book has different footers on its odd- and even-numbered pages? The even-numbered pages show the page number and part title; the odd-numbered pages show the chapter title and page number. To configure such odd/even headers (and footers) for your document, obey these steps:

1. **Create or edit a header or footer, as described elsewhere in this chapter.**

2. **Click the Header & Footer Tools Design tab.**

3. **Click the Different Odd & Even Pages check box.**

   When this feature is active, Word sets up headers and footers for odd- and even-numbered pages. The Header and Footer tags in the document reflect the change as well, saying Odd Page Footer or Even Page Footer. The tag tells you which header or footer you're editing.

4. **Create the header and footer for the odd-numbered pages.**

   Follow the suggestions listed in this chapter.

5. **On the ribbon's Header & Footer Tools Design tab, in the Navigation group, click the Next button.**

   Word displays the even-page header or footer, allowing you to create or edit its contents. The Header or Footer tag changes to reflect which header you're editing.

   If clicking the Next button does nothing, your document has only one page! Add a page to enable the even-page headers and footers.

   To return to the odd-page header or footer, click the Previous button.

6. **Close the header or footer when you're done.**

To return to using only one header and footer for a document, repeat these steps but in Step 3 remove the check mark. Any even-page header or footer you've set is removed, leaving only the odd-page header and footer.

The even-numbered page is always on the left.

REMEMBER

No header or footer on the first page

Most people don't want the header or footer on their document's first page, which is usually the title or cover page. Suppressing the header for this page is easy — if you follow these steps:

1. **Edit the document's header or footer.**

2. **Click the Header & Footer Tools Design tab.**

3. **In the Options group, place a check mark by Different First Page.**

   That's it.

The Header or Footer tag on the first page changes to read First Page Header or First Page Footer. This visual clue informs you that the first page of the document sports a different header from the ones in the rest of the document. If you don't want anything to appear on the first page's header or footer, leave it blank.

Headers, footers, and sections

One way to apply different headers and footers to your document is to use sections. This way, you can change the header and footer between sections, but only when you unlink the headers and footers. Unless you know this trick, working with headers and footers in different sections can be frustrating.

To break the link between the current section's header and footer and the previous section's header and footer, follow these steps:

1. **Edit the document's header or footer in the section that you want to be different from the previous section's header and footer.**

2. **Click the Header & Footer Tools Design tab.**

3. **In the Navigation group, click the Next button to locate the start of the next section's header or footer.**

   The Header tag or Footer tag is updated to reflect the current section, as shown in Figure 14-4. You also see the tag Same as Previous, which is your clue that the header is identical to the one in the previous section. For example, if you change something in the first section's header, the change is reflected in all linked headers.

4. **In the Navigation group, click the Link to Previous button.**

   The link is broken. The Same as Previous tag disappears, but the header or footer's content doesn't change — yet.

5. **Edit the section's header or footer.**

   Changes made apply to only the current section.

Section 2 header   Headers are linked

FIGURE 14-4:
Header in
Section 2, linked
to Section 1.

Dan Gookin   The Novel My Agent Refuses to Sell   Page 4

Header -Section 2-   Same as Previous

Linked headers and footers confuse a lot of people. The problem is that changing the header or footer in one section doesn't update text in another. This effect means that the Same as Previous link still exists between the header or footer. To fix the problem, break the link as described in the step list.

To restore the link, edit the header or footer and repeat in the section you want to link. Click the Link to Previous button a second time to reestablish the link.

TECHNICAL STUFF

>> Unlinking a header or footer may not work if the document uses different headers and footers on odd- and even-numbered pages, as described earlier in this chapter.

>> The Different First Page option, described earlier in this chapter, doesn't link the header or footer on the first page with the rest of the document.

Removing a header or a footer

You can't destroy the header or footer area in a document, but you can remove all text and other stuff: Edit the header or footer, press Ctrl+A to select everything, and press the Delete key. Poof!

The more official way to remove a header or footer is to follow these steps:

1. **Edit the document's header or footer.**

2. **Click the Header & Footer Tools Design tab.**

3. **In the Header & Footer group, click the Header button.**

4. **Choose Remove Header.**

   The header is gone.

5. **Click the Footer button and choose Remove Footer.**

   The footer is gone.

Chapter **15**

Style Formatting

originally avoided styles in Word. They seemed silly, like extra work. Then I saw their power: When I applied a specific style to text, a single change to the style affected all text where the styles are applied. For example, to change my red text quotes to blue, one change is all that's needed to affect all red text in a document. Styles are powerful. And you use styles when you create a document, whether you avoid them or not.

The Big Style Review

A *style* is a collection of text and paragraph formats, such as bold, indent, left-justified, 16-point Arial. This collection is given a name. It's applied to text just like any other format, but the style carries with it all those individual character and paragraph attributes.

The amazing thing about styles is that when you modify a style, all text in a document with the style applied is magically and instantly updated. For heavy-duty formatting, using styles saves time.

Styles are available in all documents. The default paragraph style is called Normal. It's applied to text in a new document unless you apply another style. Along with the Normal style, many other preset styles are available for your use — plus, you can create your own.

For the current version of Word, the Normal style is defined as the Calibri font, 11 points tall, left-justified paragraphs, multiple line spacing at 1.08 lines, no indenting, zero margins, and 8 points of space after every paragraph.

Other preset styles include the Heading styles and Caption. You use the Heading styles, such as Heading 1 for a document's top-level heading and the Caption style for figure and table captions. The names reflect how to use the style.

Styles are also categorized by which part of the document they affect. Five style types are available:

Paragraph: The paragraph style contains both paragraph- and text-formatting attributes: indent, tab, font, text size — you name it. This type of style is the most common.

Character: The character style applies only to characters. It uses the character formatting commands, which are mentioned in Chapter 10.

Linked: The linked style can be applied to both paragraphs and individual characters. The difference depends on which text is selected when the style is applied.

Table: The table style is applied to tables, to add lines and shading to the table cells' contents. Refer to Chapter 19 for more information on tables in Word.

List: The list style is customized for presenting lists of information. List styles can include bullets, numbers, indentation, and other formats typical for the parts of a document that present lists of information. See Chapter 21 for info on lists.

These style types come into play when you create your own styles as well as when you're perusing various styles to apply to text.

Locating styles in Word

The Style Gallery appears on the Home tab in the aptly named Styles group. The gallery can be expanded or popped out into a floating pane, as illustrated in Figure 15-1.

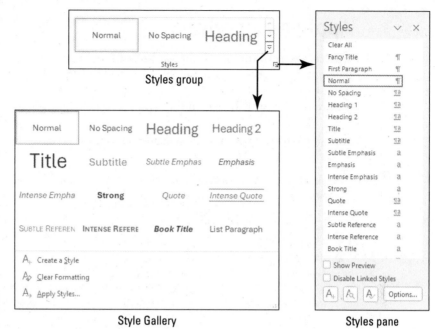

FIGURE 15-1:
Where Word
styles lurk.

Styles group

Style Gallery

Styles pane

The number of styles shown in the gallery depends on the width of the Word document window. If you click on the Expand button, you see the full gallery (refer to Figure 15-1).

The Styles pane pops up when you click the dialog box launcher in the lower right corner of the Styles group on the ribbon. This pane floats in front of the document window. To dismiss the pane, click the X (Close) button in its upper right corner.

>> To preview the styles in the Styles pane, put a check mark in the box by the Show Preview option, found at the bottom of the Styles pane.

>> Hover the mouse pointer over a style in the Styles pane to see more information about the style.

>> To view all available styles in the Styles pane, click the Options link (in the lower right corner). In the Styles Pane Options dialog box, choose All Styles from the Select Styles to Show menu. Click OK.

>> Word's predefined styles are specified in the Style Gallery, though you can customize the list to replace Word's styles with your own. See the section "Customizing the Style Gallery," later in this chapter.

Applying a style

Styles are applied to text, just like any other formatting. Select a block of text and then apply the style: Select the style from the Style Gallery or the Styles pane (refer to the preceding section). You can also choose a style and start typing. In both cases, the formats held in the style are applied to the text.

TIP

>> Some styles are assigned a keyboard shortcut. For example, the shortcut for the Normal style is Ctrl+Shift+N.

>> Heading styles play a special role in Word. They're used for document navigation and outlining as well as for creating a table of contents. See the later section "Creating heading styles" for details.

>> Applying a style replaces the previously applied style in the text.

>> If the Live Preview feature is enabled, you can hover the mouse pointer over a style in the Style Gallery to see how it affects selected text in the document. To enable this feature, click the File tab and choose Options. In the Word Options dialog box, General category, add a check mark by the Enable Live Preview item.

Identifying the current style

The Style Gallery and the Styles pane highlight the current style as you move the insertion pointer through your document's text. A more visible and detailed way to identify the current style is to use the Style Inspector. Follow these steps:

1. **Set the insertion pointer in a specific chunk of text.**

2. **Ensure that the Styles pane is visible.**

   If not, click the Home tab and, in the Styles group, click the Launcher icon.

3. **Click the Style Inspector button.**

   The Style Inspector button's icon is shown in the margin.

Upon success, you see the Style Inspector window, shown in Figure 15-2. This window discloses the text and paragraph formatting applied to the text based on the current style.

To see even more details, such as the specific formats used or attributes applied, click the Reveal Formatting button, as illustrated in Figure 15-2. Use the Reveal Formatting pane to examine all details of the style.

TIP

The shortcut key to summon the Reveal Formatting pane is Shift+F1.

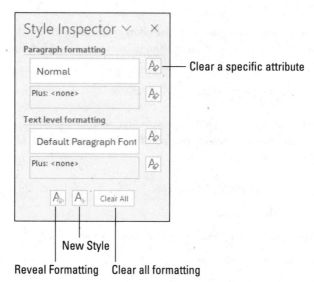

Clear a specific attribute

New Style

FIGURE 15-2:
Style Inspector. Reveal Formatting   Clear all formatting

Removing style formatting

You don't remove style formatting from text as much as you reapply another style. In Word, to remove a style, you replace it with the default style, Normal.

Because many Word users don't understand styles, Word comes with Clear Formatting commands. You can see such commands referenced in Figure 15-2, which illustrates the Style Inspector. Clicking those buttons replaces the given style with the Normal style.

>> See the later section "Changing the Normal style," for more details on setting default formatting.

>> Also see Chapter 10 for information on using the Clear Formatting command, which applies to font formats.

REMEMBER

>> "Clearing" formatting merely restores the style's original formatting. If you "remove" a style, you replace it with the Normal style. If you "clear" formatting, you remove any formatting not defined in the current style.

Make Your Own Styles

To convince you that styles are important, consider this: You create a custom format for your document's headings. You pick the right font, size, and color and add just enough space after the heading. Then you decide to change the font. When you create a style, you make only one change and then all the document's headers are updated. Otherwise, you must change each individual heading. And that sucks.

Creating a style

The easiest way to make up a new style is to format a paragraph just the way you like. After the character and paragraph formatting is applied, follow these steps to create the new style:

1. **Select the text you've formatted.**

2. **Click the Home tab.**

3. **In the Styles group, display the full Quick Styles Gallery.**

Click the down-pointing arrow in the lower right corner of the gallery (refer to Figure 15-1).

4. **Choose the Create a Style command.**

The Create New Style from Formatting dialog box appears.

5. **In the Name box, type a short and descriptive name for your style.**

For example, you might type *proposal body* for the main text of a proposal or *dialogue* for a character's lines in a play.

6. **Click the OK button to create the style.**

The style is created and applied to the selected text.

The style you create appears on the ribbon in the Style Gallery as well as in the Styles pane (if it's visible).

>> Styles you create are saved with the document, along with the text and other document info.

WARNING

>> You cannot assign the name of an existing style to your new style. Word rudely warns you when the attempt is made.

>> To make the style available in documents, build a template, as described in Chapter 16. Styles in a template are available to all documents created by using that template.

>> To fine-tune a style after it's created, see the later section "Modifying a style."

Using the Create New Style from Formatting dialog box

A more detailed way to build a style is to summon the Create New Style from Formatting dialog box, which has the same name as its tiny cousin, described in the preceding section, but offers far more controls — all in one place. If you're familiar with using Word's formatting commands, this dialog box is worth a visit to create new styles. Follow these steps:

1. **Summon the Styles pane.**

   The keyboard shortcut is Ctrl+Shift+Alt+S. If you don't want to tie your fingers in a knot, see the earlier section "Locating styles in Word" for the long way to bring up the Styles pane.

   TIP

   Because I use a lot of styles, I prefer to keep the Styles pane open in my documents. If you drag the pane over the document window's left or right edge, it docks permanently. This presentation always gives you access to styles, unlike the Styles group on the Home tab.

2. **Click the New Style button.**

   The button's icon is shown in the margin. Click it to see the Create New Style from Formatting dialog box, as shown in Figure 15-3.

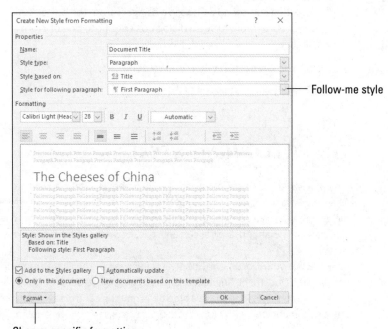

FIGURE 15-3:
The Create New
Style from
Formatting
dialog box.

Choose specific formatting

3. **Type a short, descriptive name for the new style.**

This name must be unique. Spaces and underscores are allowed.

4. **Ensure that Paragraph is chosen as the style type.**

When the format is a character style, choose Character. An example of a character style is blue, bold, Courier, 12-point — the one that I use in my documents for filenames.

5. **Choose an existing style as a base from the Style Based On drop-down list.**

Following this step saves time. If the style you're creating features similar formatting as an existing style, choose that style from the list. The formats from that style are copied over, letting you build upon them or reuse them in a different way.

Suppose that your B-level heading is the same as the A-level heading style, but 14 points instead of 18. Use the existing A-level style to quickly build your new, B-level style, modifying only the font size.

6. **Use the controls in the dialog box to set the style's format.**

The Create New Style from Formatting dialog box is brimming with style command buttons.

TIP

Use the Format button in the dialog box's lower left corner to apply specific formatting commands. Choose a category from the button's menu, such as Font or Paragraph, to see a dialog box specific to one of Word's formatting categories.

7. **Click the OK button when you're done.**

The new style is created.

THE FOLLOW-ME STYLE

A helpful way to quickly apply styles in a document is to take advantage of the Style for Following Paragraph menu, found at the top of the Create New Style from Formatting dialog box. When you choose a style from this item's menu, Word switches automatically to this style after using the current style. It's what I call the *follow-me* style.

Suppose that your Document Title style is followed by the First Paragraph style. After you type the Document Title text and press Enter, Word automatically switches to the First Paragraph style for you. This type of formatting control saves you time in formatting a document where you know that one style always follows another.

Modifying a style

Styles change. Who knows? Maybe blow-dried hair and wide lapels will creep back into vogue again, along with discos.

When you change your mind about a style and want to update a specific element, heed these steps:

1. **Summon the Styles pane.**

   Keyboard shortcut: Ctrl+Shift+Alt+S.

2. **Position the mouse pointer over the style you want to change.**

   Don't click the mouse, which applies the style. Instead, hover the pointer in the style's entry; a menu button appears on the right.

3. **Click the menu button.**

   The style's menu appears.

4. **Choose Modify.**

   The Modify Style dialog box appears, which is nearly identical to the Create New Style from Formatting dialog box (refer to Figure 15-3).

5. **Change the style's formatting.**

   Use the Format button to alter specific styles: font, paragraph, tab, and so on. You can even add new formatting options or assign a shortcut key (covered in the next section).

6. **Click OK when you're done.**

Modifying the style instantly updates all text to which the style is applied. For example, if you change the font for your Figure Caption style, all figure caption text changes at once. This power is one benefit of using styles.

Assigning a shortcut key to a style

It's tedious to apply the same style over and over, so why not assign your most beloved style a special shortcut key? Follow these steps:

1. **Press the keyboard shortcut Ctrl+Shift+Alt+S to summon the Styles pane.**

   I know: You can't use Ctrl+Shift+Alt+S for the style's shortcut key because it's already assigned to the Styles pane.

2. **In the Styles pane, click the style's menu button.**

   Position the mouse pointer over the style you want to change; the menu button appears.

3. **Choose Modify.**

   The Modify Style dialog box appears.

4. **Click the Format button and choose Shortcut Key from the menu.**

   The Customize Keyboard dialog box appears. The two items you must pay attention to are the Press New Shortcut Key box and the area just below the Current Keys list.

5. **Press the shortcut-key combination.**

TIP

   Use at least two of the shift keys — Shift, Alt, or Ctrl — when pressing the shortcut-key combination. Most of the Ctrl+Alt key combinations are unassigned in Word.

   The keys you press are named in the Press New Shortcut Key box.

   If you make a mistake, press the Backspace key and then choose another key combination.

6. **Confirm that the key combination you chose isn't already in use.**

   Look below the Current Keys list. The text there explains which Word command uses the key combination you've pressed. When you see [unassigned], it means that your key combination is available for use.

7. **Click the Assign button.**

8. **Click the Close button.**

   The Customize Keyboard dialog box skulks away.

9. **Click the OK button to dismiss the Modify Style dialog box.**

Try out your shortcut: Position the insertion pointer in a block of text and press the shortcut-key combination. The style is applied instantly.

TECHNICAL STUFF

I'll be honest: All the good shortcut keys are taken. Word uses most of them for its important commands. That leaves you with some Shift+Alt and Ctrl+Alt key combinations. Having these available is better than nothing.

Deleting a style

To peel away any style you've created, follow these steps:

1. **Display the Styles pane.**

   The keyboard shortcut is Ctrl+Shift+Alt+S.

2. **Right-click the style you want to obliterate.**

3. **Choose the Delete item.**

   The Delete item is followed by the style's name.

4. **Click the Yes button to confirm.**

   The style is removed from the document.

The Normal style is applied to the affected text.

You cannot delete any of Word's default styles, including Normal and the various heading styles.

Style Tips and Tricks

Awash in a sea of styles, it's easy to overlook some of the more subtle aspects of Word's styles. For example, the Normal style need not be stuck as the default for all new documents. And those heading styles offer more power than you may suspect.

Changing the Normal style

All documents sport the Normal style, which is the standard text-and-paragraph style and probably the style upon which all your personal styles are built. Like just about anything in Word, the Normal style can be modified — but I urge caution if you choose to do so.

To modify the Normal style's font or paragraph formats, summon the Font or Paragraph dialog boxes. (Refer to specific steps in Chapters 10 and 11, respectively, for details.) In both dialog boxes, you find a Set As Default button. Click this button to update the Normal style.

For example, to reset the Normal style's font to Times New Roman, follow these steps:

1. **Apply the Normal style to the current paragraph.**

2. **Press Ctrl+D to summon the Font dialog box.**

3. **Choose Times New Roman as the font.**

4. **Click the Set As Default button.**

   A dialog box appears.

5. **Choose the All Documents option to update the Normal template and change the Normal style for all documents.**

   If you choose the This Document Only option, the style is updated only for the current document.

6. **Click OK.**

I don't recommend making this choice unless you're determined to alter the Normal style. Mostly, people get into trouble when they accidentally change the Normal style and then want to change it back. If so, follow the steps in this section to restore the Normal style. A description of Word's current Normal style can be found in the earlier section "The Big Style Review."

Creating heading styles

Word's heading styles are numbered Heading 1, Heading 2, on down to Heading 9. You use these styles to identify different parts of a document, but they also take advantage of other Word features.

For example, text formatted with a heading style appears whenever you use the vertical scroll bar to skim a document. Headings can be expanded or collapsed, as part of Word's Outline feature, as described in Chapter 25. Headings appear in the Navigation pane when you search for text. They can be used when creating a table of contents.

TIP

You're not stuck with using Word's preset heading styles; you can create your own heading- or document-level styles. The key is to set the paragraph's outline level: In the Paragraph dialog box, use the Outline Level menu to set the heading level: Set Level 1 for top-level headings. For the next heading level (or *subheading*), choose Level 2, and so on. These paragraph formats are used by Word's document organization tools, such as the Navigation pane and the Table of Contents command.

Follow the steps in the earlier section "Using the Create New Style from Formatting dialog box" to update your heading styles to reflect the proper outline-level paragraph format.

>> Heading text is typically only one line long. Larger font sizes are usually selected. The Space After paragraph format is frequently applied.

>> Word's predefined Title style isn't a heading style.

Customizing the Style Gallery

To ensure that the styles you use the most appear in the Style Gallery, follow these steps:

1. **Summon the Styles pane.**

    Press the ungainly Ctrl+Shift+Alt+S key combination.

2. **Right-click the style you want to add to the Style Gallery.**

3. **Choose the command Add to Style Gallery.**

To remove a style from the Style Gallery, right-click the style in the gallery and choose the command Remove from Style Gallery.

REMEMBER

This trick can be useful, but the Style Gallery shows only a pittance of the styles available to a document. When you find yourself using lots of styles, use the Styles pane instead.

IN THIS CHAPTER

» **Understanding templates**

» **Using templates**

» **Attaching a template to a document**

» **Creating a document template**

» **Changing a template**

» **Understanding themes**

» **Formatting a document with a theme**

» **Creating your own themes**

Chapter **16**

Template and Themes Formatting

The smallest thing you can format in a document is text — specifically, an individual character. At the other end of the spectrum is the entire document. This container includes characters, paragraphs, page formatting, sections, styles — all of it. It's called a template.

If you believe that computers are supposed to save you time, templates are the great word processing time-saver. They contain a set of styles, perhaps even preset text and graphics, all designed to help you save time when you start creating a new document. Themes also play a role, collecting colors and other design elements. You can use preset templates and themes, or you can design your own. Or you can ignore this chapter and continue to toil in a meaningless and futile manner, which is what I did before I grew to appreciate the power of templates.

Instant Documents with Templates

A template helps you create documents that use the same styles, formatting, and common text elements without the need to re-create all the work and effort from scratch. A template saves time.

>> Choosing a specific template for a document is optional.

>> When you don't set a template, the document uses Word's default new-document template, called Normal.

REMEMBER

>> All documents in Word are based on a template. The template is attached to the document.

>> Word offers templates in two categories: Office and Personal. Office templates are those supplied by Microsoft and made available over the Internet. Personal templates are those you create.

TECHNICAL STUFF

>> Word uses three filename extensions for its document templates: .dot, .dotx, and .dotm. Older versions of Word used templates with the .dot extension. Since Word 2007, the .dotx extension is used, with macro-enabled templates using the .dotm extension. Filename extensions are normally hidden in Windows, though these extensions are referenced when choosing a file type in the Open dialog box.

Using a template to start a new document

When you press Ctrl+N to create a new, blank document in Word, you see a new document based on the Normal template. To use another template, either one supplied by Microsoft or one you've created, follow these steps:

1. **Click the File tab.**

   The File screen appears.

2. **Choose New from the left side of the File screen.**

   You see a list of template thumbnails. Atop are recently opened templates or those you've pinned to the New screen. Below this list, the templates are divided into two categories or tabs, Office and Personal, as illustrated in Figure 16-1.

3. **Choose a template.**

   Click the Personal tab to review templates you've created.

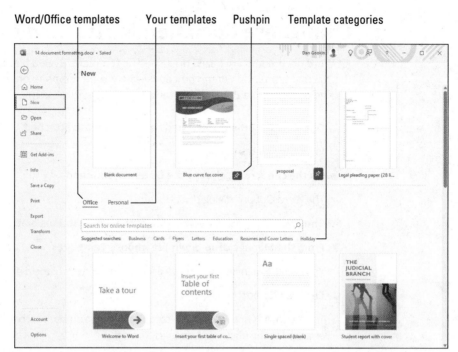

Word/Office templates · Your templates · Pushpin · Template categories

FIGURE 16-1:
Choosing a
template from
the New screen.

4. **If prompted, click the Create button.**

   The button appears when you use one of Word's predefined templates.

5. **Start working on the new document.**

   Text, graphics, headers, and footers may appear in the document, if these items are supplied with the template. You also have access to all styles saved in the template.

REMEMBER

Save your work! Saving the document doesn't overwrite the template, which remains available for you to use again. But, as with any document, you must save your work, assigning it a filename, as described in Chapter 8. Do so as soon as possible.

>> Using a template to create a new document doesn't change the template. To modify a template, see the section "Modifying a template," later in this chapter.

>> Refer to the later section "Templates of Your Own" for information on making your own templates.

TIP

>> It's possible to pin your personal templates to the Featured screen: Click the Pushpin icon, as illustrated in Figure 16-1. This way, you can quickly choose one of your own templates to quickly start a new document.

Changing a document's attached template

All Word documents are based on a specific template. Even a blank document uses the Normal template. When you choose the wrong template or suddenly desire to change or reassign a document's template, follow these steps:

1. **Open the document that needs a new template attached.**

2. **Click the File tab.**

3. **On the File screen, choose the Options command.**

   The Word Options dialog box appears.

4. **Choose Add-Ins from the left side of the Word Options dialog box.**

5. **From the Manage drop-down list, choose Templates.**

   You find the Manage drop-down list near the bottom of the dialog box.

6. **Click the Go button.**

   The Templates and Add-Ins dialog box appears. You see which template is attached to the document, such as Normal.

7. **Click the Attach button.**

   Word displays the Attach Template dialog box, which looks and works like the Open dialog box. It displays the contents of your personal template folder.

8. **Select the template you want to attach.**

9. **Click the Open button.**

   The new template is attached to your document.

10. **Ensure that the option Automatically Update Document Styles is selected.**

    Updating styles means that your document's current styles are changed to reflect those of the new template, which is what you want.

11. **Click OK.**

    The document is attached to the template. Any styles stored in the template are available.

Reassigning a template doesn't import into your document any preset text or graphics associated with the template. Only the styles, custom toolbars, and macros are merged into your document.

To unattach a template, select Normal (normal.dotm) as the template to attach in Step 8.

Templates of Your Own

If you enjoy the thrill and excitement of templates, you'll just burst with infectious glee at the thought of creating your own. Over time, you build up a collection. Custom templates greatly expedite your document production duties.

Building a template from an existing document

The easiest way to create a new template (the way I do it about 90 percent of the time) is to base the template on an existing document — for example, a document you've already written and formatted to perfection. The template retains the document's formatting and styles so that you can instantly create a new document with those same settings.

To make a template based on a document you've already created, follow these steps:

1. **Open or create a document, one that has styles or formats or text that you plan to use repeatedly.**

2. **Strip out any text that need not be in every document.**

   For example, my play-writing template has all my play-writing styles in it, but the text includes only placeholders — enough to get me started.

3. **Press the F12 key.**

   The F12 key is the ancient keyboard shortcut to the Save As dialog box. By using this key, you save about four other, tedious steps.

4. **Type a name for the template.**

   Type the name in the File Name box. Be descriptive. You don't need to use the word *template* when naming this file.

5. **From the Save As Type drop-down list, choose the option Word Template (*.dotx).**

   Ah-ha! This is the secret. The document must be saved in a document template format, which makes it different from a typical, boring Word document.

   Don't worry about setting the document's location. Word templates are saved in a predefined folder, which is chosen for you automatically.

6. **Click the Save button.**

   Your efforts are saved as a document template.

7. **Close the template.**

   The reason for closing it is that any changes you make from now on are saved to the template. If you want to *use* the template to start a new document, choose it from the New window, as described earlier in this chapter.

I perform this task for each of my books, writing Chapter 1 and then creating a new template based upon it.

REMEMBER

>> You don't change a template by using it.

>> You can create a new template from scratch by starting a new document, creating the necessary styles, and adding necessary text or graphical elements. Then follow the steps in this section starting at Step 3. This approach works best when you keenly know Word's formatting commands and are well-versed in creating templates.

Modifying a template

You have two options for changing a template. The first is to start a new document by using the template. Make the changes you want. Then save the document as a template file, overwriting the original template file.

The second way is to use Word's Open command to open the template file directly. This approach is more difficult because Word keeps the template files in a special folder that's not easy to find. Put on your nerd goggles to view the following:

```
%USERPROFILE%\Documents\Custom Office Templates
```

In your home, or user profile, folder, open the Documents folder and then open the Custom Office Templates folder. Use the Open dialog box to open a template file held in this location.

REMEMBER

>> You must open the template file directly to modify it. Use the Open command. Do not start a new document based on the template, which doesn't change the template.

>> If you use Word's Open command to open a template but no templates appear to be in the folder, don't panic! Instead, click the File Type menu button and choose Word Template. You should see the lot.

WARNING

>> Changing a template has a widespread effect. When you update or modify a template, you change all documents using the template. Although such a change can be beneficial, and one of the best reasons for using a template, be mindful of your changes!

» A second, secret location exists for Word (and all Microsoft Office) templates in a hidden folder buried under your user profile folder:

```
%USERPROFILE%\AppData\Roaming\Microsoft\Templates
```

The contents of this folder are duplicated in the folder mentioned earlier in this section.

The Theme of Things

Themes supply a palette of decorative styles, such as fonts and colors, to a document, giving your written efforts a professionally formatted feel while keeping hordes of graphic designers unemployed.

A theme consists of these elements:

Colors: A set of colors is chosen to format the text foreground and background, any graphics or design elements in the theme, plus hyperlinks.

Fonts: Two fonts are chosen as part of the theme — one for the heading styles and a second for the body text.

Paragraph spacing: This effect enhances paragraph line spacing, as well as spacing before and after, by adjusting these values uniformly. The spacing can be increased or decreased throughout the document.

Graphical effects: These effects are applied to any graphics or design elements in your document. The effects can include 3D, shading, gradation, drop shadows, and other design doodads.

Each of these elements is organized into a theme, given a name, and placed on the Design tab's Themes menu for painless application in your document.

» A professionally licensed, certified mentally stable graphic designer creates a theme's fonts, colors, and design effects so that they look good and work well together.

» A theme doesn't overrule styles chosen for a document. Instead, it accents the styles. The theme may add color information, choose different fonts, or present various graphical elements.

» The graphical effects of a theme are only applied to any graphics in the document; applying a theme doesn't insert graphics into your text. See Chapter 22 for information on playing with graphics in Word.

REMEMBER

>> Choosing a theme affects the entire document all at once. To affect individual paragraphs or bits of text, apply a style or format manually. Refer to Chapter 15.

Applying a document theme

To apply a theme to a document, obey these directions:

1. **Click the Design tab.**

2. **Click the Themes button.**

   Built-in themes are listed along with any custom themes you've created. Figure 16-2 illustrates the Themes menu.

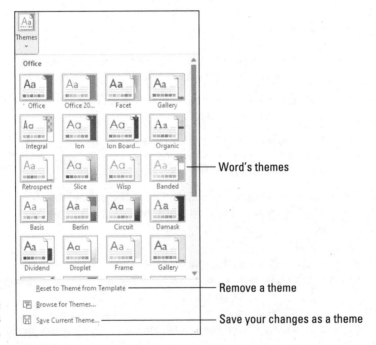

Word's themes

Remove a theme

Save your changes as a theme

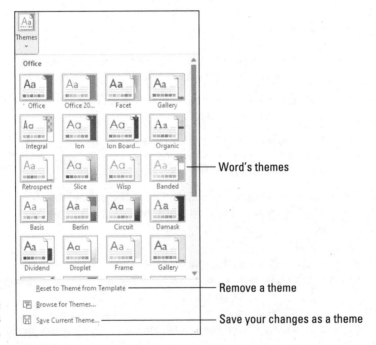

FIGURE 16-2:
The Themes
menu.

Each built-in theme controls all three major theme elements (colors, fonts, graphical effects), changing your document's contents accordingly. Hover the mouse pointer over a theme to visually preview its effect on theme elements (if any are present). Click a theme to choose it.

>> Because a document uses only one theme at a time, choosing a new theme replaces the current theme.

>> To remove a theme from your document, choose the menu command Reset to Theme from Template (refer to Figure 16-2).

>> If you would rather change only one part of a theme, such as a document's fonts, use the Colors, Fonts, Paragraph Spacing, or Effects command buttons on the Design tab.

Modifying or creating a theme

You can't create your own themes from scratch, but you can modify existing themes to make your own, custom theme. You start by selecting an existing theme. Choose one of these options while viewing the Design tab:

To create a custom color theme, choose Colors ⇨ Customize Colors. Use the Create New Theme Colors dialog box to pick and choose which colors to apply to text or various graphical elements in your document.

To create a custom font theme, choose Fonts ⇨ Customize Fonts. Use the Create New Theme Fonts dialog box to select fonts — one for the headings and another for the body text.

To create a custom paragraph-spacing theme, choose Paragraph Spacing ⇨ Custom Paragraph Spacing. Use the Manage Styles dialog box to set paragraph position and spacing.

For the Color and Font options, give the new theme a name and save it. You can then choose the theme from the Custom area of either the Colors or Fonts menu.

After customizing various elements, on the Design tab, click the Themes menu button and choose Save Current Theme. Use the Save Current Theme dialog box to give your theme a proper descriptive name and save it. The theme you create then appears in the Custom area of the Themes menu.

To remove a custom theme, right-click it on the Themes menu and choose the Delete command. Click the Yes button to confirm and remove the theme.

IN THIS CHAPTER

» Using fancy text formatting

» Swiping text formats

» Creating automatic lists and borders

» Formatting quotes, fractions, and stuff

» Centering a title page

Chapter **17**

Everything Drawer Formatting

E ven neatniks who proudly profess to be organized have one: It's the random-stuff drawer where you toss everything that doesn't belong anywhere else. Maybe it's in the kitchen or a desk drawer in your home office. Perhaps you have several such drawers. These are necessary because everyone needs a location for stuff that just doesn't fit anywhere else.

Welcome to the everything-drawer formatting chapter. Here you find formatting commands various and sundry. They just don't fit in well with the other formatting chapters found in this part of the book.

Weird and Fun Text Effects

On the Home tab, in the Font group, is a button adorned with a fuzzy, blue *A*, as shown in the margin (but not the blue part). It's the Text Effects and Typography button. Click this button to view the Text Effects menu, as shown on the far left in Figure 17-1. This menu lists special text decorations, well beyond the standard text attributes covered in Chapter 10. Choose an effect from the menu to apply it to your text.

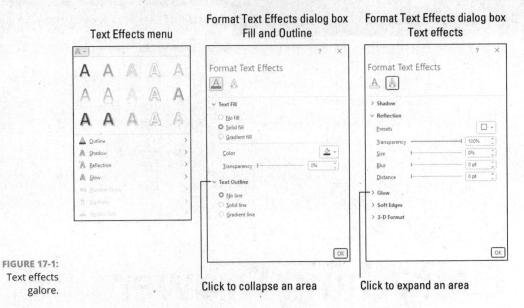

Text Effects menu

Format Text Effects dialog box
Fill and Outline

Format Text Effects dialog box
Text effects

FIGURE 17-1:
Text effects
galore.

Click to collapse an area

Click to expand an area

If the effects on the Text Effects menu aren't exactly what you want, you can build your own: Choose custom effects from the submenus on the Text Effects and Typography menu. If these effects don't sate your desires, you can summon the Format Text Effects dialog box, shown in the center and on the right in Figure 17-1. To access this dialog box, follow these steps:

1. **Press Ctrl+D.**

   The Font dialog box appears.

2. **Click the Text Effects button.**

   The Format Text Effects dialog box appears. It features two categories: Text Fill & Outline and Text Effects, shown in the center and on the right in Figure 17-1, respectively.

3. **Manipulate the controls in the dialog box to customize text effects.**

   Choose a category and then click a chevron to expand items in a subcategory. Controls appear, as illustrated in Figure 17-1, which let you customize each effect. Sadly, the dialog box lacks a preview window, so you must make your best guess about the results.

4. **Click the OK button to dismiss the Format Text Effects dialog box.**

5. **Click the OK button to close the Font dialog box.**

The options you choose affect any selected text in the document or any text you type from this point onward.

>> Font effects are best used for document headings and other decorative text. Seriously: Don't otherwise tax your reader with unnecessary text effects.

TECHNICAL STUFF

>> The Text Effects button is unavailable (dimmed) if you're editing an older Word document. See Chapter 24 for information on converting such documents. If the document is based on an older template, you must also update the template and then reattach the document to that template. It's a bother. See Chapter 16.

Steal This Format!

It's not a whisk broom, and it's not a shaving brush. No, it's a paintbrush. Not only that, it's a *special* paintbrush — one that steals text and paragraph formatting, lifting it from one place in your document and splashing it down in another. It's the Format Painter, and here's how it's used:

1. **Place the insertion pointer in the midst of the text that has the formatting you want to thieve.**

   Think of this step as dipping a brush into a bucket of paint.

2. **Click the Home tab.**

3. **In the Clipboard group, click the Format Painter command button.**

   The mouse pointer changes to a paintbrush/I-beam, as depicted in the margin. Use it to select and reformat text.

4. **Hunt for the text you want to change.**

5. **Select the text.**

   Drag over the text you want to change — to "paint" it.

Voilà! The text format is changed.

>> The Format Painter works with character and paragraph formatting, but not with page formatting.

TIP

>> To change the formatting of multiple bits of text, double-click the Format Painter. The Format Painter mouse pointer stays active, ready to repaint lots of text. Press the Esc key to cancel your Dutch Boy frenzy.

TECHNICAL STUFF

>> If you tire of the mouse, you can use the Ctrl+Shift+C key combination to copy the character format from one location to another. Use the Ctrl+Shift+V key combination to paste the character format.

>> You can sorta kinda remember to use Ctrl+Shift+C to copy character formatting and use Ctrl+Shift+V to paste, because Ctrl+C and Ctrl+V are the copy-and-paste shortcut keys. Sorta kinda.

Automatic Formatting

Part of Word's AutoCorrect feature (covered in Chapter 7) is a tool named Auto-Format. Whereas AutoCorrect fixes typos and common spelling boo-boos, Auto-Format fixes formatting fumbles.

Enjoying automagical text

AutoFormat controls some minor text formatting as you type. All its settings are visible in the AutoCorrect dialog box's AutoFormat As You Type tab, as shown in Figure 17-2.

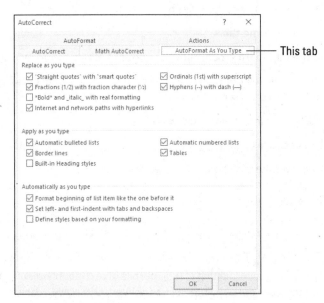

FIGURE 17-2: AutoFormat As You Type settings.

To display the AutoCorrect dialog box and access the AutoFormat As You Type features, heed these steps:

1. **Click the File tab.**

2. **Choose Options.**

   The Word Options dialog box appears.

3. **Select Proofing from the left side of the window.**

4. **Click the button labeled AutoCorrect Options.**

   The AutoCorrect dialog box says hello.

5. **Click the AutoFormat As You Type tab.**

   This part of the dialog box is where you find all the AutoFormat options. (Well, aside from the AutoFormat tab, which is redundant.) Add or remove a check mark to turn an option on or off, respectively.

The best way to demonstrate the AutoFormat-as-you-type concept is to have a Word document on the screen and then type the examples in the following sections. These samples demonstrate only a few of the tricks AutoFormat can perform.

Smart quotes

The quote keys on the keyboard generate *tick mark* characters: " and ' . AutoFormat converts them into the more stylish open and closed curly quotes. Type hither:

```
I'm a politician! There's a difference between
a promise and a "promise."
```

Both the single and double quotes are converted.

Real fractions

You can format a fraction by formatting the first value in superscript and the second value in subscript. Or you can let AutoFormat do it for you. Here's an example:

```
Every day I eat ½ of my body weight
in peanut butter.
```

The characters 1/2 are converted into the single character ½. This trick works for some, but not all, common fractions. When it doesn't work, use superscript/subscript formatting, as described in Chapter 31.

Hyperlinks

Word can underline *and* activate hyperlinks that are typed in your document, such as

```
Well, I've never been to heaven, but I've
been to https://www.oklahoma.gov/.
```

The website `https://www.oklahoma.gov` is automatically underlined, colored, and turned into an active web page link for you. (To follow the link, Ctrl+click the text.)

Ordinals

You're guessing wrong if you think that *ordinals* are a baseball team or a group of religious leaders. They're numbers that represent an order (get it?), such as first, second, third, and so on. Here's how AutoFormat deals with ordinals:

```
Yes, even with only two pies in the contest,
the judges awarded you 3rd place.
```

Word's AutoFormat feature automatically superscripts ordinal numbers, making them look oh-so-spiffy.

Em dashes

An *em dash* is the official typesetting term for a long dash, longer than the hyphen (or its evil twin, the en dash). Most people type two hyphens to emulate the *em dash*. Word fixes that problem:

```
A red one is a slug bug—not a punch buggy.
```

After you type the – – ("dash dash") and then the word that follows, AutoFormat replaces it with the official em dash character.

>> The keyboard shortcut for typing an em dash is Ctrl+Alt+minus sign, where the minus sign (–) is the minus key on the numeric keypad.

>> The single hyphen is also converted into an en dash when you follow it with a word.

>> The keyboard shortcut for typing an en dash is Ctrl+minus sign.

>> The en dash is approximately the width of the letter *N* in the current font. Likewise, the em dash is the width of the letter *M*.

TECHNICAL STUFF

Formatting tricks for paragraphs

At the paragraph level, AutoFormat helps you quickly handle some otherwise irksome formatting issues. Some folks enjoy this feature, some despise it. The following sections provide a few examples of what AutoFormat is capable of.

Numbered lists

Anytime you start a paragraph with a number, Word assumes (through AutoFormat) that you need all your paragraphs numbered. Here's the proof:

```
Things to do today:
1. Refuel the nuclear reactor.
```

 Immediately after typing 1., you see the infamous AutoCorrect Lightning Bolt icon and notice that your text is reformatted. Darn, this thing is quick! The AutoFormat feature is guessing that you're about to type a list. Go ahead and finish typing the line; after you press Enter, you see the next line begin with the number 2.

Keep typing until the list ends or you get angry, whichever comes first. To end the list, press the Enter key twice to erase the final number and restore the paragraph formatting to unnumbered.

>> The AutoCorrect Lightning Bolt icon won't appear when you've mercifully disabled this feature.

TIP

>> This numbering trick works also for letters (and Roman numerals). Just start something with a letter and a period, and Word picks up on the next line by suggesting the next letter in the alphabet and another period.

>> Bulleted lists can also be created in this way: Start a line by typing an asterisk (*) and a space to see what happens.

>> See Chapter 21 for more information on Word's numbered and bulleted list formats.

TECHNICAL STUFF

>> You don't press the Enter key twice to end a typical paragraph in a document, but pressing Enter twice to terminate an AutoFormat list is completely acceptable. Doing so doesn't add an empty paragraph to your document.

Borders (lines)

A line above or below a paragraph is typographically called a *rule*, but Word uses the term *border*. Most folks call them lines. Here's how to use AutoFormat to whip out a border:

```
- - -
```

Type three hyphens and press the Enter key. Word instantly transmutes the three wee hyphens into a solid line that touches the left and right paragraph margins.

>> To create a double line, type three equal signs (=) and press Enter.

>> To create a bold line, type three underlines (_) and press Enter.

>> Refer to Chapter 18 for details on borders and boxes around the text.

Undoing an AutoFormat

You have two quick ways to undo autoformatting. The first, obviously, is to press the Ctrl+Z keyboard shortcut for the Undo command. Easy.

You can also use the Lightning Bolt icon to undo autoformatting. Click the icon to display a drop-down menu, shown in Figure 17-3. Use the options displayed to control the AutoFormat options as you type.

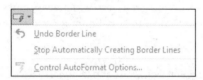

FIGURE 17-3: AutoFormat options.

Choosing the first option, Undo *whatever* (refer to Figure 17-3), is the same as pressing Ctrl+Z on the keyboard.

Selecting the second option, Stop Automatically *doing whatever*, disables the specific AutoFormat feature so that it never happens again. People enjoy selecting this option.

Choosing the final option, Control AutoFormat Options, summons the AutoCorrect dialog box's AutoFormat As You Type tab, which is shown earlier, in Figure 17-2.

Also see Chapter 33 for more details on disabling AutoFormat features.

Center a Page, Top to Bottom

Nothing makes a document title nice and crisp like having it sit squat in the center of a page, as shown in Figure 17-4. The title is centered from left to right, which is a paragraph formatting trick, but how can it be centered from top to bottom on the page?

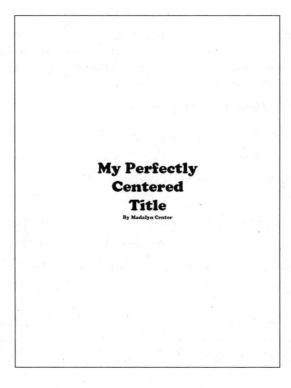

My Perfectly Centered Title

By Madalyn Center

If you're thinking about whacking the Enter key 17 times in a row to center a title from top to bottom, stop! Let Word do the math to make the title perfectly centered vertically on a page. Here's how:

1. **Press the Ctrl+Home key combination.**

   The insertion pointer jets to the start of the document.

2. **Type and format the document's title.**

   It can be on a single line or on several lines.

   To center the title paragraph, apply center paragraph justification: Press Ctrl+E. Apply any additional font or paragraph formatting as necessary.

   If the title is split between two or more lines, use Ctrl+Enter to break a line, which reduces the spacing.

   Avoid the temptation to press the Enter key to add space above or below the title. Such space is unneeded and wrecks Word's automatic centering powers.

REMEMBER

3. **Set the title page into its own section (if you haven't already).**

   Chapter 14 covers creating sections, but here are the CliffsNotes: To create a separate section for the title page, position the mouse pointer at the end of the title: Press the End key on the last line of the title, or the author line (refer to Figure 17-4). Click the Layout tab and, in the Page Setup group, choose Breaks ⇨ Next Page. With a next-page section break inserted into the document, the title now sits on its own page as its own section.

4. **Click the document's first page.**

   You need to be on the page you want to format.

5. **Click the Layout tab.**

6. **Click the dialog box launcher in the lower right corner of the Page Setup area.**

7. **In the Page Setup dialog box, click the Layout tab.**

8. **Click the Vertical Alignment drop-down list and choose Center.**

9. **Confirm that the Apply To drop-down list shows This Section.**

10. **Click OK.**

The first page of the document is centered from top to bottom. Because the title page is its own section, the top-to-bottom centering applies to only this page and not the rest of the document.

4

Spruce Up a Dull Document

Chapter **18**

They're Called Borders

I f you try to use any of these characters to draw a line or box in a Word document, your computer will explode: – = _ + |

Well, maybe not explode, but it gets angry with you. That's because Word hosts a collection of line-drawing tools to artfully place borders in and around your text. You have no need to pore over the keyboard and scout out the best character to box some chunk of text in your document. All you must know is that the text format is called a border and the graphical element is a line.

» This chapter covers the *border,* which is a linear graphical doojobbie applied to text.

» *Lines* are graphical elements that you can set in your document. See Chapter 22.

» To create a fill-in-the-blank underline, refer to Chapter 12.

» Terms aside, graphics designers refer to any line in the text as a *rule.*

The Basics of Borders

A border is a paragraph-level format. Yes, it's a line. People call it a line. But as a paragraph format, a *border* is coupled to a paragraph on the top, bottom, left, or right or some combination thereof. The line can be thick, thin, doubled, tripled, dashed, or painted in a variety of colors.

Like any paragraph style, a border sticks to the paragraph it's applied to: When you add a border to the left of the current paragraph and press Enter, the next paragraph inherits the same border.

Borders can also be part of a style, applied to text like any other format.

 To control the border format, on the Home tab, in the Paragraph group, look for the Borders button. The button's icon reveals the current paragraph's border style, such as Bottom Border, shown in the margin. Click this button to apply the format shown. To choose another border style, and view other options, click the downward-pointing chevron next to the button to view the Borders menu, shown in Figure 18-1.

Bottom Border
Top Border
Left Border
Right Border
No Border
All Borders
Outside Borders
Inside Borders
Inside Horizontal Border
Inside Vertical Border
Diagonal Down Border
Diagonal Up Border
Horizontal Line
Draw Table
View Gridlines
Borders and Shading...

FIGURE 18-1:
The Borders and Shading menus.

The final item on the Borders menu summons the Borders and Shading dialog box, covered in the later section "The Borders and Shading Dialog Box." Use this dialog box to gain more control when formatting paragraph borders.

Other sections in this chapter describe how to use the Borders button to apply borders (lines) to paragraphs in a document.

Putting borders around a paragraph

To apply a border to any or all sides of a paragraph, follow these steps:

1. **Place the insertion pointer in a paragraph.**

2. **Click the Home tab.**

3. **In the Paragraph group, click the triangle next to the Borders command button.**

   The Borders menu appears.

4. **Choose a border style from the menu.**

   For example, to place a line atop the paragraph, choose Top Border. Its icon is shown in the margin.

The border is applied using the line style, thickness, and color set in the Borders and Shading dialog box. See the later section "The Borders and Shading Dialog Box" for details.

> » Horizontal borders stretch between the paragraph's left and right margins. These margins are different from the page margins. See Chapter 11 for information on setting a paragraph's left and right margins.

> » A common use of paragraph borders is to set off a document title or heading. See the later section "Creating a fancy title" for formatting tips.

REMEMBER

> » When multiple paragraphs are selected, the border is applied to all paragraphs as a group. Therefore, a top or bottom border appears on only the first or last paragraph in the selected block. To set lines between paragraphs, see the next section. Likewise, when you press Enter to end a paragraph, any border formatting is applied to the following paragraph. For top and bottom borders, the effect is that only the first or last paragraph displays the border line.

Boxing multiple paragraphs

To stick a box around a paragraph, use the Outside Borders command, found on the Borders menu and shown in the margin. When multiple paragraphs are selected, the box wraps around the group.

If you desire to box several paragraphs in a row and keep lines between the paragraphs, use the All Borders command instead of Outside Borders. The All Borders icon is shown in the margin.

>> More fancy options for boxing paragraphs can be found in the Borders and Shading dialog box. See the later section "The Borders and Shading Dialog Box."

>> Before you go paragraph-boxing crazy, what you might need in your document instead is a table. See Chapter 19 for information on tables.

Removing borders

To peel away the border format from one or more paragraphs of text, apply the No Border format: Select the paragraph(s), click the Borders button, and then choose No Border, as shown in the margin.

TIP To remove specific parts of a border, use the Borders and Shading dialog box, covered — why, it's in the next section!

The Borders and Shading Dialog Box

To fully flex Word's border bravado, summon the Borders and Shading dialog box:

1. **Click the Home tab.**

2. **In the Paragraph group, click the chevron by the Borders button to display the Borders menu.**

3. **Choose the Borders and Shading command.**

The Borders and Shading dialog box appears, as shown in Figure 18-2.

Unlike the Borders menu, additional and custom border-setting options are available in the Borders and Shading dialog box. Most notably, you can set the border line style, thickness, and color.

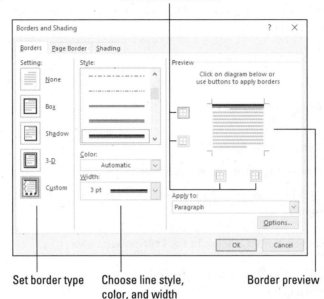

Set individual borders

FIGURE 18-2:
The Borders
and Shading
dialog box.

Set border type   Choose line style,   Border preview
                    color, and width

>> The Borders and Shading dialog box also allows you to place a border around a page, which is covered in the later section "Applying a page border."

>> You can use the commands in the Borders and Shading dialog box to format a table. See Chapter 19 for information on tables in Word.

Creating a fancy title

To create custom titles for newsletters, documents, or anything else you want to pretend is painfully important, click to select a paragraph and then go nuts in the Borders and Shading dialog box. You may end up with a result like the one shown in Figure 18-3.

Zolezzi's
Gym & Pizzeria

FIGURE 18-3:
Fancy borders.

714 Galactic Road, Hedonist, WI 53702 ~ (608) 555-6797

"Calories go in, calories go out! It's a wash!"

To properly apply a special border, follow these general steps in the Borders and Shading dialog box:

1. **Choose a line style in the Style list.**

    Scroll the list to view the full variety of styles (refer to Figure 18-2).

2. **Set the color in the Color list.**

    The Automatic color uses black, or the standard color as set by the document's theme (usually, black).

3. **Choose a width in the Width list.**

4. **Click in the Preview part of the dialog box to place the line: top, bottom, right, or left.**

To remove a border, click it in the Preview window.

TIP

To start out quickly, select a preset design from the list of icons on the left side of the dialog box (refer to Figure 18-2).

Click the OK button to apply the customized border to your document's text.

Boxing text

The border is primarily a paragraph-level format, though you can also wrap borders around tiny tidbits of text as a character format. To do so, follow these steps:

1. **Select the text.**

2. **Summon the Borders and Shading dialog box.**

    Directions are found earlier in this chapter.

3. **Set the border style you desire.**

    Only the Box and Shadow options are available, although you can set the color and line thickness.

4. **Ensure that the Apply To menu shows Text.**

    Normally, it shows Paragraph (refer to Figure 18-2).

5. **Click OK.**

Also see Chapter 10 for information on shading text. From a design point of view, I believe that shading text is a better option than wrapping it in a box.

Applying a page border

One gem hidden in the Borders and Shading dialog box is the tool to place a border around an entire page of text. The border sits at the page's margins and is in addition to any paragraph borders you might apply.

Here are the secret directions to set a page border:

1. **Place the insertion pointer on the page you want to border.**

   For example, you might put it on the first page in the document.

2. **Summon the Borders and Shading dialog box.**

3. **Click the Page Border tab.**

4. **Set the border style.**

   Choose a preset style, line style, color, and thickness.

TIP

   Use the Art drop-down list to choose a funky pattern for the border.

5. **Click the Apply To menu button to select which pages you want bordered.**

   Choose Whole Document to put borders on every page. To select the first page, choose the This Section — First Page Only item. Other options let you choose other pages and groups, as shown in the drop-down list.

   And now, the secret:

6. **Click the Options button.**

   The Border and Shading Options dialog box appears.

7. **In the Measure From drop-down list, choose the Text option.**

   The Edge of Page option just doesn't work with most printers. Text does.

TIP

   To add more "air" between the text and the border, increase the values in the Margin area.

8. **Click OK.**

9. **Click OK to close the Borders and Shading dialog box.**

To remove the page border, choose None under Settings in Step 4 and then click OK.

A page border is a page-level format. If you desire borders to sit on only certain pages, split the document into sections. Use the Apply To drop-down menu (refer to Step 5) to select the current section for the page border. See Chapter 14 for more information on section formatting.

Stick a Thick Line Between Paragraphs

It's not a border, nor is it a paragraph-level format. No, it's a horizontal line, which is used to break up paragraphs of text. To add a horizontal line, follow these steps:

1. Position the insertion pointer where you want the horizontal line to appear.

A horizontal line works best as its own paragraph; otherwise, it appears wherever the insertion pointer blinks. It can split a paragraph — if that's what you want.

2. Click the Home tab.

3. In the Paragraph group, click the Borders button.

4. Choose Horizontal Line.

Word inserts a line stretching from the left to right margins.

Click the line to adjust its size: Use the mouse to drag one of the six handles (top and bottom and the four corners) to set the line's width or thickness.

To format the horizontal line, double-click it. Use the Format Horizontal Line dialog box to set the width (as a percentage), height, color, alignment, and stuff like that.

To remove the horizontal line, click once to select it and then press the Delete key.

Chapter **19**

Able Tables

n olden times, writers used the Tab key to build a table and rows and columns. They toiled setting various tab stops and cleverly formatting the text. This approach worked, but Word offers a better way: the Table command.

Set a Table in Your Document

Tables are ideal for storing information in a grid, organizing text into cells stacked as rows and columns. Each cell is formatted with its own margins, spacing, or paragraph style. The cells can contain text or graphics. Lines and background colors complete the table design palette. Truly, Word lets you set a mean table.

Working with tables in Word

To begin your table-making journey, click the ribbon's Insert tab. In the Tables group, the only item is the Table button. Click this button to behold the Table menu, shown in Figure 19-1.

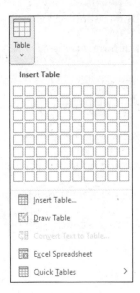

FIGURE 19-1:
The Table menu.

The Table menu features multiple methods for slapping down a table in the document, each of which is covered in this chapter. As a bonus, if you already used the Tab key to create tabular text, you can convert the clumsy concoction into a talented table; see the later section "Convert tab-formatted text into a table."

See the later section "Typing text in a table" for details on adding text to a table.

To help you modify tables and make them look pretty, two new tabs appear on the ribbon when a table is selected: Table Tools Design and Table Tools Layout. Details about using the commands on these two table tabs are offered throughout this chapter.

Creating a table

Word offers a slate of tools to create a table, from right brain to left brain with options between. These choices allow for more flexibility but also to make this chapter longer than it would be otherwise.

TIP

» I recommend placing the table on a blank line by itself. Furthermore, add a second blank line *after* the table. This blank line makes it easier to start typing text below the table.

» Don't worry about getting the table dimensions wrong. You can easily add or remove rows or columns after creating the table. See the later section "Adding or removing rows or columns."

The quick way to create a table

The fastest way to make a table in Word is to use the grid on the Table button's menu. Follow these steps:

1. **Click the mouse at the location in the document where you want the table to appear.**

2. **On the Insert tab, click the Table button.**

3. **Drag through the grid to set the number of rows and columns.**

   In Figure 19-2, a 4-column-by-3-row table is created. As you drag the mouse pointer on the menu, the table's grid magically appears in the document, as shown in the figure.

4x3 Table selected

Table button   Table preview in document

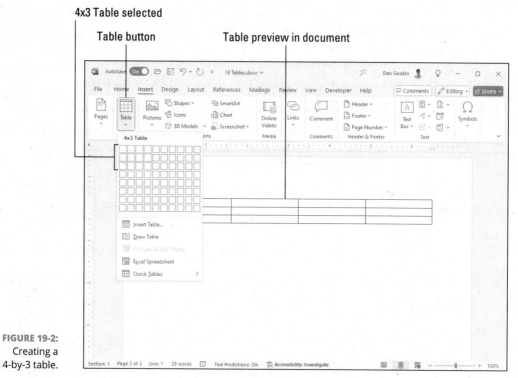

FIGURE 19-2:
Creating a
4-by-3 table.

4. **Release the mouse button to begin working on the table.**

See the later section "Text in Tables" to continue the table creation task.

The right-brain way to create a table

When dialog boxes make more sense than using menus and graphical goobers, follow these steps:

1. **On the Insert tab, click the Table button.**

2. **From the Table menu, choose the Insert Table command.**

   The Insert Table dialog box appears.

3. **Enter the number of rows and columns.**

4. **Click the OK button to plop down the table.**

The left-brain way to create a table

Free your mind from the constraints of conventionalism, clutch a crystal, and use the mouse to draw a table inside your document:

1. **Click the Table button and choose Draw Table.**

   The mouse pointer changes to a pencil, as shown in the margin.

2. **Drag the mouse to draw the table's outline in the document.**

   Start in the upper left corner and drag to the lower right corner, which tells Word where to insert the table. You see an outline of the table as you drag down and to the right, as shown in Figure 19-3.

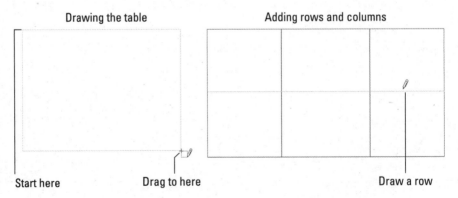

FIGURE 19-3: Drawing a table in a document.

Drawing the table   Adding rows and columns

Start here   Drag to here   Draw a row

3. **Draw horizontal lines to create rows; draw vertical lines to create columns.**

   Refer to Figure 19-3 (on the right) for an example of drawing a row.

While the mouse pointer resembles a pencil, you can use it to draw the rows and columns in the table.

4. **Press the Esc key when you've finished drawing the table.**

Convert tab-formatted text into a table

If you've used the Tab key to create rows and columns of text, hide your shame and quickly snap this part of the document into an official Word table. Follow these steps:

1. **Select the tab-formatted text.**

   If columns are separated by tabs, great. If they aren't, each paragraph you select becomes a row in a single-column table.

2. **Click the Insert tab.**

3. **Choose Table ⇨ Convert Text to Table.**

4. **Confirm the values in the Convert Text to Table dialog box.**

   Word has guessed at the proper number of columns and rows for the new table. If the columns are separated by tabs, ensure that Tabs is chosen at the bottom of the dialog box.

   Use the mouse to relocate the Convert Text to Table dialog box so that you can better see the text in the document.

   TIP

5. **Click OK.**

   A table is born.

See the later section "Table Modification" for details on fixing a freshly created table.

The "I can't do anything — please help" approach to creating a table

Word comes with an assortment of spiffy predefined tables. Plopping one down in a document is as easy as using the Quick Tables submenu: Click the Table button and, from the menu, choose Quick Tables. Select a table type from the submenu.

After the table is inserted, you can add or edit the existing text, add more rows or columns, or otherwise modify the table. Refer to directions elsewhere in this chapter for specifics.

A Quick Table is the fastest way to create a calendar in Word.

TIP

Converting a table to text

At some point, you may surrender the notion of needing a table, and desire the text to be freed from the table's confines. To perform such a jailbreak, obey these steps:

1. **Click inside the table you want to convert.**

    Don't select anything — just click the mouse.

2. **Click the Table Tools Layout tab.**

3. **From the Table group, choose Select ⇨ Select Table.**

4. **From the Data group, choose Convert to Text.**

    The Convert to Text dialog box appears. It guesses how you want the table converted, such as using tabs or paragraphs.

5. **Click OK.**

    Bye-bye, table. Hello, ugly text.

Some post-table-destruction clean-up might be necessary, but generally the conversion goes well. The only issue you may have is when a cell contains multiple paragraphs of text. In this case, undo the operation (press Ctrl+Z) and choose Paragraph Marks from the Convert to Text dialog box (before Step 5).

Deleting a table

To utterly remove the table from a document, text and all, heed these destruction directions:

1. **Click inside the table.**

2. **Click the Table Tools Layout tab.**

3. **In the Rows & Columns group, choose Delete ⇨ Delete Table.**

    The table is blown to smithereens.

WARNING

Deleting the table zaps its contents as well. If you must save the contents, I recommend converting the table instead of deleting it. See the preceding section.

Text in Tables

Text fills a table on a cell-by-cell basis. A cell can be empty or contain anything from a single letter to multiple paragraphs — or nothing at all. The cell size automatically adjusts to accommodate larger swaths of text.

>> Within a cell, text is formatted just as it is elsewhere in Word, including margins and tabs.

WARNING

>> Although a single cell can deftly handle vast quantities of text, graphic artists don't put a lot of text into a single cell. Consider another way to present such information.

>> I don't recommend formatting text inside a cell with first-line indents. Although it's possible, such formatting is a pain to manipulate.

TIP

>> Show the ruler when you work with formatting text in a table: Click the View tab and, in the Show group, place a check mark by the Ruler item. The ruler reflects the cell's margins and indents, and it's used to adjust a cell's width as well.

Typing text in a table

Text appears in whichever cell the insertion pointer is blinking. Type some text and it wraps to fill the cell. Don't worry if it doesn't look right; you can adjust the cell size after you type the text, as described in the later section "Adjusting row and column size."

>> To move to the next cell, press the Tab key.

>> To move back one cell, press Shift+Tab.

>> Pressing Tab at the end of a row moves the insertion pointer to the first cell in the next row.

TIP

>> Pressing the Tab key while the insertion pointer is in the table's lower right cell adds a new row to the table.

>> To produce a tab character within a cell, press Ctrl+Tab. Even so:

>> I don't recommend putting tabs into table cells. It makes the cell formatting all funky.

>> When you press the Enter key in a cell, you create a new paragraph in the cell, which probably isn't what you want.

>> Use the Shift+Enter key combination (a soft return) to break up long lines of text in a cell.

Selecting in a table

Selecting within a table refers to selecting text but also cells, rows, columns, and the entire table. Here are my suggestions:

>> Triple-click in a cell to select all text in that cell.

>> Select a single cell by positioning the mouse pointer in the cell's lower left corner. The pointer changes to a northeastward-pointing arrow, as shown in the margin. Click to select the cell, which includes the cell's text but also the cell itself.

>> Move the mouse pointer into the left margin and click to select a row of cells.

>> Move the mouse pointer above a column and click to select that column. When the pointer is in the sweet spot, it changes to a downward-pointing arrow (shown in the margin).

>> Clicking the table's handle selects the entire table. The handle is visible whenever the mouse points at the table or when the insertion pointer blinks inside the table.

If you have trouble selecting any part of a cell, click the Table Tools Layout tab. In the Table group, the Select button's menu provides commands to select the entire table, a row, a column, or a single cell.

Aligning text in a cell

Text in a cell sports some special, table-specific alignment options. To adjust the position of text in a cell, follow these steps:

1. **Click in the cell's text.**

2. **Click the Table Tools Layout tab.**

3. **In the Alignment group, click an icon representing the desired alignment.**

The Alignment group features nine icons representing nine position combinations: left, center, and right with top, middle, and bottom.

 Click the Alignment group's Text Direction button (shown in the margin) to change the way text reads in a cell. Keep clicking the button to reset the orientation.

Table Modification

No table is perfect. You may need to add or remove a row or column, adjust the width or height, or otherwise fine-tune and format the table. The tools to help you are found on two special tabs on the ribbon: Table Tools Design and Table Tools Layout. To summon these tabs, click anywhere in a table. Then start making adjustments.

TIP

The best time to format and fix a table is *after* you add text.

Adding or removing rows or columns

You can add rows and columns to any of a table's four sides or squeeze in new rows and columns, and even cells inside a table. The secret is to click the Table Tools Layout tab. In the Rows & Columns group, use the Insert buttons to add new rows and columns relative to the current row or column.

To remove a row or column, click to position the mouse and then click the Table Tools Layout tab. In the Rows & Columns group, choose the proper command from the Delete button menu.

>> Rows and columns are added or removed relative to the insertion pointer's position or any selected rows and columns.

>> When you choose the Delete ➪ Delete Cells command, you see a dialog box asking what to do with the other cells in the row or column: Move them up or to the left. Also see the later sections "Merging cells" and "Splitting cells."

 >> A mousey way to add a new row is to position the mouse pointer outside the table's left or right edge. A Plus (+) button appears, as shown in the margin. Click this button to insert a new row.

 >> Likewise, if you position the mouse pointer at the table's top edge, click the Plus (+) button, shown in the margin, to insert a new column.

Adjusting row and column size

To adjust row height and column width to best present the information, wait until *after* you've added text. Then position the mouse pointer at the left side of the column, just on the vertical border. The mouse pointer changes to the icon shown in the margin. Double-click and the column width is adjusted.

To adjust all column widths, put the mouse pointer at the far-left vertical border in the table and double-click.

To evenly distribute row and column sizes, click the Table Tools Layout tab. In the Cell Size group, click the Distribute Rows and Distribute Columns command buttons.

To oddly distribute row and column sizes, click the Auto Fit button, also found in the Cell Size group on the Table Tools Layout tab. Use the commands on the Auto Fit menu to choose how to adjust a table's row and column size.

The most common way to adjust rows and columns in a table is to use the mouse: Position the mouse pointer at the vertical or horizontal border within a table. When the pointer changes to a left–right or up–down pointy thing, drag to the left, right, up, or down to change the border's position. You can also use the ruler to adjust columns, providing that the ruler is visible.

Merging cells

The completely rational way to combine two cells into one or to split one cell into two is to use the table drawing tools and erase the line that separates them. Follow these steps:

1. **Click the Table Tools Layout tab.**

2. **In the Draw group, choose Eraser.**

    The mouse pointer changes to a bar of soap, shown in the margin, but it's supposed to be an eraser.

3. **Click the line between the two cells.**

    The line is gone.

4. **Click the Eraser tool again to quit merging.**

    Or you can tap the Esc key.

To merge a clutch of cells, select them and click the Merge Cells button. This button is found on the Table Tools Layout tab, in the Merge group, and shown in the margin.

Splitting cells

The easy way to turn one cell into two is to draw a line separating the cell. Follow these steps:

1. **Click the Table Tools Layout tab.**

2. **In the Draw group, click the Draw Table button.**

   The mouse pointer changes to the pencil pointer.

3. **Draw a line in the table to split a cell.**

   You can draw horizontally or vertically.

4. **Click the Draw Table button again when you're done.**

Any text in the cell you split goes to one side of the drawn line.

You can also split cells by selecting a single cell and then choosing the Split Cells command from the Merge group on the Table Tools Layout tab. Use the Split Cells dialog box to determine how to best mince up the cell.

Making the table pretty

Unless you want the table to look like it was made from hog wire, I recommend applying some table formatting. You can set line thickness, color, and style and apply color to the various rows and columns. The commands necessary are found on the Table Tools Design tab; click anywhere within a table to summon this tab on the ribbon.

TIP

Rather than get bogged down with details, you should know that the spiffiest way to spruce up a table is to choose a preset format from the Table Styles gallery: Click inside the table, and then position the mouse pointer at a thumbnail in the gallery to see a preview. Click the thumbnail to apply that format to the table.

>> More thumbnails are available in the Table Styles gallery than are shown on the ribbon: Scroll the list or click the down-pointing arrow (below the scroll bar on the left) to view the full gallery.

>> If you'd rather format the table in a more painful manner, use the Shading button as well as the commands located in the Borders group. These are the same borders applied to a paragraph, as revealed in Chapter 18.

TIP

>> To remove the table's borders, select the table and choose No Border from the Borders menu. If you choose this format, the borders vanish, and working with the table becomes more difficult. Therefore, I recommend that you also select the table and choose the View Gridlines command from the Borders menu. Unlike borders, a table's gridlines show up in the document window, but they don't print.

Adding a table caption

The best way to stick a title or caption on a table is to use Word's Insert Caption command. Don't bother trying to find that command on any of the Table Tools tabs. Instead, follow these steps:

1. **Click in the table you want to caption.**

2. **Click the References tab.**

3. **Click the Insert Caption button.**

The Caption dialog box appears.

4. **Type the table's caption in the Caption text box.**

The text *Table 1* might already appear. You cannot remove this text, so type a space after it and continue typing the table's caption.

TIP

If the text says *Figure 1* instead of *Table 1*, click the Label menu and choose Table. Or you can click the New Label button and concoct your own label.

5. **Click the Position menu and choose whether to place the caption above or below the table.**

6. **Click OK to set the caption.**

A benefit of using Word's Insert Caption command is that you can easily create a list of tables for a document. See Chapter 21 for details on building such a list.

IN THIS CHAPTER

» **Understanding columns**

» **Breaking text into columns**

» **Creating a three-column brochure**

» **Returning to one-column text**

» **Switching column layouts in a document**

» **Breaking up a column on a page**

Chapter **20**

Columns of Text

I f you're a reader, you might think of columns as a review written in a news-paper by a grizzled reporter. If you're a historian, the word *columns* may bring up the visions of Doric, Ionic, and Corinthian. If you're a military buff, you may think of rows of marching soldiers or rolling tanks. These are interesting interpretations of columns, but they have nothing to do with this chapter's topic, which is the folding of text in a Word document into columns.

All about Columns

Here's a shocker: All Word documents sport a column format. Even when you fail to see it, a page of text in Word is formatted as a single column of text. Otherwise, the only time you notice the column format is when you cleave a document's text into more than a single column on a page.

Column duty is handled by using Word's Columns command: Click the Layout tab and, in the Page Setup group, click the Columns button. A menu appears, listing common column-formatting options, as shown on the left in Figure 20-1.

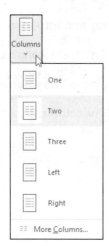
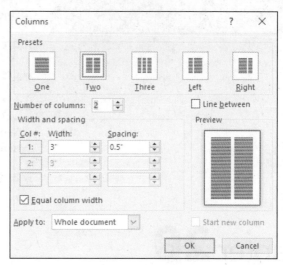

Columns menu   Columns dialog box

FIGURE 20-1:
The Columns
menu and
dialog box.

To be more specific with column layout, choose the More Columns command, at the bottom of the Columns menu. The Columns dialog box appears, as shown on the right in Figure 20-1.

The Columns dialog box helps you create and design multiple columns not available on the Columns menu: Use the Number of Columns box to set the quantity of columns desired. Use the Preview window to determine how the page is formatted. Click the OK button to apply the column format to the text.

TIP

» When multiple columns are set in a document, the keyboard's cursor movement keys operate in an unpredictable manner. I recommend clicking the mouse to position the insertion pointer in the text when you work with columns.

» The column is a page format. Choosing a column format from the Columns button menu affects the entire document, reformatting every page to the number of columns specified.

» When you need to set different column formats on different pages, split the document into sections and apply the column format to only the current section. See Chapter 14 for more information on sections.

REMEMBER

» Word can become fussy and slow when a document features multiple columns of text. Therefore, I recommend that you save your work often.

>> The maximum number of columns per page depends on the page size. Word's minimum column width is half an inch, so a typical sheet of paper can have up to 12 columns — not that such a layout would be appealing or anything.

>> Columns look best when using Print Layout view. Use this view when formatting columns.

TIP

>> To quickly adjust column widths, show the ruler: On the View tab, ensure that a check mark appears by the Ruler item (in the Show group). You can use controls on the ruler to adjust column width and position.

Making two-column text

When you desire to impress someone with your word processing prowess, I suggest putting two columns on the page. Any more columns and the line width becomes too skinny and difficult to read. Two columns, however, is a great way to get fancy and remain legible. Follow these steps:

1. **Click the Layout tab.**

2. **Click the Columns button and choose Two.**

You're done.

If the document already has text, it flows into two columns. If you create text after setting the number of columns, you see your scribblings flow down the left side of the page and then hop up to the upper right to start a new column.

TIP

>> To restore the document to one column, choose One from the menu (in Step 2).

>> Columns look best when full justification is applied to all paragraphs. The keyboard shortcut is Ctrl+J. See Chapter 11 for more information on paragraph alignment.

>> You can make specific column adjustments in the Width and Spacing area of the Columns dialog box (refer to Figure 20-1).

>> If you want an attractive line to appear between the columns of text, visit the Columns dialog box and put a check mark in the Line Between box.

TECHNICAL STUFF

>> The space between columns is the *gutter*. Word sets a gutter width at half an inch (0.5"). This amount of white space is pleasing to the eye without being too much of a good thing.

Building a trifold brochure

The three-column text format works nicely on standard-size paper in Landscape mode. This method is how most trifold brochures are created. Obey these steps after you've written the document's text:

1. **Click the Layout tab.**

2. **Choose Orientation ⇨ Landscape.**

The document's pages appear in landscape orientation, which is best for three columns of text and traditional for trifold brochures, programs, and documents.

3. **Click the Columns button and choose Three.**

Your trifold brochure is effectively formatted. Three columns are evenly spaced across the page, as illustrated in Figure 20-2.

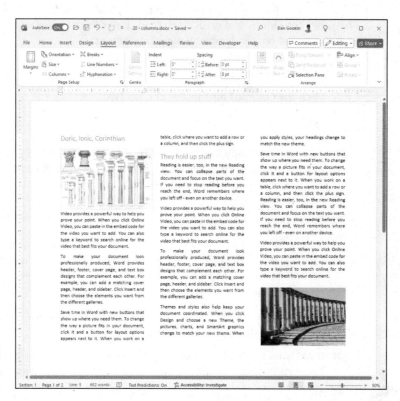

FIGURE 20-2:
Trifold brochure in Word.

For more sprucing up, use the Columns dialog box: On the Layout tab, click the Columns button and choose More Columns from the menu. In the dialog box, adjust the spacing between columns, add a line between, and perform other magic.

See Chapter 22 for information on sticking graphics into a document, such as those shown in Figure 20-2.

Giving up on columns

Columns can't be removed from a document, because all Word documents feature at least one column. The key to "removing" columns is to reset multiple columns back to that single column:

1. **Click the Layout tab.**

2. **Click the Columns button and choose One.**

   The document's text layout is restored.

When these steps don't work, summon the Columns dialog box (refer to Figure 20-1) and choose One from the list of presets. Ensure that Whole Document is chosen from the Apply To menu and then click the OK button. The columns are gone.

REMEMBER

Removing columns from a document doesn't remove sections or section breaks. See Chapter 14 for information on deleting section breaks.

Column Tricks

Columns need not march uninterrupted. You can conjure some magic to change the column format in a document or halt a column halfway down a page. These tricks give you more control over columns in a document, and they will dutifully impress historians and architects.

Changing column formats

As with other page-level formats, you can change column formats throughout a document: Part of the document is in one column and another part is in two columns and then maybe another part goes back to one column. The secret is to follow these steps:

1. **Click to place the insertion pointer at the spot where you need the column format to change.**

2. **Click the Layout tab.**

3. **Click the Columns button and choose More Columns.**

   The Columns dialog box appears.

4. **Choose the new column format.**

   Click one of the presets or use the clicker-thing to set a specific number of columns.

5. **From the Apply To drop-down list, choose This Point Forward.**

6. **Click OK.**

The text is broken at a specific point in the document (which you set in Step 1). Above this point, one-column format is used; after this point, the format chosen in Step 4 is used.

TIP

>> To help you pull off this feat, Word inserts a continuous section break in the document.

>> If you choose to manually insert the continuous section break, choose This Section from the Apply To drop-down list in Step 5.

>> Refer to Chapter 14 for more information on section breaks.

Placing a column break

Just as you can break a page of text, you can break the vertical flow of a column. This *column break* works only on multicolumn pages. It forces the column's text to stop at some point down the page and then continue at the top of the next column.

In Figure 20-3, you see an example of a column break, added at the end of the left column. This column break stops the left side column and then continues the text at the top of the right column.

To break a column, heed these steps:

1. **Click to place the insertion pointer in the document.**

   The insertion pointer's location becomes the start of the next column.

2. **Click the Layout tab.**

3. **In the Page Setup group, click the Breaks button.**

   A menu appears.

4. **Choose Column.**

   The text hops to the top of the next column.

Text continues here

Doric, Ionic, Corinthian

Video provides a powerful way to help you prove your point. When you click Online Video, you can paste in the embed code for the video you want to add. You can also type a keyword to search online for the video that best fits your document.

To make your document look professionally produced, Word provides header, footer, cover page, and text box designs that complement each other. For example, you can add a matching cover page, header, and sidebar. Click Insert and then choose the elements you want from the different galleries.

Save time in Word with new buttons that show up where you need them. To change the way a picture fits in your document, click it and a button for layout options appears next to it. When you work on a table, click where you want to add a row or a column, and then click the plus sign.

They hold up stuff

Reading is easier, too, in the new Reading view. You can collapse parts of the document and focus on the text you want. If you need to stop reading before you reach the end, Word remembers where you left off - even on another device.

Video provides a powerful way to help you prove your point. When you click Online Video, you can paste in the embed code for the video you want to add. You can also type a keyword to search online for the video that best fits your document.

To make your document look professionally produced, Word provides header, footer, cover page, and text box designs that complement each other. For example, you can add a matching cover page, header, and sidebar. Click Insert and then choose the elements you want from the different galleries.

Themes and styles also help keep your document coordinated. When you click Design and choose a new Theme, the pictures, charts, and SmartArt graphics change to match your new theme. When you apply styles, your headings change to match the new theme.

Save time in Word with new buttons that show up where you need them. To change the way a picture fits in your document, click it and a button for layout options appears next to it. When you work on a table, click where you want to add a row or a column, and then click the plus sign. Reading is easier, too, in the new Reading view. You can collapse parts of the document and focus on the text you want. If you need to stop reading before you reach the end, Word remembers where you left off - even on another device.

Video provides a powerful way to help you prove your point. When you click Online Video, you can paste in the embed code for the video you want

FIGURE 20-3: Column break.

Column break inserted here

REMEMBER

A column break doesn't terminate the column format. Instead, it splits a column, ending text at a certain point on a page and starting the rest of the text at the top of the next column.

TIP

Use the Show/Hide command in the Home group (the Paragraph Mark button) to spy exactly where to place the column break. You might want to insert the column break *after* a paragraph mark (¶) to have the columns line up at the top of the page.

To remove a column break, use the Show/Hide command, found on the Home tab in the Paragraph group. Click this button (its icon is shown in the margin) to reveal hidden codes in the document, including the column break. It appears in the text as a line by itself. Delete this line. Click the Show/Hide button again to hide the messy codes.

IN THIS CHAPTER

» **Automatically bulleting or numbering text**

» **Building a multilevel list**

» **Numbering lines on a page**

» **Adding a TOC to a document**

» **Creating an index**

» **Using footnotes and endnotes**

Chapter **21**

Lots of Lists

Y ou need not get fancy when writing a simple list, such as items to pick up at the hardware store to assemble a robot. Other types of lists in a document may require more work, such as creating a table of contents or an index for instructions on how to build the robot. Word provides tools to help you easily create both types of lists, plus it offers the capability to keep lists formatted and numbering updated automatically. Robots appreciate such features.

Lists with Bullets and Numbers

A list of items can be presented in multiple ways. A to-do list may feature check marks. A list of steps may have numbers. A list of points in an argument may feature letters, especially uppercase letters for angry arguments. Multilevel lists may mix numbers, letters, and the outlined shapes of insects. All these options are made possible by using Word's list-making tools.

» Word's list commands are found on the Home tab, in the Paragraph group.

» You might find Word overly eager to format a list for you. The feature is called AutoFormat. See Chapter 33 for information on disabling this potentially annoying feature.

TIP

Making a bulleted list

In typesetting, a *bullet* is a graphical element, such as a ball or a dot, that high-lights items in a list. The word *bullet* comes from the French word *boulette*, which has more to do with food than with round pieces of lead hurtling from a firearm, like this:

>> Bang!

>> Bang!

>> Bang!

 To apply bullets to the text, drop the gun and select several paragraphs. On the Home tab, in the Paragraph group, click the Bullets button, shown in the margin. Instantly, the text is not only formatted with bullets but also indented and made all neat and tidy.

TIP

>> To choose a different bullet style, click the menu chevron next to the Bullets command. Select a new bullet graphic from the list, or use the Define New Bullet command to concoct your own bullet style, such as that of a squashed insect.

>> The bullet is a paragraph format. As such, bullets *stick* to the paragraphs you type until you remove the format.

>> Bulleted paragraphs automatically are assigned a hanging indent, keeping the bullet away from the rest of the paragraph's text.

>> To remove bullets from the text, select the bulleted paragraphs and click the Bullet command button. You can stop applying bullets as you type by pressing the Enter key twice.

Numbering a list

To have Word number a list, heed these directions:

1. **Write the text, the items in the numbered list.**

   Don't write the numbers at the start of each paragraph. Word does this task for you in Step 3.

2. **Select the paragraphs as a block.**

1 ⸺
2 ⸻
3 ⸺

3. **On the Home tab, in the Paragraph group, click the Numbering command button.**

The button's icon is shown in the margin. The Numbering command assigns a number to each paragraph — plus, it formats the paragraphs with a hanging indent, which looks nice.

You can also click the Numbering command button and then type the list. Press the Enter key twice or click the Numbering command button again to turn off automatic numbering.

As a bonus, when you add or rearrange paragraphs in the list, Word automatically renumbers the list for you. This trick makes using the Numbering command better than trying to manually number and format your text.

» To choose another numbering format, click the menu triangle next to the Numbering command button. You can choose letters or Roman numerals, or you can concoct a numbering scheme by choosing the Define New Number Format command.

» To remove the numbering from a paragraph, choose None from the Numbering menu (refer to Step 3).

Creating a multilevel numbered list

A *multilevel* list consists of items and subitems all properly indented, as presented in Figure 21-1. Word automatically formats such a list, but it's a tricky thing to do. Pay attention!

1. **Start typing the list.**

Type the first, top-level item, such as the line that reads *Purpose* in Figure 21-1. You do not need to type the number (or letter) before this initial item.

1 ⸺
a ⸺
i -

2. **On the Home tab, in the Paragraph group, click the Multilevel List button.**

The button is shown in the margin. Immediately, the first line grows one number or letter, depending on the list format.

3. **Continue typing the list.**

Press the Tab key to indent and create a sublevel. Press Shift+Tab to unindent and promote an item to a higher level. Word labels the paragraphs according to the multilevel list format.

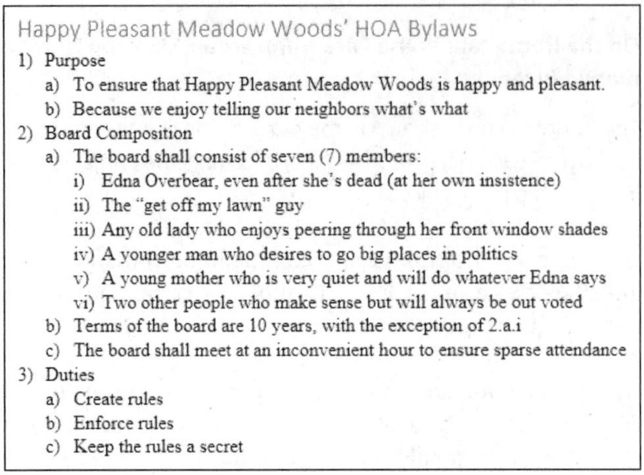
Happy Pleasant Meadow Woods' HOA Bylaws

1) Purpose
   a) To ensure that Happy Pleasant Meadow Woods is happy and pleasant.
   b) Because we enjoy telling our neighbors what's what
2) Board Composition
   a) The board shall consist of seven (7) members:
      i) Edna Overbear, even after she's dead (at her own insistence)
      ii) The "get off my lawn" guy
      iii) Any old lady who enjoys peering through her front window shades
      iv) A younger man who desires to go big places in politics
      v) A young mother who is very quiet and will do whatever Edna says
      vi) Two other people who make sense but will always be out voted
   b) Terms of the board are 10 years, with the exception of 2.a.i
   c) The board shall meet at an inconvenient hour to ensure sparse attendance
3) Duties
   a) Create rules
   b) Enforce rules
   c) Keep the rules a secret

FIGURE 21-1: A multilevel list.

You can also write the entire list in advance, select it, and then click the Multilevel List button to format it. Providing that you use Tab and Shift+Tab to organize the topics, and that you don't break the format, the list stays intact.

- To change the list's format, select all paragraphs and then choose a new presentation from the Multilevel List menu.
- WARNING: Where you can get into trouble is when you try to edit the list, insert new items, or move items around. Unless you remember the trick about pressing Tab and Shift+Tab to format the list, things can get screwy. If so, reapply the multilevel list format, as explained in the preceding bullet.
- TIP: If you're creating a complex, hierarchical list, use Word's Outline view instead of the multilevel list format. See Chapter 25.

Numbering lines on a page

Word lets you slap down numbers for every line on a page, a popular feature with those in the legal profession. Here's how it goes:

1. **Click the Layout tab.**
2. **In the Page Setup group, click the Line Numbers command button to display its menu.**
3. **Choose a numbering format.**

   For example, to number lines on each page 1 through whatever, choose the Restart Each Page option. Or, to number all lines on all pages cumulatively, choose Continuous.

To remove the line numbers, choose None from the Line Numbers command button. Or choose Suppress for Current Paragraph if you don't want the selected paragraph numbered.

REMEMBER

Line numbering is a page-level format. It sticks to each page in the document. If you prefer to number only one page, set aside that page as its own section. See Chapter 14 for more information on sections.

Document Content Lists

One reason to obey some of Word's silly rules is that when things are done just so, you can easily construct a useful document content list. For example, when you use Word's heading styles (or properly created heading styles of your own), you can quickly create a table of contents. You can mark specific tidbits of text for inclusion in an instant index. And, if you bother with Word's Caption command, you can build a list of figures or tables. These feats would be excruciatingly difficult if attempted on your own in a manual manner.

Creating a table of contents

The trick to creating a quick table of contents, or TOC, for your document is to use Word's heading styles. Use Heading 1 for main heads, Heading 2 for subheads, and Heading 3 for lower-level heads and titles. Word's Table of Contents command relies upon these formats to build a table-of-contents field, which reflects the heading names and their page numbers.

Providing that you've used the heading (or equivalent) styles in your document, follow these steps to create a table of contents:

1. **Create a separate page for the TOC.**

   Word places the TOC field at the insertion pointer's location, though I prefer to have the thing on its own page. Refer to Chapter 13 for information on creating pages; a blank page near the start of the document is ideal for a TOC.

2. **Click the mouse to place the insertion pointer on the blank page.**

   The TOC field is inserted at that point.

3. **Click the References tab.**

4. **In the Table of Contents group, click the Table of Contents button.**

   The Table of Contents menu appears.

5. **Choose a format.**

   The TOC is created and placed in the document, page numbers and all.

A preset title may be applied, such as *Contents*. Feel free to edit this text to make it clever, such as *Table of Contents*. Don't format this text as a heading unless you want it included in the table of contents.

>> When the steps in this section don't produce the effect you intended, it means that the document doesn't use the proper heading styles.

>> If your document uses your own heading styles, ensure that the paragraph format specifies the proper outline level. See Chapter 15 for more information.

>> If, instead of the TOC, you see a field such as **{ TOC \o "1-3" \h \z\ u }**, click the mouse in that ugly monster and press Alt+F9.

>> The TOC field is static, so it doesn't reflect further edits in the document. To update the field, click once to select it. On the References tab, in the Table of Contents group, click the Update Table button. Use the Update Table of Contents dialog box and choose to update the TOC. Click OK.

>> Cool people in publishing refer to a table of contents as a *TOC,* pronounced "tee-oh-see" or "tock."

>> See Chapter 23 for more information about fields in a document.

Building an index

An index is yet another document reference or list, one that Word helps you build and format. The secret is to mark text in a document for inclusion in the index. After words and phrases are marked, an index field is inserted, which displays the index.

Select index entries

To flag a bit of text for inclusion in an index, follow these steps:

1. **Select the text you want to reference.**

   The text can be a word or a phrase or any old bit of text.

2. On the References tab in the Index group, click the Mark Entry button.

The selected text appears in the Mark Entry dialog box.

3. If the entry needs a subentry, type that text in the Mark Index Entry dialog box.

The subentry further clarifies the main entry. For example, the word you select (the main entry) might be *boredom* and you type **In a waiting room** as the subentry.

4. Click one of the buttons, either Mark or Mark All.

The Mark button marks only the selected text. The Mark All button directs Word to include all matching instances of the text in the document.

TECHNICAL STUFF

When you mark an index entry, Word activates the Show/Hide command, where characters such as spaces, paragraph marks, and tabs appear in the document. Don't let it freak you out.

Because Show/Hide is on, the Index code appears in the document. It looks something like this:

```
{·XE·"boredom"·}
```

5. Continue scrolling the document and looking for items to mark for the index.

The Mark Index Entry dialog box remains open as you continue to build the index.

6. Click the Close button when you're done, or just tired, to banish the Mark Index Entry dialog box.

7. Press Ctrl+Shift+8 to cancel the Show/Hide command.

Use the 8 key on the keyboard, not on the numeric keypad.

Place the index in the document

After you mark bits and pieces of text for inclusion in the index, the next step is to build and place the index. Do this:

1. Position the insertion pointer where you want the index to appear.

TIP

If you want the index to start on a new page, create a new page in Word (see Chapter 13). I also recommend putting the index at the *end* of the document, which is what the reader expects.

2. Click the References tab.

3. **In the Index group, click the Insert Index button.**

   The Index dialog box appears. Here are my recommendations:

   - The Print Preview window is misleading. It shows how the index might look but doesn't use the actual index contents.

   - Use the Formats drop-down list to select a style for the index. Just about any choice from this list is better than the From Template example.

   - The Columns setting tells Word how many columns wide to make the index. The standard is two columns. I usually choose one column, which looks better on the page, especially in shorter documents.

   - I prefer to use the Right Align Page Numbers option.

4. **Click the OK button to insert the index into the document.**

   What you see is an index field, displayed using the information culled from the document. See Chapter 23 for more information on fields.

Review the index. Do it now. If you dislike the layout, press Ctrl+Z to undo and start over. Otherwise, you're done. But:

REMEMBER

When you modify your document, update its index: Click the index field and then choose the Update Index command button from the Index group. Word updates the index to reference any new page numbers and includes freshly marked index entries.

>> Feel free to add a heading for the index, because Word doesn't do it for you.

>> Use a heading style for the index header so that it's included in the document's table of contents. See the earlier section "Creating a table of contents."

TECHNICAL STUFF

>> Word uses continuous section breaks to place the index field in its own document section. Refer to Chapter 14 for more information on sections.

Adding a list of figures

The References tab's groups help you insert other document lists, but only if you've created the list appropriately.

For example, you can create a table of figures, providing you've used the References tab's Insert Caption button. To build the table of figures, click the Insert Table of Figures button (found in the Captions group). The process works similarly to inserting a table of contents or an index, but it works only when you use the Insert Caption comment to create captions.

Footnotes and Endnotes

Both footnotes and endnotes contain bonus information, clarifications, or asides to supplement text on a page. Each is marked by a superscripted number or letter in the text.[1]

The difference between a footnote and an endnote lies in its placement: A *footnote* appears at the bottom of the *page*, and an *endnote* appears at the end of the *document*. Otherwise, both references are created in a similar way:

1. **Click the mouse so that the insertion pointer sits immediately to the right of a word or some text that you want the footnote or endnote to reference.**

   There's no need to type the note's number; it's done automatically.

2. **Click the References tab.**

3. **From the Footnotes group, choose either the Insert Footnote or Insert Endnote command button.**

   A superscripted number is inserted into the text, and you're instantly whisked to the bottom of the page (footnote) or the end of the document (endnote).

4. **Type the footnote or endnote.**

5. **To return to the spot where you last edited the document, press Shift+F5.**

Here are some footnote/endnote notes:

>> The keyboard shortcut for inserting a footnote is Alt+Ctrl+F (F for *footnote*).

>> The keyboard shortcut for inserting an endnote is Atl+Ctrl+D (D for *da* endnote).

TECHNICAL STUFF

>> If you're curious, know that the keyboard shortcut Alt+Ctrl+E, which should be the Endnote command keyboard shortcut, instead enables and disables Word's revision marks feature, covered in Chapter 26.

>> As you add new footnotes or endnotes, all footnotes and endnotes are updated to be numbered sequentially in the document.

>> To browse footnotes and endnotes, click the References tab. In the Footnotes group, use the Next Footnote button's menu to browse the footnote and endnote references.

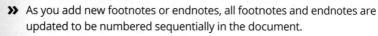

[1]Made you look!

» You can preview a footnote's or endnote's contents by hovering the mouse pointer at the superscripted number in the document's text.

» Use the Show Notes button (References tab, Footnotes group) to examine footnotes or endnotes as they appear on the page.

» To delete a footnote or an endnote, highlight its reference number in the text and press the Delete key. Word magically renumbers any remaining footnotes or endnotes.

TIP

» To convert a footnote to an endnote, right-click the footnote's text at the bottom of the page. Choose the Convert to Endnote command. Likewise, you can convert endnotes to footnotes by right-clicking the endnote text and choosing the Convert to Footnote command.

» For additional control over footnotes and endnotes, click the Dialog Box Launcher button in the Footnotes group. Use the Footnote and Endnote dialog box to customize the reference text location, format, starting number, and other thrilling options.

Chapter **22**

Here Come the Graphics

ord processing is supposedly only about words, but not always. Historically speaking, medieval Europe's scriptoriums had monks not only writing text but also illuminating manuscripts with illustrations. Typewriters could draw crude images, what we call *ASCII art* today. But Word firmly crosses the text-only Rubicon.

It's possible to mix and mingle text with graphics in Microsoft Word, almost broaching upon the software realm of desktop publishing. You can insert images, create them, and edit them to the point of Word pretending that it's some sort of graphics application. The tricks presented in this chapter might just save you 1,000 words.

Graphical Goobers in the Text

The door to Word's graphical goober closet is found on the Insert tab. The command buttons nestled in the Illustrations group place various graphical goodies into the text. Here's how the process works:

1. **Click the mouse at the spot in the text where you desire the image to appear.**

   You don't need to be precise, because you can always relocate the image.

2. **Click the Insert tab.**

3. **Use one of the command buttons to choose which type of graphical goober to add.**

   You can also paste a previously copied image, as described in the next section.

Figure 22-1 illustrates how a freshly added image looks, highlighting some of its features.

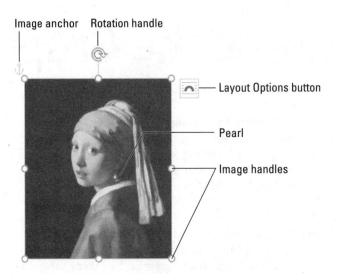

Image anchor   Rotation handle

Layout Options button

Pearl

Image handles

FIGURE 22-1: An image in a document.

While the image is selected, a new tab appears on the ribbon. For pictures, it's the Picture Format tab; for other types of graphics, the Shape Format tab appears. Both tabs offer similar tools to help you perfect the recently inserted graphic. Later sections in this chapter cover using those tools, as well as the controls illustrated in Figure 22-1.

» Right-click an image or a graphic to gain quick access to common graphical formatting commands.

TIP

>> To remove an image, click to select it and then tap the Delete key. If the graphical object, such as a shape, contains text, ensure that you've clicked the object's border before you tap the Delete key.

>> How the image sits in the document is important, and you should consider making these adjustments after adding the image. Refer to the later section "Image Layout" for information on precise image placement.

>> The more graphics you add in Word, the more sluggish it becomes. My advice: Write first. Add graphics last. Save often.

Copying and pasting an image

A simple way to thrust an image into a document is to paste it in from elsewhere. Follow these steps:

1. **Select the image in another program or from the web.**

2. **Press Ctrl+C to copy the image.**

   For a web page image, right-click and choose the Copy command or the Copy Image command. This command may not be available on all websites.

3. **Switch to the Word document window.**

4. **In Word, position the insertion pointer where you want the image to dwell.**

5. **Press Ctrl+V to paste the image into the document.**

If the image doesn't paste, it might be in a graphical format incompatible with Word.

You can also obtain an image from the web directly, by performing a web image search from within Word: On the Insert tab, in the Illustrations group, choose Pictures ⇨ Online Pictures. Use options in the Insert Pictures window to locate an online image, courtesy of Microsoft's Bing search engine.

Plopping down a picture from a file

Your computer is most likely littered with picture files. No matter how the image was created, if it's found somewhere on your PC, you can stick it into your document. Follow these steps:

1. **Click the mouse in the text where you want the image to appear.**

2. **On the Insert tab, in the Illustrations group, click the Pictures button.**

   The Pictures button icon is shown in the margin.

3. **From the Pictures menu, choose This Device.**

4. **Use the Insert Picture dialog box to hunt down and select the image.**

5. **Click the Insert button.**

   The image is slapped down in the document.

A nifty picture to stick at the end of a letter is your signature. Use a desktop scanner to digitize your John Hancock. Save the signature as an image file on your computer, and then follow the steps in this section to insert that signature picture in the proper place in the document.

Slapping down a shape

Word comes with a library of common shapes ready to insert in a document. These include basic shapes, such as squares, circles, geometric figures, lines, and arrows — plus popular and unpopular symbols. Graphics professionals refer to these types of images as *line art.*

To place some line art in a document, follow these steps:

1. **Click the Insert tab.**

2. **In the Illustrations group, click the Shapes button.**

   The button, shown in the margin, holds a menu that lists shapes organized by type.

3. **Choose a predefined shape.**

   The mouse pointer changes to a plus sign (+) in preparation for you to draw the shape in the document.

4. **Drag to create the shape.**

   The shape is placed into the document, floating in front of the text.

At this point, you can adjust the shape: Change its size, location, or colors. Use the Shape Format tab, conveniently appearing on the ribbon while the shape is selected, to effect those changes.

>> Instantly change the image by using the Shape Styles group on the ribbon's Shape Format tab. Choose a new style from the Shape Gallery. Styles are related to the document's theme; see Chapter 16 for information on themes.

TIP

>> Other items in the Shape Styles group affect the selected shape specifically: Click the Shape Fill button to set the fill color; use the Shape Outline button to set the shape's outline color; choose an outline thickness from the Shape Outline button's menu, on the Weight submenu; use the Shape Effects button to apply 3D effects, shadows, and other fancy formatting to the shape.

>> To more effectively format a shape, click the launcher in the lower right corner of the Shape Styles group. Use the Format Shape pane to manipulate settings for any selected shape in the document.

Sticking things into a shape

Shapes need not be colorful distractions. You can use a shape to hold text or frame a picture, which makes it one of the more flexible graphical goobers to add to a document.

To slip a smidgen of text into a shape, right-click the shape and choose the Add Text command. The insertion pointer appears within the shape. Type and format the text.

To place a picture into a shape, select the shape. Click the Shape Format tab. In the Shape Styles group, click the Shape Fill button and choose the Picture menu item. Use the Insert Pictures window to hunt down an image to frame inside the shape.

>> Yes, it's possible to have both a picture and text inside a shape. It may not look good, but it's possible.

>> To further deal with text in a shape, click the shape and then click the Shape Format tab on the ribbon. The Text group contains buttons to manipulate the shape's text.

>> To remove text from a shape, select and delete the text.

>> To remove a picture, choose a solid color from the Shape Fill menu.

>> Also see Chapter 23 for information on text boxes, which work like shapes with text inside.

Using WordArt

Perhaps the most overused graphical goober that's stuck into any Word document is WordArt. This feature is almost too popular. If you haven't used it yourself, you've probably seen it in a thousand documents, fliers, and international treaties. Here's how it works:

1. **Click the Insert tab.**

2. **In the Text group, click the WordArt button to display the WordArt menu.**

The WordArt button is shown in the margin.

3. **Choose a style from the WordArt gallery.**

A WordArt graphical placeholder appears in the document. It's a graphical element that holds specially formatted text.

4. **Type the (short and sweet) text that you want WordArt-ified.**

If you've selected text before Step 2, the text is converted into the WordArt format.

Use the WordArt Styles group on the Shape Format tab to customize WordArt's appearance. If you don't see the Shape Format tab, select the WordArt graphic.

TIP

Image Layout

To keep text and graphics living in harmony within a document, you must provide the proper layout options. These options control how the text and graphics interact, creating a visually impressive presentation where things don't look dorky.

In Word, layout options fall into three categories:

» **Inline:** The image is inserted directly into the text, just like a large, single character. It stays with the text, so you can press Enter to place it on a line by itself or press Tab to indent the image, for example.

» **Wrapped:** Text flows around the graphic, avoiding the image like cheerleaders at a high school dance avoid the guys in the chess club.

» **Floating:** The image appears in front of or behind the text. Shapes (or line art) inserted in the document appear floating in front of the text by default.

To set image layout options, click to select an image and then click the Layout Options button. It appears to the upper right of a selected image (refer to Figure 22-1) and is shown in the margin. The Layout Options menu lists various layout settings, as illustrated in Table 22-1.

TABLE 22-1   **Image Layout Options**

Icon	Setting	What It Does
	Inline	The image acts like a character, moving with other text on the page.
	Square	Text flows around the image in a square pattern, regardless of the image's shape.
	Tight	Text flows around the image and hugs its shape.
	Through	Text flows around the image but also inside the image (depending on the image's shape).
	Top and Bottom	Text stops at the top of the image and continues below the image.
	Behind Text	The image floats behind the text, looking almost like the image is part of the paper.
	In Front of Text	The image floats on top of the text, like a photograph set on the page.

Wrapping text around an image

For smaller images, or images that otherwise break up a document in an inelegant manner, choose one of the text-wrapping layout options. Heed these steps:

1. **Click to select the image.**

   A selected image appears with eight handles, as shown earlier, in Figure 22-1.

2. **Click the Layout Options button.**

   Word features four text-wrapping options, found in the With Text Wrapping area of the Layout Options menu. These options are Square, Tight, Through, and Top and Bottom, described earlier, in Table 22-1.

3. **Choose a text wrapping option.**

Examine the image to see how text wraps around. If you're displeased, repeat these steps and choose another layout option in Step 3.

 To remove text wrapping, choose the Inline option from Step 3.

Floating an image

When you want an image to be placed in the document independently of the text, you float the image. The image can float in front of the text, like some little kid pasted a sticker on the page, or float behind the text, as though the image were part of the paper.

 To float an image, select it and then click the Layout Options button, shown in the margin. Choose Behind Text or In Front of Text. Refer to Table 22-1 for the appropriate icons.

After choosing either Behind Text or In Front of Text, you see the image released from the confines of the text. The image floats freely, either behind or in front of the text.

Keeping an image with a paragraph

Images in your document are often referenced in the text, such as "Refer to Figure 22-1." As such, it's good to keep the image close to that paragraph, if not right next to it. You could say that it's nice to anchor the image to the text, which is something Word lets you do.

 Paragraphs associated with an image feature an Anchor icon at their top right corner, as shown in the margin. This paragraph is where the image is "anchored," and it moves with the paragraph as you edit and mangle your document's text.

To change anchor paragraphs, drag the Anchor icon to another paragraph — hopefully, one that references the image. This way, if the paragraph moves to another page, the image moves with it.

 To keep an image pasted to the same spot on a page, select the image and then click the Layout Options button. Choose the Fix Position on Page setting. The image becomes "stuck" on the page at a specific location, regardless of how the text flows around it.

TIP

Image Editing

Word is neither a graphics application nor a photo editing program. Still, it features a handful of commands to control and manage pictures and images in a document. For serious work, however, I recommend that you use an image editing program or any application designed to manipulate graphics.

» Use the Undo command, Ctrl+Z, to undo any image editing boo-boos.

» Document theme effects are automatically applied to any graphic inserted into your document. Refer to Chapter 16 for more information on themes.

Resizing an image

To make an image larger or smaller, heed these steps:

1. **Select the image.**

   Click the image and it grows handles, as shown earlier, in Figure 22-1.

2. **Drag one of the image's four corner handles inward or outward to make the image smaller or larger, respectively.**

TIP

   The image is proportionally resized when you use a corner handle to drag and resize. Use the edge handles to resize in a specific direction only, though not proportionally.

On the Picture Format tab, in the Size group, you can use the Height and Width controls to nudge the image size vertically or horizontally or to type specific values for the image's size.

Cropping an image

In graphics lingo, *cropping* works like taking a pair of scissors to the image: You make the image smaller, but by doing so, you eliminate some content, just as an angry, sullen teen would use shears to remove his cheating former girlfriend from a prom picture. Figure 22-2 shows an example.

To crop an image in a document, put away those shears and obey these directions:

1. **Click the image once to select it.**

   The Picture Format tab appears on the ribbon.

2. **On the Picture Format tab, in the Size group, click the Crop button and choose Crop.**

   The button is shown in the margin. After you choose the Crop command, the image grows eight thick crop handles.

3. **Drag one of the crop handles to discard a portion of the image.**

4. **Press the Enter key to crop the image.**

   The portion of the image not contained within the crop handles is eliminated.

Portion discarded   Portion kept   Crop handles

FIGURE 22-2:
Cropping
an image.

TIP

Images aren't completely altered by Word's Crop command; only a portion of the image is hidden. If you re-crop the image, it's possible to restore the originally cropped portion.

>> I use the edge (left, right, top, or bottom) handles to crop. The corner handles never crop quite the way I want them to.

>> Items other than Crop on the Crop menu let you crop the image to a pre-defined shape or aspect ratio.

REMEMBER

>> You can set an image inside a shape, if you want to perform some fancy cropping.

Rotating an image

You have two handy ways to rotate an image, neither of which involves turning the computer's monitor or craning your neck to the point of chiropractic necessity.

To freely rotate an image, use the mouse to "grab" the rotation handle at the top of the image (refer to Figure 22-1). Drag the mouse to orient the image to any angle.

For more precise rotation, on the Picture Format tab in the Arrange group, click the Rotate command button. From its menu, you can choose to rotate the image 90 degrees to the left or right or to flip the image horizontally or vertically.

Changing an image's appearance

To manipulate a selected image, click the Picture Format tab and use the tools in the Adjust group. Specifically, use these tools: Corrections, Color, and Artistic Effects. As a bonus, each tool's button shows a menu full of options previewing how the changes will affect the image. To make the change, choose an option from the appropriate button's menu. Here are some suggestions:

>> Brightness and contrast settings are made from the Corrections button menu.

>> To wash out a picture you placed behind the text, click the Color button and choose the Washout color from the Recolor area.

>> To convert a color image to monochrome (black-and-white), click the Color button and choose the first item on the menu: Saturation 0%.

>> A slew of interesting, artistic brushstrokes and other effects are found on the aptly named Artistic Effects button menu.

Image Arrangement

Managing more than one image on a page can be toilsome, especially when the images overlap. You may find yourself unable to click an image to select it. Or, maybe you prefer one image to be in front of the other, perfectly aligned, or you must move two images together. All these image arranging tasks are made easier, thanks to magical graphics tools available in Word, providing you know where to find them and how to incant the spells.

>> To arrange images, click a graphic to summon either the Picture Format tab or Shape Format tab. For either tab, the tools you need are located in the Arrange group.

>> To select multiple images, press and hold the Shift or Ctrl key as you click each one.

TIP

Moving an image hither and thither

To relocate an image to a better spot, point the mouse at the image. The mouse pointer changes to a 4-way arrow, as shown in the margin. When you see this mouse pointer, drag the image nigh and yon.

>> Point the mouse at the center of the image to drag. If you accidentally point at one of the image's handles, you resize the image.

» Depending on the layout option chosen, you can use the keyboard's cursor keys to nudge a selected image by teensy increments.

» When an image floats behind the text, you may need to open a spot in the text so that you can grab the image. To do so, position the mouse pointer by or on the same line as the image and then whack the Enter key a few times. After moving the image, delete the extra blank paragraphs you created when you pressed the Enter key.

Aligning graphics

Image alignment is necessary to keep two or more graphical objects looking neat and tidy on the page. Especially when the images use a floating or wrapped layout, you want to ensure that they line up by the top edges, side to side, or centered.

To align graphics, follow these steps:

1. **Click the first image to select it.**

2. **Hold down the Shift or Ctrl key and click to select the rest of the images.**

3. **On the Picture Format tab, in the Arrange group, click the Align Object button.**

   The button is shown in the margin. Click that button to display a menu of alignment choices.

4. **Choose an alignment command.**

   For example, choose Align Top to ensure that the top edges of both pictures are aligned on the page.

If you'd rather eyeball the arrangement, activate the grid: Click the Align Object button and choose View Gridlines from the menu. Instantly, the page looks like it's a sheet of graph paper. Use the grid to help position multiple images. Choose the View Gridlines command again to hide the grid.

Another handy tool found on the Align Object button menu is Use Alignment Guides. When it's selected, green lines appear in the text to show page and paragraph margins. Use these lines to help precisely position the graphic.

The Distribute commands on the Align Object menu help you organize multiple images evenly across a page. For example, if you have three images left-to-right and you want to space them evenly, first align the images by choosing Align Middle. Then choose Distribute Horizontally to evenly space the images.

Shuffling images front or back

Graphics are plunked down on a page one atop the other. This arrangement is difficult to notice unless two images overlap, as shown in Figure 22-3. To change the order and shuffle images in front of or behind each other, click the Picture Format tab, and in the Arrange group, use the Bring Forward or Send Backward commands.

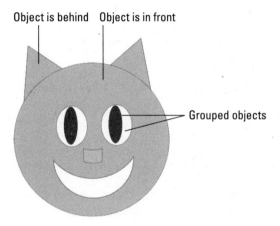

Object is behind   Object is in front

Grouped objects

FIGURE 22-3:
Working with
multiple images.

To move one image in front of another, first click that image. Choose Bring Forward ⇨ Bring Forward to shuffle that image forward one position. To bring the image in front of all other images, choose Bring Forward ⇨ Bring to Front.

Likewise, use the Send Backward ⇨ Send Backward or Send Backward ⇨ Send to Back commands to shuffle an image to the background.

Grouping images

When you use smaller shapes to cobble together a complex image, use the Group command to keep those items together. This way, you can move them as a single unit, copy and paste them, and apply image effects to the entire group. The eyeballs in Figure 22-3 are grouped and then duplicated on the cat image. (Yes, that's a cat.)

To group two or more graphical objects in a document, select the images: Click the first one, and then press and hold the Shift key as you click other images. When the group is selected, on the Picture Format tab, in the Arrange Group, click the Group button and choose the Group command. The images are then treated as a unit.

To ungroup, click the grouped images and then choose the Ungroup command from the Group menu.

Chapter **23**

Insert Tab Insanity

A side from formatting, everything from text to graphics that finds its way into a Word document is inserted. This approach makes me curious why the magicians at Microsoft sought to dedicate a tab on the ribbon to the topic of Insert. The weird and wonderful buttons that crowd this tab's various groups are covered in this chapter.

Characters Foreign and Funky

The computer's keyboard provides all letters of the alphabet, numbers, a smattering of symbols, and punctuation thingies. Writers weave these characters into a tapestry of text heretofore unseen in literary history. As if this feat weren't enough, you can sprinkle even more characters into the document, those not directly found on a computer keyboard, spicing up your document like garlic in a salad.

Nonbreaking spaces and hyphens

The space and the hyphen characters are special in Word. They're used to wrap a line of text: The *space* splits a line between two words, and the *hyphen* (using hyphenation) splits a line between a word's syllables.

When you don't want a space or hyphen to split a line of text, you use one of the unbreakables:

>> The nonbreaking hyphen character is Ctrl+Shift+ – (hyphen).

>> The nonbreaking space is Ctrl+Shift+spacebar.

For example, if you don't want a phone number split between two lines, press Ctrl+Shift+– (hyphen) instead of using a standard hyphen. And when two words must remain together in a paragraph, use Ctrl+Shift+spacebar to marry them.

Typing characters such as Ü, ç, and Ñ

You can be boring and type *deja vu* or be all fancy and type *déjà vu* or *café* or *résumé*. Such tricks make your readers think that you know your stuff, but what you really know is how to use Word's diacritical mark keys.

Diacritical is not an urgent medical situation. Instead, it's a term that refers to symbols appearing over certain letters. Foreign languages use diacritical marks, such as the examples used in the preceding paragraph.

To create a diacritical mark in Word, you press two keys: first a special Ctrl-key combination prefix and then the character to adorn with the mark.

The Ctrl-key combination prefix key somewhat represents the diacritical mark you need, such as Ctrl+' to produce the ' diacritical mark. Table 23-1 lists the prefixes and their associated character hats and tails.

For example, to insert an é into a document, press Ctrl+' and then type uppercase E for É or lowercase e for é. This shortcut makes sense because the apostrophe (') is essentially the diacritical mark you're adding to the vowel.

REMEMBER

>> The apostrophe (or *tick*) and the accent grave (or *back tick*) are two different characters, found at two different locations on the keyboard.

>> For the Ctrl+@, Ctrl+:, Ctrl+^, and Ctrl+~ key combinations, you must also press the Shift key. Therefore, Ctrl+~ is really Ctrl+Shift+`.

>> Word's AutoCorrect feature recognizes a few special characters. For example, when you type *café,* Word automatically sticks the whoopty-doop over the *e.*

TABLE 23-1	**Those Pesky Foreign Language Characters**

Prefix Key	Characters Produced
Ctrl+'	á é í ó ú
Ctrl+`	à è ì ò ù
Ctrl+,	ç
Ctrl+@	å
Ctrl+:	ä ë ï ö ü
Ctrl+^	â ê î ô û
Ctrl+~	ã õ ñ
Ctrl+/	ø

Inserting special characters and symbols

On the right end of the Insert tab dwells the Symbols group. One of the two items residing in this group is Symbol. Click this button to see some popular or recently used symbols and characters. Choose one from the menu to insert it directly into your text.

To see the complete host of available symbols and characters, click the Symbol button and choose the More Symbols command. The Symbol dialog box appears, as shown in Figure 23-1. Choose a decorative font, such as Wingdings, from the Font menu to see strange and unusual characters. To see the gamut of what's possible with normal text, choose (normal text) from the Font drop-down list. Use the Subset drop-down list to see specific symbols and such.

To stick a character into the document from the Symbol dialog box, select the symbol and click the Insert button.

Click the Cancel button when you're done using the Symbol dialog box.

>> The Insert button plops a character into the document each time you click the Insert button. For example, to thrust three Σ (sigma) symbols into the document, you must locate the symbol on the grid and then click the Insert button three times.

>> Symbols you choose from the Symbol dialog box later appear on the Symbol menu's palette of recently chosen characters.

>> Some symbols have shortcut keys. Look at the bottom of the Symbol dialog box (refer to Figure 23-1) to find them. For example, the degree symbol (°)

uses the Ctrl+@, spacebar keyboard shortcut: Press Ctrl+@ (actually, Ctrl+Shift+2) and then type a space.

TECHNICAL STUFF

>> The character code shown in the Symbol dialog box (refer to Figure 23-1) is used with the Alt+X keyboard shortcut to generate the symbol. For example, the character code for Σ (sigma) is 2211: Type **2211** in the document and then press Alt+X. The number 2211 is magically transformed into the Σ character.

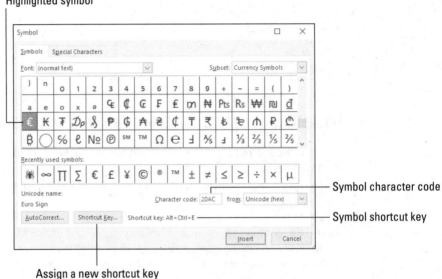

Highlighted symbol

Symbol character code

Symbol shortcut key

Assign a new shortcut key

FIGURE 23-1:
The Symbol dialog box.

Spice Up a Document with a Text Box

A *text box* is a graphical element that contains — hold your breath, wait for it, wait — *text*. The text is used as a decorative element commonly called a *pull quote* or *callout*, or it can be an information box or an aside, like a list of household items you can use to construct a robot. The primary purpose of the text box is to prevent the document from becoming what graphics designers refer to as the dreaded Great Wall of Text.

To shove a text box into a document, follow these steps:

1. **Click the Insert tab.**

2. **In the Text group, choose Text Box.**

3. **Choose a preformatted text box from the list.**

The text box is splashed onto the current page in your document.

4. **Rewrite the box's placeholder text.**

Despite its purpose, a text box is a graphical element in Word. As such, the Shape Format tab appears on the ribbon when the text box is selected. Use this tab to modify the text box, apply a layout, and so on.

TIP

>> You can set the layout options for the text box just as you would for any graphical goober in the document; options are presented in Chapter 22.

>> It's common to copy and paste text from the document into the box, which is how pull quotes work.

>> To change text orientation within the text box, click the box and then click the Shape Format tab. In the Text group, click the Text Direction button to peruse orientation options.

>> To remove a text box, click its edge (so that the box is selected, not its text) and press the Delete key.

Fun with Fields

What you write in Word isn't carved in stone — well, unless you have a cool printer I've not heard of. Still, the text you scribble remains static until you change it or until the computer crashes and messes up everything.

To liven things up a tad, Word lets you add dynamic elements to a document. Unlike the text you normally compose, *dynamic* text changes to reflect certain document details. To add these dynamic elements to a document, you use a Word feature called *fields*.

Understanding fields

The Field command is found on the Insert tab, in the Text group, on the Quick Parts menu. To add a field to a document, click the Quick Parts button, icon shown in the margin, and choose the Field command. The Field dialog box appears, shown in Figure 23-2.

Specific fields

Narrow down field names by choosing a category   Even more options!

FIGURE 23-2:
The Field
dialog box.

Options for the selected field

The scrolling list on the left side of the Field dialog box shows categories. These represent various dynamic nuggets you can insert in a document. Choose a specific category to narrow the list of field names.

The center and right parts of the dialog box contain formats, options, and other details for a selected field. (Examples are described in the sections that follow.)

To insert the field, click the OK button. The field appears just like other text, complete with formatting and such, but the information displayed changes to reflect whatever the field represents. For example, the current page-number field always shows the current page.

TIP

When the insertion pointer is placed inside a field, the text is highlighted with a dark gray background. It's your clue that the text is a field and not plain text. Also see the later section "Deleting fields."

Adding some useful fields

Word offers an abundance of fields you can shove into a document. Of the lot, you might use only a smattering. My favorites are listed in this section, which assumes that the Field dialog box is open, as described in the preceding section.

Page numbers

To ensure that the document accurately reflects the current page number, insert a current page–number field:

1. **In the Field dialog box, select Numbering from the Categories drop-down list.**
2. **Select Page from the Field Names list.**
3. **In the Field Properties section of the Field dialog box, select a format for the page number.**
4. **Click OK.**

The current page number appears in the document. No matter how you edit or modify the document, this number reflects the current page number.

Total number of pages

To insert the total number of pages in a document, heed these directions:

1. **Select Document Information from the Categories drop-down list.**
2. **Select NumPages from the Field Names list.**
3. **Select a format.**
4. **Click OK.**

Word count

Are you getting paid by the word? Stick an automatic word count at the end of the document:

1. **From the Categories list, select Document Information.**
2. **Select NumWords from the Field Names list.**
3. **Click OK.**

Document filename

Many organizations place the document's filename into a document header or footer. Even when the filename changes, the field is updated to contain the exact name. Do this:

1. **From the Categories list, select Document Information.**
2. **Select FileName from the Field Names list.**

3. In the Field Properties list, choose a text case format.

4. Optionally (though recommended), put a check mark by the option Add Path to Filename.

5. Click OK.

Updating a field

Page number fields update automatically, but other fields require some encouragement. To perform a manual update and freshen a field's contents, right-click the field and choose the Update Field command. The field's text is refreshed.

REMEMBER

Printing fields update only when the document is printed.

Changing a field

When you don't get the field's text quite right — for example, when you desire a date format that displays the weekday name instead of an abbreviation — right-click the field and choose the Edit Field command. Use the Field dialog box to make whatever modifications you deem necessary.

Viewing a field's raw data

TECHNICAL STUFF

Just as those mutants at the end of *Beneath the Planet of the Apes* removed their human face masks, you can remove a field's mask by right-clicking it and choosing the Toggle Field Codes command. For example, the FileSize field looks like this:

```
{ FILESIZE \* MERGEFORMAT }
```

To restore the field to human-readable form, right-click it again and choose the Toggle Field Codes command. The keyboard shortcut is Alt+F9. All praise be to the bomb.

Deleting fields

Removing a field works almost like deleting text. Almost. The difference is that you must press the Delete or Backspace key twice.

For example, when you press Backspace to erase a field, the entire field is highlighted. This visual update is your clue that you're about to erase a field, not regular text. Press Backspace again to remove the field.

THE MYSTERY OF CONTENT CONTROLS

Word's fields aren't the only dynamic text gizmos you can stick into a document. Another changing goober is the content control. It's not really a field, though it can be inserted and updated in a similar manner. The primary difference is how a content control looks, which is something like this:

$$V = \frac{4}{3}\pi r^3$$

Content controls are usually inserted by Word commands, such as those that automatically create headers or footers or insert page numbers. On the Insert tab, in the Text group, you can choose Quick Parts ⇨ Document Property to insert a property control. The Equation menu, found in the Insert tab's Symbols group, also inserts content controls.

The Date and Time

With few exceptions, time travelers are the only ones who bother asking for the current year. Otherwise, people merely want to know the month and day or just the day of the week. Word understands these people (but not time travelers), so it offers a slate of tools and tricks to insert date-and-time information into a document.

Adding the current date or time

Rather than look at a calendar and type the date, follow these steps:

1. **Click the Insert tab.**

2. **In the Text group, click the Date and Time button.**

   The button may say Date & Time, or you may see only the icon, shown in the margin.

3. **Use the Date and Time dialog box to choose a format.**

4. **If desired, click the Update Automatically option so that the date-and-time text remains current with the document.**

   Setting the Update Automatically option ensures that the date-and-time values are updated when you open or print the document.

5. **Click the OK button to insert the current date or time into the document.**

The keyboard shortcut to insert the current date is Alt+Shift+D. To insert the current time, press Alt+Shift+T.

Using the PrintDate field

TIP

The date field I use most often is PrintDate. This field reflects the current date (and time, if you like) when a document prints. Include this marvelous field in a letterhead template or in any document you print frequently. Here's how it works:

1. **Click the Insert tab.**

2. **In the Text group, click Quick Parts ⇨ Field.**

   The Field dialog box, which is covered earlier in this chapter, appears.

3. **Select Date and Time from the Categories drop-down list.**

4. **Select PrintDate from the Field Names list.**

5. **Choose a date-and-time format from the Field Properties area.**

6. **Click OK.**

The field looks odd until you print the document, which makes sense. Also, the field reflects the last day the document was printed. It's updated when you print again.

5
Famous Last Words

Chapter **24**

Multiple Documents, Windows, and File Formats

You need not toil with one document at a time. No! In Word, you can toil with multiple documents open at the same time or struggle viewing a single document in two windows or two documents in one window. Word even accommodates documents in strange and alien file formats. It's nuts, but potentially useful if you can multitask or just enjoy toiling.

Multiple Document Mania

Word can work on more than one document at a time, depending on how you open the documents. Here are some options:

>> **Keep using the Open command to open documents.** No limit exists on the number of documents Word can have open, but please consider your sanity at some point.

>> **In the Open dialog box, select multiple documents to open.** Press and hold the Ctrl key as you click to select documents. Click the Open button, and all the documents open like flowers, each in its own pot (window).

>> **From any folder window, select multiple Word document icons.** Lasso them with the mouse, or Ctrl+click to select multiple documents. Press the Enter key to open the lot.

Each document dwells cozy in its own window. To switch between windows, click one (if you can see it), choose one from the Windows taskbar, or follow these steps in Word:

1. Click the View tab.

2. In the Window group, click the Switch Windows button.

The Switch Windows button is shown in the margin.

3. Choose a document from the menu.

When you have the mental capacity to handle more than nine open documents at a time, the final command on the Switch Windows menu is More Windows. Choose this item to view the Activate dialog box, which lists *all* open document windows. Select a document from the window and click OK to switch to it.

WARNING

>> Should you spy any document in the list named Document1, Document2, or similar, immediately switch to that window and save before it's too late!

>> Refer to Chapter 8 for details on opening and saving Word documents.

Viewing multiple documents

A nifty way to review two documents is to arrange them side by side. Both documents are visible on the screen, and their scrolling is locked so that you can peruse them in parallel. Here's how to accomplish this trick:

1. Open both documents.

2. On the View tab, in the Window group, click the View Side by Side button.

After you click this button (icon shown in the margin), Word arranges both documents in vertical windows.

3. Scroll either document.

Scrolling one document also scrolls the other. In this mode, you can compare the documents.

To disable synchronous scrolling, click the Synchronous Scrolling button, found in the View tab's Window group.

4. **When you're done, choose View Side by Side again.**

Another way to work with multiple documents is to click the Arrange All button, found in the Window group (icon shown in the margin). Choose this button in Step 2 to see all open document windows arranged like patches of fabric in a quilt. Be aware that this command works only with visible windows on the desktop, not minimized windows on the taskbar.

>> Though you can see more than one document at a time, you can *work* on only one at a time. The document with the highlighted title bar is the one "on top." Click a document to put it on top. Merely looking at the window doesn't do squat.

>> The fewer documents you arrange, the easier it is to view their contents.

>> Also see Chapter 26, which covers reviewing changes made to a document.

Showing a single document in multiple windows

Editing a document involves a lot of hopping around, which can be devastating for your calf muscles. Rather than suffer cramps and irritability, consider viewing a single document in two windows. To open a second window on a single document, obey these steps:

1. **Click the View tab.**

2. **In the Window group, click the New Window button.**

   After you click the New Window button, shown in the margin, a second window opens, showing the current document.

To confirm that the same document is open in two windows, check the title bar: The first window's filename is followed by :1, and the second window's filename is followed by :2.

When you no longer need the second window, close it. You can close either window :1 or :2; it doesn't matter. The document is still open and available for editing in the remaining window.

>> Don't be fooled by the two windows! You're still working on only one document. The changes you make in one window are reflected in the other.

>> This feature is useful for cutting and pasting text or graphics between sections of a long document.

>> You can even open a third window by choosing the New Window command again, but that's just nuts.

Using the old split-screen trick

Splitting the screen allows you to view two parts of a document in the same window. No need to bother with extra windows — or scissors. When active, the top part of the window shows one part of the document and the bottom part another. Each window split scrolls individually, so you can peruse different parts of the same document without switching windows.

To split a window, heed these directions:

1. **Click the View tab.**

2. **In the Window group, click the Split Window button.**

   A line bisects the document, slicing it from side to side, as illustrated in Figure 24-1. If the ruler is visible, a copy appears for both document splits.

Drag up or down   Word's window commands   Double-click to close

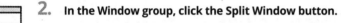

FIGURE 24-1:
Splitting a
document
window.

282   PART 5 Famous Last Words

You can scroll the top or bottom part of the document independently. This way, you can peruse or edit different parts of the document in the same window.

To undo the split, choose the Remote Split command from the Window group. (This command replaces the Split command). Or you can double-click the line separating the document.

TIP

The split line is adjustable; drag it up or down to change the split proportions.

Other Document Types

When you save a document, Word places the document's text, formatting, and other details into a file. To keep the information organized, Word uses a specific file format. The *file format* makes a Word document unique and different from other types of files lounging on your computer's storage system.

Word's document format is popular, but it's not the only word processing document format available. Other word processors, as well as document utilities such as Adobe Acrobat (PDF), use their own formats. Word permits you to open documents saved in those formats as well as save your Word documents in the alien formats. I'm not certain whether the software is pleased to do so, but it's capable.

» Basic document opening and saving information is found in Chapter 8.

» The best way to save a file in another format is to use the Export command, discussed in Chapter 9.

TECHNICAL STUFF

» The standard Word document format uses the .docx filename extension. This extension is applied automatically to all Word documents you save, though it may not be visible when viewing files in a folder. The older Word document format used the .doc filename extension. See the later section "Updating an older Word document."

Opening a non-Word document

Word can magically open and display a host of weird, non-Word documents. Here's how it works:

1. **Press Ctrl+F12 to summon the traditional Open dialog box.**

2. **Choose a file format from the File Type menu button.**

The menu button is illustrated in Figure 24-2.

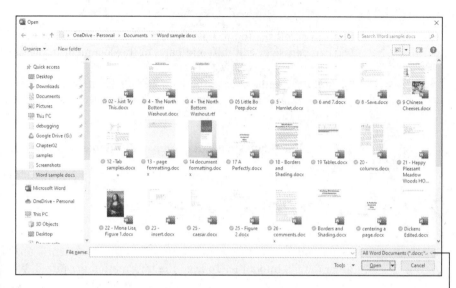

FIGURE 24-2:
Change file types
in the Open
dialog box.

File Type menu

When you select a specific file format, Word narrows the number of files displayed in the Open dialog box to match only the specific file format.

If you don't know the format, choose All Files from the drop-down list.

TIP

3. **Work the controls in the dialog box to hunt down and select the file.**

4. **Click the Open button.**

The alien file appears onscreen, ready for editing, just like any other Word document — or not. Word tries its best to open alien file formats, but it may not get everything 100 percent okey-doke.

>> For some document types, Word displays a file conversion dialog box. Use its controls to preview the document, though clicking the OK button is usually your best bet.

>> The Recover Text from Any File option is useful for peering into unknown files, especially from antique and obscure word processing file formats.

WARNING

>> Word *remembers* the file type! When you use the Open dialog box again, the same file type is already chosen from the Files of Type drop-down list. That means your regular Word document could be opened as a plain text document, which looks truly ugly. Remember to check the Files of Type drop-down list if such a thing happens to you.

REMEMBER

» Accordingly, when you open a Word document after opening an HTML document, or especially when using the Recover Text from Any File option, you *must* choose Word Documents from the list. Otherwise, Word may open documents in a manner strange and loathsome.

» You may see a warning when opening a document downloaded from the Internet. Word is just being safe; the document is placed into Protected view. You can preview the document, but to edit it, you need to click the Enable Editing button.

» Don't blame yourself when Word is unable to open a document. Many, many file formats are unknown to Word. When someone is sending you this type of document, ask the person to resend it using a common file format, such as HTML, PDF, or RTF.

Updating an older Word document

Microsoft Word has used the same .doc file format since the early days, back when Word ran on steam-powered computers that took three people to hoist onto a table.

In 2007, Word changed its document file format. Gone was the .doc format, replaced by the .docx format. Because many people still use older versions of Word, and given the abundance of older .doc files still available, it became necessary to work with and convert these older documents. Ever since then, Word has secretly updated its document file.

Working with an older Word document is cinchy: Open the document. You see the text *[Compatibility Mode]* after the filename at the top of the window. This text is a big clue that you're using an older Word document. Another clue is that some of Word's features, such as the capability to preview format changes and document themes, don't work when editing an older document.

To update an older document, follow these steps:

1. **Click the File tab.**

2. **Choose Info.**

3. **Click the Convert button.**

Convert

The Convert button is shown in the margin. After you click it, a descriptive dialog box appears. If not, skip to Step 6.

4. **In the Microsoft Word dialog box, click to place a check mark by the item Do Not Ask Me Again about Converting Documents.**

5. **Click the OK button.**

6. **Click the Save button to save the document.**

   Use the Save As dialog box, as covered in Chapter 8. If you look at the File Type menu, you see that the chosen file format is Word Document (*.docx). The document is updated.

In some instances, the document is instantly converted. Otherwise, the older .doc file is retained. You're free to delete it.

See Chapter 8 if you desire to save a current document in the older Word file format.

TECHNICAL STUFF

Some very old Word documents cannot be opened due to potential security issues. If you're certain that the document is safe, visit the Trust Center in Word to open the file. I've created a YouTube video to assist in this operation: www.youtube. com/watch?v=kyTUfhqrTzY.

Chapter **25**

Word for Writers

The word processor is the best tool for writers since the ghostwriter. Of course, cobbling together words in a word processor doesn't make you a writer any more than working with numbers in a spreadsheet makes you an accountant. Even so, beyond its basic word processing capabilities, Word comes with an armada of tools for making a writer's job easier. Whether you're writing your first guest piece for the church newsletter or crafting your 66th horror-thriller, you'll enjoy Word's features for writers.

Organize Your Thoughts

Good writers use an outline to organize their thoughts. Back in the old days, outlines were scribbled on a stack of 3-by-5 index cards. Today, outlines are electronic, stored as a Word document. This update makes it easier not to confuse your outline with grandma's recipes.

Word's Outline view presents a document in a unique way: It takes advantage of Word's heading styles to help you group topics, ideas, or plotlines in a hierarchical fashion. Outline tools make it easy to shuffle around topics, make subtopics, and mix in text to help organize your thoughts. Even if you're not a writer, you can use Word's Outline mode to create lists, work on projects, or look busy when the boss comes around.

The outlining feature is missing from the online version of Word.

Entering Outline view

To enter Outline view, click the View tab and, in the Views group, click the Outline button, shown in the margin. The document's presentation changes to show Outline view, and the Outlining tab appears on the ribbon, as shown in Figure 25-1.

To exit Outline view, click the View tab and choose another document view. You can also click the big, honkin' Close Outline View button (labeled in Figure 25-1).

TIP

>> The keyboard shortcut for entering Outline view is Ctrl+Alt+O (the letter O).

>> A squat, horizontal bar marks the end of the outline. You cannot delete this bar.

>> All basic Word commands behave in Outline view. You can use the cursor keys, delete text, check spelling, save, insert oddball characters, and so on.

>> Don't worry about the text's appearance in Outline view; outlining isn't about formatting.

>> Word uses the Heading 1 through Heading 9 styles for the outline's topics. Main topics are formatted in Heading 1, subtopics in Heading 2, and so on.

>> Use the Body style or Normal style to make notes or add text to the outline. See the section "Adding a text topic," later in this chapter.

REMEMBER

>> An outline isn't a special type of document; it's a document *view*. You can switch between Outline view and any other view, and the document's contents don't change.

Text topic

Open/Close topic

Move topic

Set topic level

Big, honkin, Close Outline View button

Outlining tab   Set which levels appear

End of the outline

No subtopics

FIGURE 25-1:
A typical outline.   Subtopics hidden

Typing topics in the outline

Outlines are composed of topics and subtopics. *Topics* are main ideas; *subtopics* describe the details. Subtopics can contain their own subtopics, drilling down to several levels of detail. The amount of detail used depends on how organized you want to be.

To create a topic, type the text. Word uses a specific heading style to format the topic based on its level. To start, main topics are at the highest level, as shown in Figure 25-2.

- Arrakis
- Caprica
- Floston
- Gallifrey
- Krypton
- LV-426
- Minbar
- Pandora
- Tatooine
- Vulcan

FIGURE 25-2:
Topics in
an outline.

Keep the main topic levels short and descriptive. Deeper topics can go into more detail. Press the Enter key when you're done typing one topic and you want to start another.

>> Use the Enter key to split a topic. For example, to split the topic Pots and Pans, replace the word *and* with a press of the Enter key.

>> To join two topics, press the End key to send the insertion pointer to the end of the first topic. Then press the Delete key. This method works just like joining two paragraphs in a regular document.

TIP

>> Don't worry about organizing the outline when you first create it. In Word's Outline view, you can rearrange topics as your ideas solidify. My advice is to start writing things down first and concentrate on organization later.

Rearranging topics

The power of Word's Outline view is that you can rearrange topics as you go. This feature keeps the outline fluid: Organize the outline by moving topics up or down as you think about the subject and how best to present the information. Use these commands found on the Outlining tab:

>> Click the Move Up button (or press Alt+Shift+↑) to move a topic up a line.

>> Click the Move Down button (or press Alt+Shift+↓) to move a topic down a line.

You can also drag a topic up or down: Point the mouse pointer at the circle to the topic's left. When the mouse is positioned just right, the mouse pointer changes to a 4-way arrow (see the margin). I recommend using this trick only when you're moving topics a short distance; dragging beyond the current screen can prove unwieldy.

To move a topic and all its subtopics, first collapse the topic. When the topic is expanded, only the topic itself is moved. See the later section "Expanding and collapsing topics."

Demoting and promoting topics

Outline organization also includes demoting and promoting topics. For example, you demote a topic because it's really a subtopic of a main topic. Likewise, when a subtopic becomes hefty enough, you promote it to a main topic. Commands to organize the outline in a hierarchical manner are found on the Outlining tab on the ribbon:

>> Click the Demote button (or press Alt+Shift+→) to demote a topic into a subtopic.

>> Click the Promote button (or press Alt+Shift+←) to promote a topic.

New topics you type are created at the same level as the topic above them (where you pressed the Enter key).

>> To instantly make any topic a main-level topic, click the Promote to Heading 1 button.

>> You can use the mouse to promote or demote topics: Drag the topic's circle left or right. I admit that this move can be tricky, which is why I use the keyboard shortcuts or buttons on the ribbon to promote or demote topics.

>> You don't *create* subtopics in Word as much as you *demote* higher-level topics.

>> Promoting or demoting a topic changes the text's paragraph format. For example, demoting a top-level topic changes the style from Heading 1 to Heading 2. The subtopic also appears indented on the screen (refer to Figure 25-1).

>> The Level menu in the Outlining tab's Outline Tools group changes to reflect the current topic level. You can also use this item's drop-down list to promote or demote the topic to any specific level in the outline.

>> Unlike with main topics, you can get wordy with subtopics. After all, the idea here is to expand on the main topic.

>> According to Those Who Know Such Things, you must have at least two subtopics for them to qualify as subtopics. When you have only one subtopic, either you have a second main topic or you've created a text topic. See the later section "Adding a text topic" for information.

Expanding and collapsing topics

A detailed outline is wonderful, the perfect tool to help you write that novel, organize a meeting, or plot against your enemies. To help you pull back from the detail and see the Big Picture, you can collapse all or part of an outline. Even when you're organizing, sometimes it helps to collapse a topic to help keep it in perspective.

Any topic with subtopics shows a plus sign (+) in its circle. To collapse this topic and temporarily hide its subtopics, you have several choices:

» Click the Collapse button (the Minus icon, shown in the margin) on the Outlining toolbar.

» Press the Alt+Shift+_ (underline) keyboard shortcut.

» Double-click the plus sign to the topic's left (in the circle).

When a topic is collapsed, it features a fuzzy underline, in addition to a plus sign in the icon to the topic's left. To expand a collapsed topic, you have several choices:

» Click the Expand button (the Plus icon shown in the margin) on the Outlining toolbar.

» Press Alt+Shift++ (plus sign).

» Click the topic's plus sign (in the circle).

Show Level: The fastest way to display an outline at a specific topic level is to choose that level from the Show Level drop-down list. To find this command, look on the Outlining toolbar, in the Outline Tools group. For example, to show only Level 1 and Level 2 topics, choose Level 2 from the Show Level button's menu. Topics at Level 3 and higher remain collapsed.

To see the entire outline, choose Show All Levels from the Show Level menu.

When some of the subtopics get wordy, place a check mark by the Show First Line Only option. This option is found on the Outlining tab in the Outline Tools group. When this option is active, Word displays only the first line of text in any topic.

ENJOYING OUTLINE COMMANDS OUTSIDE OF AN OUTLINE

Word's outlining commands affect paragraphs and headings in a document — even when you're not viewing the document in Outline view.

For example, a tiny triangle button appears to the left of a heading-style paragraph whenever a document is shown in Print Layout view. Click this button to expand or collapse the heading and all its contents — including any subheadings. Using this trick is a great way to collapse parts of a document without having to switch to Outline view.

You can also use the topic rearrangement commands to move paragraphs in a document: Alt+Shift+↑ moves a paragraph up; Alt+Shift+↓ moves a paragraph down.

Adding a text topic

Creating an outline can potentially include writing text. After all, if the mood hits you, write! Rather than write your prose as a topic, use the Demote to Body Text command:

1. Press the Enter key to start a new topic.

2. On the Outlining tab, in the Outline Tools group, click the Demote to Body Text button (shown in the margin).

The keyboard shortcut is Ctrl+Shift+N, which is also the keyboard shortcut to apply the Normal style.

These steps change the text style to Body Text. Use this trick to write text for a speech, some instructions in a list, or a chunk of dialogue from your novel and not have it appear as a topic or subtopic.

Printing an outline

Printing an outline works just like printing any other document in Word but with one big difference: Only visible topics are printed. Yes, the print preview shows all the topics printing. It's a lie.

OUTLINE-MANIPULATION SHORTCUT KEYS

I prefer using Word's shortcut keys whenever possible. Especially when working on an outline, when I'm typing more than mousing, it helps to know these outline-manipulation shortcut keys:

Key Combo	What It Does
Alt+Shift+→	Demotes a topic
Alt+Shift+←	Promotes a topic
Alt+Shift+↑	Moves a topic up one line
Alt+Shift+↓	Moves a topic down one line
Ctrl+Shift+N	Demotes a topic to body text
Alt+Shift+1	Displays only top-level topics
Alt+Shift+2	Displays first- and second-level topics
Alt+Shift+n	Displays all topics up to Level n, such as Alt+Shift+4 for Level 4
Alt+Shift+A	Displays all topics
Alt+Shift++ (plus sign)	Displays all subtopics in the current topic
Alt+Shift+_ (underline)	Hides all subtopics in the current topic

To control visible topics, use the Show Level menu, as discussed earlier, in the section "Expanding and collapsing topics." For example, to print the entire outline, choose All Levels from the Show Level menu and then print.

To print only the first two levels of an outline, choose Level 2 from the Show Level drop-down list and then print.

>> Word uses the heading styles when it prints the outline, though it doesn't indent topics.

>> See Chapter 9 for more information on printing documents in Word.

Humongous Documents

The first novel I wrote (and never published, of course) was several hundred pages long. It was saved as a single document. Word documents can be *any* length, but putting everything into one document can be impractical. Editing, copying and pasting, searching and replacing, and all other word processing operations become less efficient the larger the document grows.

A better solution for long documents is to store each chapter, or large chunk, as its own file. This is how publishers I work with prefer to see submissions. When you're done writing, you assemble the individual chapters. But for writing, editing, and organizing, using individual chapter files makes more sense.

>> What qualifies as a large document? Anything over 100 pages qualifies, as far as I'm concerned.

TIP

>> When writing a novel, create each chapter as its own document. Keep these documents in their own folder. Further, use clever filenames to help with organization. For example, I name chapters by using numbers: The first chapter is 01, the second is 02, and so on.

WARNING

>> Word has a feature called Master Document. Avoid it. Instead, use my suggestions in this section to create a larger document by combining smaller chapter documents.

Stitching together chapter documents

If you choose to write your book as separate chapter documents, good! I believe you'll find it easier to work with the material, especially should you need to rearrange things. Above all, ensure that all these chapter documents use the same template. When you use a different template for each document (chapter), you must labor through more formatting when it comes time to assemble all the documents.

When it's time to stitch together the chapter documents, start with a new document using the same template file as all the chapter files. One at a time, insert the chapters:

1. **From the Insert tab, in the Text group, click the chevron by the Object button to display its menu.**

   The Object button icon is shown in the margin.

2. **Choose the Text from File command.**

3. **Use the Insert File dialog box to locate, select, and insert a chapter document file.**

   I recommend inserting the chapters in order, but not doing so may improve the readability of your book.

4. **On the Layout tab, in the Page Setup group, choose Breaks, Odd Page.**

   An odd-page section break is inserted into the document after the chapter's text. This step ensures that the next chapter starts on a righthand page.

   If you're creating an eBook, just choose Next Page from the Breaks menu. This choice is better than Odd Page because eBooks aren't printed.

5. **Repeat Steps 1 through 4, once for each document/chapter in the manuscript.**

Once the document is assembled, you can mess with headers and footers and page numbering as well as build the index, TOC, and other document references.

TIP

Keep the original chapter documents! Just in case anything goes awry or you need to start over for some reason, having the original documents is easier than working with a long manuscript document. Even so, continue to complete your book using the larger document.

Splitting a document

If your Great American Novel already exists as a single document, it's possible to split it into separate chapter document chunks. Doing so isn't a requirement, but the separate chapter documents may help maintain your sanity when you have a lot of reorganization to do; for example, it's easier to rearrange a book's chapters when they're separate documents.

Here's how to split a document:

1. **Select the portion of the document you want to split into a new document.**

   For example, split the document at the chapter breaks or a main heading break.

2. **Cut the selected block.**

   Press Ctrl+X to cut the block.

3. **Summon a new, blank document.**

   Ctrl+N does the trick. Or, if you're using a template (and you should be), start a new document by using that template. See Chapter 16.

4. Paste the document portion.

Press Ctrl+V to paste. If the text doesn't paste in with the proper formatting, click the Home tab and, in the Clipboard group, click the Paste button (shown in the margin). Choose the Keep Source Formatting option.

5. Save the new document.

Continue splitting the larger document by repeating these steps.

Dan's Writing Tips

Nothing beats advice from someone who has been there and done that. As a professional writer, I'm excited to pass along my tips, tricks, and suggestions to any budding scrivener.

Choosing the best word

When two words share the same meaning, they're said to be *synonyms* — for example, *big* and *large*. Synonyms are helpful in that they allow you to find better, more descriptive words and, especially, to avoid using the same tired old words over and over. Obviously, knowing synonyms is handy for any writer.

TIP

To find a word's synonym, right-click the word in the document. From the pop-up menu, choose the Synonyms submenu to see a list of words that have a similar meaning. Choose a word from the menu and it replaces the word in the document.

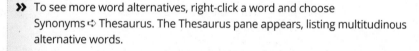

TIP

>> To see more word alternatives, right-click a word and choose Synonyms ⇨ Thesaurus. The Thesaurus pane appears, listing multitudinous alternative words.

>> To use a word from the Thesaurus pane, right-click the word and choose the Insert command. The word is placed in the document at the toothpick cursor's location.

>> *Antonyms,* or words that mean the opposite of the selected word, might also appear on the Synonyms submenu.

>> For more research on a specific word, right-click and choose the Search command. The Search pane appears, which lists sources from online references to help you determine whether you're using the best word. The Search command, as well as its companion, the Researcher command, are both available on the References tab in the Research group.

Counting every word

You pay the butcher by the pound. The barkeep is paid by the drink. Salespeople keep a percentage of their sales. Writers? They're paid by the word.

If you're lucky enough to be paid for your writing, you know that word count is king. The best way to see how many words dwell in a document is to view the status bar. The word count appears by the *Words* label, and the count is updated as you type. If you don't see this data tidbit, right-click the status bar and choose Word Count.

 To obtain more than a word count, click the Review tab. In the Proofing group, click the Word Count button (shown in the margin). The detailed Word Count dialog box appears, listing all sorts of word counting trivia.

Also see Chapter 23 for information on inserting a Word Count field in a document.

Writing for writers

Here's a smattering of tips for any writer using Word:

>> Thanks to the AutoFormat feature, Word fixes ellipses for you. When you type three periods in a row, Word inserts the ellipsis character (. . .). Don't correct it! Word is being proper. When you don't want to use the ellipsis character, separate the three periods with spaces.

>> You can format paragraphs by separating them with a space or by indenting the first line of each paragraph. Use one or the other, not both.

>> Use Outline view to collect your thoughts. Keep working on the outline and organizing your thoughts. When you find yourself writing text-level topics, you're ready to write.

>> Use the soft return (Shift+Enter) to split text into single lines. I use the soft return to break up titles and write return addresses, and I use it at other times when text must appear one line at a time, such as in a chapter heading or title.

>> Word is configured to select text one word at a time. This option isn't always best for writers, where it's often necessary to select text by character. To fix that setting, from the File tab menu, choose Options. In the Options dialog box, click the Advanced item. Remove the check mark by the When Selecting, Automatically Select Entire Word item. Click OK.

Chapter **26**

Let's Work This Out

Writing isn't a team sport, but it can be. Eventually, writers encounter collaboration, welcome or not. Often, it comes after the writing is done in the form of an editor. In today's connected society, collaboration can happen at any time and with just about anyone. Word recognizes this challenge and, to help you cope, provides some useful work-it-out-together tools.

Comments on Your Text

Have you ever written a comment to yourself in a document? For example, used a different font color or typed a note in ALL CAPS? Such tricks work, but better — especially when collaborating with others — is to use the commenting tools on the ribbon's Review tab.

Adding a comment

To gently thrust a comment into a document, heed these steps:

1. **Select the chunk of text upon which you desire to comment.**

    The more contextual you are with your selection, the more effective the comment.

2. **From the Mini toolbar, choose the New Comment button.**

The New Comment button is shown in the margin. Click it to see the Comments box appear to the right of the current page. It shows your account icon (if available) and name, plus a text box. The side of the page where the comment appears is called the *markup area*.

If you've disabled the Mini toolbar, click the View tab. In the Comments group, click the New Comment button to view the Comments box.

3. **Type a comment.**

Tag a collaborator in the comment by prefixing their name with the @ character.

4. **Press Ctrl+Enter or click the Send icon to post the comment.**

The Send button is shown in the margin.

Your comment is time-stamped after sending, as shown in Figure 26-1. Also, the three icons appear in the comment box: An Overflow icon (three dots), an Edit icon (pencil), and a Thumbs Up icon.

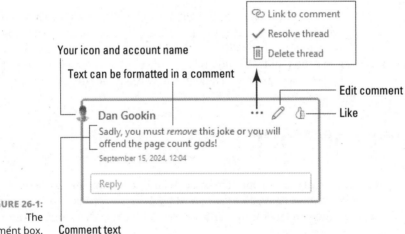

FIGURE 26-1:
The comment box.

The Overflow icon hosts these commands:

Link to Comment: Share the comment with others, but only when the document is available on OneDrive.

Resolve the Thread: The comment's subject matter has been dealt with.

Delete Thread: Remove the comment.

Use the Edit icon to edit the comment (duh). Use the Thumbs Up icon when you agree with a comment made by someone else.

Perusing comments

As comments litter your document like the pox, you can use the handy tools on the Review tab's Comments group to quickly peruse the lot.

 Click the Next Comment button to jump to the next comment in the document.

 Click the Previous Comment button to jump to the previous comment in the document.

Clicking either button displays the Comments pane on the right side of the document's window.

 You can also click the Show Comments button (shown in the margin) to view all comments. Choose the Contextual item to view a comment, as shown earlier, in Figure 26-1. Choose List to view the Comments pane with the comments listed sequentially. Click a comment in the Comments pane to view the relative part of the document.

The quick way to view comments is to click the Comments button found in the upper right corner of the document window.

TIP

Dealing with a comment

With a comment poised in your document, you have two duties. First, you can reply, which starts a conversation on the topic. Second, and more commonly, you deal with the issue raised by the comment and then mark the comment as resolved.

To reply to a comment, type your reply in the comment box's Reply text box (refer to Figure 26-1). Make your counterpoint, rebuttal, or curse.

 When the commented issue is no longer an issue, mark it as resolved: Click the Overflow icon (refer to Figure 26-1) and choose Resolve Thread. The comment still exists but is marked as "resolved." The Resolved Comment icon (shown in the margin) appears in the document to the right of the commented text.

When you're collaborating online, the jerk who originally made the comment is informed of your reply or resolution.

Deleting comments

All comments, even resolved ones, remain in the document until you delete them. In a comment box (refer to figure 26-1), click the Overflow icon and choose the Delete Thread command to remove the comment. For a resolved comment, show the Comments pane, as described in the earlier section "Perusing comments." Click the Delete (Trash icon) button to remove a resolved comment thread.

 When viewing a comment, you can click the Delete Comment button found in the Comments area of the Review tab. Its icon is shown in the margin.

To remove all comments from a document in a single massive retaliatory act, use the Delete Comment button's menu: Choose Delete ⇨ Delete All Comments in Document.

The Yellow Highlighter

Word comes with a digital pen that lets you highlight and colorize the text in a document without damaging the computer's monitor. To highlight text, abide by these steps:

1. **Click the Home tab.**

 2. **In the Font group, click the Text Highlight button.**

The mouse pointer changes to a — well, I don't know what it is, but the point is that Word is now in Highlighting mode.

3. **Drag the mouse over the text you want to highlight.**

The text becomes highlighted — just as though you used a highlighter on regular paper but minus the felt pen smell.

4. **Click the Text Highlight button again or press the Esc key to return the mouse to normal operation.**

The highlight need not be yellow. Click the menu chevron to the right of the Text Highlight button and choose a different highlighter color from the palette that's displayed.

To remove highlighting from the text, highlight it again in the same color or choose No Color as the highlight color.

>> To highlight multiple chunks of text, double-click the Text Highlight button. The mouse pointer stays in Highlighting mode until you click the Text Highlight button again or press the Esc key.

>> To highlight a block of text, mark the block and then click the Highlight button that appears on the Mini toolbar.

>> Highlighting isn't the background color, nor is it a text format. See Chapter 10 for information on setting the text background color.

Look What They've Done to My Text, Ma

All good writers enjoy feedback. Still, I'd like to know what's been done to my text, to not only see the effect but also learn something. Word's revision tracking tools make such a review possible.

Comparing two versions of a document

You have the original copy of your document — the stuff you wrote. You also have the copy that Debby, the soulless automaton from the legal department, has worked over. Your job is to compare them to see exactly what's been changed from the original. Here's what to do:

1. **Click the Review tab.**

2. **In the Compare group, choose Compare ➪ Compare.**

   The Compare Documents dialog box shows up.

3. **Choose the original document from the Original Document drop-down list.**

   The list shows recently opened or saved documents. Choose one, or use the Browse item to summon the Open dialog box and hunt down the original document.

4. **Choose the edited document from the Revised Document drop-down list.**

   Choose the document from the list, or use the Browse item to locate the changed, altered, or mangled document.

5. **Click OK.**

Word compares the two documents. The changes are displayed in a quadruple-split window, as illustrated in Figure 26-2. What you see is a third document, titled Compare Result.

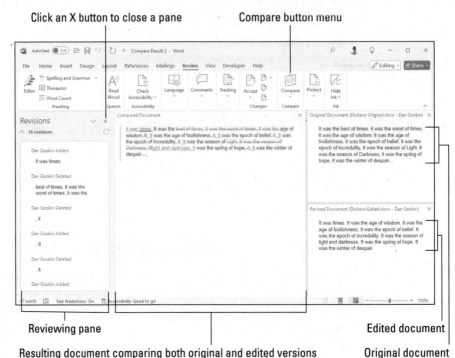

Click an X button to close a pane   Compare button menu

FIGURE 26-2:
The shameful changes show up here.

Reviewing pane

Resulting document comparing both original and edited versions

Edited document

Original document

Peruse the edits made to your pristine prose by the barbarian interlopers: Added text is underlined. Removed text is shown in strikethrough style. Color codes match your evil editors.

Scrolling is synchronized between all three documents: original, edited, and compared. Click a change in the Reviewing pane (shown on the left in Figure 26-2) to quickly see which part of your document was folded, spindled, or mutilated.

To confirm or reject the changes, see the upcoming section "Reviewing changes."

Tracking changes as they're made

To be a kind and gentle collaborator, activate Word's Tracking feature *before* you make changes to someone else's text: Click the Review tab and, in the Tracking group, click the Track Changes button, shown in the margin.

As with comparing documents, additions to the text appear colored and underlined, and deletions appear colored with strikethrough marks. The main difference is that these modifications appear as they're made.

Click the Track Changes button again to disable this feature.

TIP

>> When doing heavy editing, activate the revision marks (Track Changes) but choose No Markup from the Display for Review button's menu. This approach makes it easier to concentrate on editing and not be distracted by the cross-outs and underlines.

>> Once revision marks are activated on a document, it opens with revision marks visible and the tracking feature active. Even after accepting and rejecting changes, this feature remains enabled.

>> Use the Editing button in the upper right corner of the document window to switch between editing, reviewing, and viewing a document. This button is specifically suited for remote collaboration, as covered later in this chapter.

TIP

>> I recommend activating the Track Settings option on the status bar. To set this option, right-click the status bar and choose Track Changes. This item appears on the status bar when revision marks are active. You can, as a bonus, click this item on the status bar to activate or deactivate revision marks in the document.

Viewing revision marks (and comments)

Once tracking is activated, any changes made to the document appear like scars in the text. You can use the Display for Review button (shown in the margin) to set one of four visibilities for these modifications:

Simple Markup: Choose this item to display markup items as vertical lines in the margin on the left side of the document. This setting affects any comments in the document.

All Markup: Choose this item to display the full markup area, where all comments and revisions are shown. This setting also affects any comments in the document.

No Markup: Choose this item to hide the markup area. Any revisions are hidden in the text.

Original: Choose this item to hide the markup area as well as any revisions made to the document.

Regardless of these settings, Word continues to track changes and edits in the document until you deactivate Track Changes.

Reviewing changes

After your poor, bruised document is returned to you, the best way to review the damage inflicted is to use the commands on the Review tab, located in the Changes group and illustrated in Figure 26-3. Depending on the window size, you may not see their names.

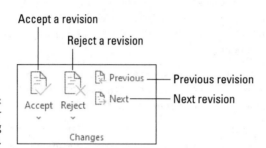

To review changes sequentially, click the Next button. The next change is highlighted in the document, though it's best to choose the All Markup command from the Display for Review menu button to see the changes.

Upon arriving at a change, you can:

>> Click the Accept button when you tolerate the change.

>> Click the Reject button to remove the change, restoring your original text.

After clicking either button, you instantly see the next change in the document, until all the changes are dealt with.

The Accept and Reject buttons host menus with commands that accept or reject all changes in a document in one fell swoop. The only thing missing is the "swoop!" sound when you use these commands.

WARNING

It's easy to get confused when reviewing changes. For example, rejecting a deletion restores the text. Carefully peruse each choice as you review the document. Remember that Ctrl+Z can undo the Accept or Reject commands.

Printing revisions (and comments)

Yes, it's horrible, but comments print with the document. This output probably isn't what you intended, so follow these steps:

1. **Press Ctrl+P to view the Print screen.**

2. **Click the Print All Pages button.**

   A menu appears.

3. **Remove the check mark by the Print Markup menu item.**

   This setting controls whether the revision marks as well as comments appear in the printed output. You can check the print preview to confirm that the markup is gone.

4. **Click the big Print button to print the document.**

REMEMBER

You must follow these steps every time you print the document; otherwise, the comments print.

See Chapter 9 for more information on printing documents in Word.

Remote Collaboration

Most document changes are made sequentially: You write something, and save, and then someone else works on the document. If this chaos isn't enough for you, Word allows you to invite people to edit a document as you're working on it. This collaboration feature is called Sharing, probably because a better name wasn't available or Microsoft was pressed for time.

To make document sharing work, save your document to OneDrive storage. Then follow these steps to make the document available for collaboration:

1. **Click the Share button.**

   The Share button is shown in the margin. Locate it in the upper right area of the document's window. Clicking this button displays a menu where you can choose to share the document directly, copy a link to the document, or manage who has access and their permissions.

2. **Choose Share.**

   The Send Link dialog box appears, shown in Figure 26-4. Fill it in to send a link to the document for a collaborator to join you; use suggestions in the figure for what to set.

3. **Click the Send button to whisk off the invite(s).**

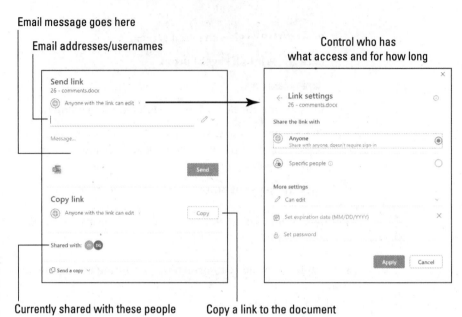

Email message goes here

Email addresses/usernames

Control who has
what access and for how long

Currently shared with these people

Copy a link to the document

FIGURE 26-4:
Inviting strangers
on the Internet to
abuse your work.

Eventually, the recipients receive the email invite. To access the shared document, they click the link in the email message. The document may be available on their copy of OneDrive, or they can edit it on a web browser.

To stop sharing, click the Share button and choose Manage Access. Adjust the access for any shared users in the Manage Access dialog box, removing them from the list or demoting their access to View only.

TIP

» When collaborating remotely, I recommend activating revision marks, as described earlier in this chapter.

» When others are editing your document at the same time you are, their edits appear on the screen. The other editor's insertion pointer looks like the one shown in the margin, in a unique color. As the cursor moves, the other editor's initials appear at the top of their insertion pointer.

» See Chapter 8 for details about OneDrive.

Chapter **27**

Mail Merge Mania

ere's a little quiz: What do these things have in common? Rocket science. Quantum mechanics. Brain surgery. Levitation. The answer: They're all a lot easier to accomplish than attempting mail merge in Word.

It's not that mastering mail merge is impossible. True, it's an ancient word processing tradition — something that just about everyone toys with at one time or another. Yet the way Word handles mail merge can be frustrating to any sane person. This reason is why I wrote this chapter.

As you might come to expect, the mail merge feature isn't available in the online version of Microsoft Word.

About Mail Merge

The term *mail merge* is given to the process of opening a single document, stirring in a list of names and other information, and then combining *(merging)* everything. The result is a sheaf of personalized documents, email messages, envelopes, and more. The process seems simple, but don't underestimate the power of Word to make simple concepts complex.

Understanding Word's mail merge jargon

I prefer to use descriptive, understandable, and relatable terms when describing something strange and scary. Word ignores such common sense. So take a deep breath and review the following jargon that applies to the mail merge process:

Main document: This document is just like any other document in Word, complete with formatting, layout, and all the fancy stuff that goes into a document. The document also contains various fill-in-the-blanks items, which is what makes it the main document.

Recipient list: This list contains the information that creates the customized documents. It's a type of *database*, with rows and columns of information used to fill in the form letters.

Field: Each of these fill-in-the-blanks items inside the main document is a placeholder that's filled in by information from the recipient list. Fields are what makes mail merge possible.

Persuading these three elements to work together is the essence of the mail merge operation. All the commands necessary are located on the ribbon's Mailings tab. In fact, the Mailings tab's five groups are organized from left to right in the order you use them in the mail merge process. The remainder of this chapter describes the details.

REMEMBER

>> The key to the mail merge operation is the recipient list. If you plan to create a mail merge as part of your regular routine, build a recipient list that you can use again and again.

>> A mail merge document can have as many fields as it needs. These are the parts of the document that change in the output. In fact, any item you want to change can be a field: the greeting, name, address, insult — whatever.

>> Fields are also known as *merge fields*.

TIP

>> You can use information from the Outlook program, also a part of Microsoft Office, as a recipient list for a mail merge in Word. You must have a healthy contact list in Outlook, which is the key to the operation.

MAIL MERGE DOCUMENT TYPES

In addition to a form letter, the main document in a mail merge can be an email message, envelopes, a set of labels, or anything else you want mass-produced. Here are the official Word mail merge document types:

Letter: The traditional mail merge document is a letter, a document in Word.

Email messages: Word can produce customized email messages, which are sent electronically rather than printed.

Envelopes: You can use mail merge to create a batch of customized envelopes, each printed with its own address.

Labels: Word lets you print sheets of labels, each of which is customized with specific information from the mail merge. See Chapter 28 for specifics.

Directory: A directory is a list of information, such as a catalog or an address book.

Reviewing the mail merge process

The typical mail merge nightmare involves five steps. These steps are presented in more detail throughout this chapter:

I. Build the main document.

Choose the document type — usually, a letter, though other document types are listed in the nearby sidebar, "Mail merge document types." As you create the document, you decide which fields are needed. This decision is the key to building an effective recipient list.

II. Create the recipient list — the data for the mail merge.

The recipient list is a table, consisting of rows and columns. Each column is a field containing information to go into the fill-in-the-blanks parts of the main document. Each row represents data for each different custom document created by the mail merge process.

III. Insert fields into the main document.

The fields are placeholders for information that's eventually supplied from the recipient list.

IV. **Preview the merge results.**

You don't just merge — first, you must preview how the document looks. This step helps you clean up any formatting, check for errors, and make other corrections.

V. **Merge the information from the recipient list into the main document.**

The final mail merge process creates the customized documents. These can then be saved, printed, emailed, or dealt with however you like.

WARNING

Mail merge involves coordination between multiple documents and various Windows technologies. When you open a mail merge document that you've already created, you may see an alert dialog box. You're informed that opening the document also runs an SQL command. This command is what links the recipient list to the main document. Click Yes to proceed.

Using the Mail Merge Wizard

If all this mail merge malarkey is just too intense for you, consider an alternative: Word offers the Mail Merge Wizard, which guides you through the entire ordeal, one step at a time.

To run the wizard, click the Mailings tab and choose Start Mail Merge ⇨ Step-by-Step Mail Merge Wizard. You see the Mail Merge pane on the right side of the document's window. Answer the questions, choose options, and click the Next link to proceed.

The rest of this chapter assumes that you're brave enough to do mail merge the macho way.

I. The Main Document

Mail merge begins with the *main document.* It's the prototype for all the individualized documents you eventually create, so it contains only common elements.

The following sections discuss different types of main documents. Read the section that relates to the type of mail merge you're attempting, and then proceed with the later section "II. The Recipient List."

Creating a mail merge form letter

The most common item to mail-merge is the standard, annoying form letter. Here's how you begin this journey:

1. **Start a new, blank document.**

    Press Ctrl+N.

2. **Click the Mailings tab.**

3. **In the Start Mail Merge group, choose Start Mail Merge ⇨ Letters.**

4. **Type the letter.**

    You type only the common parts of the letter, the text that doesn't change for each copy.

REMEMBER

5. **Type the fields you need in ALL CAPS.**

    This step is my idea, not Word's. For text that changes for each letter, type in ALL CAPS — for example, FIRST NAME or HAT SIZE. Use short, descriptive terms. Figure 27-1 shows an example.

6. **Save the main document.**

    If you already saved the document as you were writing it, give yourself a treat.

After you create the letter, the next step is to create or use a recipient list. Continue with the section "II. The Recipient List," later in this chapter.

Creating mail merge email messages

To spew out custom email messages, use Word's E-Mail option for mail merge. This option works only when you configure the Microsoft Outlook program on your computer. After doing so, obey these steps to start the main document for your email merge:

1. **Press Ctrl+N to create a fresh document.**

2. **On the Mailings tab, choose Start Mail Merge ⇨ E-Mail Messages.**

    Word changes to Web Layout view, a mode rarely used for creating web page documents.

3. **Create your email message.**

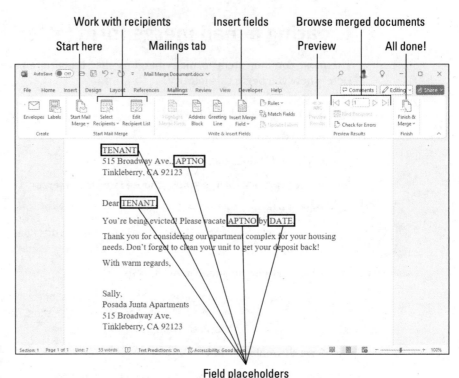

Work with recipients

Start here

Insert fields

Mailings tab

Browse merged documents

Preview

All done!

Field placeholders

FIGURE 27-1:
A mail merge
main document.

4. **If you anticipate inserting fields in the message, type them in ALL CAPS.**

An email mail merge is mostly about sending a message to multiple email addresses, though it might have a few fields, such as the person's name. If you plan to add fields, refer to Step 5 in the preceding section.

5. **Save the document.**

Unlike other fields, the email address field need not be specified in the document (the email's message). You add the recipient's email address during the final stage in the process.

REMEMBER

You can't do an email merge without the recipient's email address. Continue your mail merge adventure in the later section "II. The Recipient List."

Creating mail merge envelopes

To create a stack of mail merge envelopes, which is far classier than using peel-and-stick mailing labels, abide by these steps:

1. **Start a new document.**

2. **On the Mailings tab, choose Start Mail Merge ⇨ Envelopes.**

   The Envelope Options dialog box appears. Set the envelope size and font options, if necessary. The document page format is reset to look like the envelope type chosen.

3. **Click OK.**

4. **Edit or create the return address.**

   TIP

   The insertion pointer is set in the envelope's upper left corner. Type and format the return address, pressing Shift+Enter to place a soft return at the end of each line.

5. **Save the envelope.**

Not readily visible in the envelope document is a large text box (lower center). This location is where fields for the recipient's name are inserted.

Your next task is to use a recipient list to gather the information for your mailing. Keep reading in the next section.

II. The Recipient List

To make mail merge work, you need a list of items to merge, rows and columns, as in a database. This information, called the *recipient list,* contains the field data used to build the individual documents, email messages, envelopes, and other items.

Your options include creating a new recipient list, reusing an existing list, and pulling in information from the Outlook program.

Building a new recipient list

I won't lie: Building a recipient list is time-consuming, data-input drudgery. Still, it beats creating multiple individual documents, which is the point of a mail merge. Here are the general steps:

1. **Direct Word to create a new recipient list.**

2. **Edit and add fields.**

3. **Type in the recipient data.**

The last step is the most time-consuming. If you're an intern at a major organization, Step 3 is why you were given the mail merge task.

Create the new recipient list

Before you can create a new recipient list, you must have created and saved the main document. Refer to the earlier section "I. The Main Document." The steps for creating a new recipient list apply to all mail merge document types:

1. **Click the Mailings tab.**

2. **In the Start Mail Merge group, choose the Select Recipients ⇨ Type a New List command.**

   You see the New Address List dialog box, ready for you to edit the fields.

Edit the fields

The New Address List dialog box comes stocked with standard fields — the columns you see marching atop the dialog box (Title, First Name, Last Name, and so on). If you can use these, great! Otherwise, follow these steps to remove those you don't need:

1. **Click the Customize Columns button.**

   The Customize Address List dialog box appears, displaying fields that Word assumes you need. Such foolishness cannot be tolerated.

REMEMBER

2. **Click to select a field that you *do not* need.**

   When you're merging an email message, you need the E-Mail Address field, whether it appears in the message body or not. Word uses this field so that it knows where to send the message. Don't delete the E-Mail Address field!

3. **Click the Delete button, and then click Yes in the confirmation dialog box to confirm.**

   The keyboard shortcut for the Yes button is the Y key.

4. **Repeat Steps 2 and 3 for each field you don't need.**

   Yes, it's tedious, but it makes building the list easier.

   After removing the fields you don't need, add those that you do. The clues to which fields you need are found in the main document. Specifically, use the ALL CAPS text you added as placeholders. You need a field in the recipient list for each of these ALL CAPS items.

5. **In the Customize Address List dialog box, click the Add button to add a needed field.**

The teeny Add Field dialog box pops into view.

6. **Type the field name and click the OK button.**

Follow these rules for naming a field:

- Though a field may be used twice in the main document, you need only one field in the recipient list.

- No two fields can have the same name.

- Field names can contain spaces but cannot start with a space.

- Field names can be quite long, though shorter is best.

- The following characters are forbidden in a field name: . ! ` [ ].

7. **Repeat Steps 5 and 6 for each new field needed in the main document.**

Don't worry if you miss a field; you can always add fields later.

8. **Click OK.**

Your customized fields now appear as column headings in the New Address List dialog box.

TIP

Rather than delete fields you don't need, you can rename them: Select a field and click the Rename button. For example, I renamed *First Name* to *First*; *Last Name* to *Last*; and so on.

Add the recipient data

After customizing the fields, your final job is to fill in the recipient list. You need to input records, one for each merged document you plan to create. Perform these steps in the New Address List dialog box:

1. **Type the first record's data.**

Type the information that's appropriate to each field: name, title, evil nickname, planet of origin, and so on.

2. **Press Tab to move to the next field.**

After filling in the last field, you'll probably want to add another record:

3. **To add a new record, press the Tab key after typing in the last field.**

A new record is automatically created and added on the next line. Keep filling in data!

4. Review your work when you're done.

Figure 27-2 shows a completed recipient list.

Records   Fields   Click to sort the list

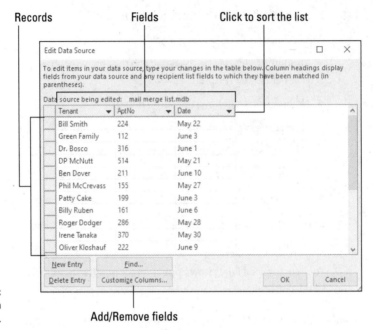

Add/Remove fields

FIGURE 27-2:
Making a
recipient list.

To edit any field, click to select it.

TIP

If you accidentally add a blank record at the end of the list, select it and then click the Delete Entry button. Deleting a blank record ensures that a blank document isn't printed during the merge.

5. Click OK.

The Save Address List dialog box pops up, allowing you to save the recipient list.

**TECHNICAL
STUFF**

Recipient lists dwell in the folder named My Data Sources, found in your account's Documents folder. Word selects this folder for you, creating it if it doesn't exist.

6. Type a name for the recipient list file.

Descriptive names are best. After all, you might use the same list again.

7. Click the Save button to save the list and return to the main document window.

The next step in the mail merge agony is to stir the fields from the recipient list into the main document. Refer to the later section "III. Fold In the Fields."

Using an already created recipient list

To use an existing recipient list for your mail merge, follow these steps after creating the main document:

1. From the Mailings tab, choose Select Recipients ⇨ Use an Existing List.

The Select Data Source dialog box appears. It works like the Open dialog box, though it's designed to display recipient lists that Word can use or that you previously created and saved.

Word stores recipient lists in the My Documents folder, in the My Data Sources subfolder.

2. Choose an existing recipient list from the displayed files.

I hope you used a descriptive name when you first saved the recipient list, which I recommend in the preceding section.

3. Click the Open button.

That's it: The recipient list is now associated with the main document.

Refer to the later section "III. Fold In the Fields" for information on inserting fields into your document, which is the next step in the mail merge nightmare.

You can tell when a recipient list is associated with the main document because the Insert Merge Field button is available. Look on the Mailings tab in the Write & Insert Fields group for this button.

Grabbing a recipient list from Outlook

If you use Microsoft Outlook, you can follow these steps to create a recipient list:

1. On the Mailings tab, in the Start Mail Merge group, choose Select Recipients ⇨ Choose from Outlook Contacts.

2. If necessary, select your profile from the Choose Profile dialog box and click OK.

3. If you have multiple accounts, choose an account from the Select Contacts dialog box and click OK.

The number of contacts for each account is listed in the Count column.

4. **Use the Mail Merge Recipients dialog box to filter the recipient list.**

    If the list isn't too long, remove the check marks by the names of the individuals you don't want in the list. You can also click the Filter link in the dialog box to do more advanced filtering, which I'm loath to describe right now.

5. **Click OK when you're done culling the recipient list.**

Editing a recipient list

No damage is done if you goof when creating the recipient list. Editing it is a cinch:

1. **On the Mailings tab, in the Start Mail Merge group, click the Edit Recipient List button.**

    The button isn't available unless the main document is associated with a recipient list, as described earlier in this chapter.

2. **Select the data source.**

    In the lower left corner of the Mail Merge Recipients dialog box, select the data source filename.

3. **Click the Edit button.**

    You can now use the Edit Data Source dialog box to edit records, to add or remove fields, and to perform other chaos:

    - *Click the Delete Entry button to remove the selected record.*

    - *Click the New Entry button to create a new record.*

    - *Click the Customize Columns button to add or remove fields.*

4. **Click the OK button when you're done editing; click Yes if you're prompted to update the list.**

5. **Click the OK button to dismiss the Mail Merge Recipients dialog box.**

This process may not be without its hiccups. The file may be "in use" or unavailable to edit. You may be prompted to save the recipient list before editing.

III. Fold In the Fields

With the main document prepared and the recipient list ready, the next step in the mail merge process is to insert the fields: Replace your silly ALL CAPS placeholders in the main document with the proper fields from the recipient list. Obey these directions:

1. **Position the mouse pointer where you want the field to appear in the main document.**

   If you followed my advice from the earlier section "Creating a mail merge form letter," select a placeholder, such as FIRST NAME.

2. **On the Mailings tab, click the Insert Merge Field button.**

   When the Insert Merge Field button isn't available, a recipient list isn't associated with the document. See the earlier section "II. The Recipient List."

3. **Choose the field to add to the main document.**

   For example, to replace the FIRST NAME placeholder, choose the First Name field to stick it into the document.

   After the field is inserted, you see its name hugged by angle brackets, like this:

   «First_Name»

   If the field doesn't look like this, press Alt+F9 to toggle the field codes from the raw format to the angle bracket presentation.

4. **Repeat Steps 1–3 to add fields to the document.**

   When adding fields to an address, press Shift+Enter to end each line.

5. **Save the main document.**

   Always save! Save! Save! Save!

TIP

The next step in your journey is to preview the results and fix any mistakes. Continue reading with the next section.

IV. Preview the Merged Documents

Rather than just plow ahead with the merge, take advantage of the buttons in the Mailings tab's Preview Results group. This way, you can peruse the merged documents without wasting a lot of paper.

To preview, click the Mailings tab and, in the Preview Results group, click the Preview Results button, shown in the margin. The fields in the main document vanish! They're replaced by information from the first record in the recipient list. What you see on the screen is how the first customized mail merge document appears. I hope everything looks spiffy.

Use the left and right triangles in the Preview Results group to page through each document. As you page, look for these problems:

» Formatting mistakes, such as text that obviously looks pasted in or not part of the surrounding text

» Punctuation errors, missing commas, extra or no spaces, or absent periods

» Double fields or unwanted fields, which happen when you believe that you've deleted a field but haven't

» Awkward text layouts, strange line breaks, or margins caused by missing or long fields

To fix any boo-boos, leave Preview mode: Click the Preview Results button again. Edit the main document to correct the mistakes. Then repeat the preview process.

Once everything looks up to par, you're ready to perform the merge, covered in the next section.

V. Mail Merge, Ho!

 The final step in the mail merge ordeal is to create the personalized documents. The gizmo that handles this task is the Finish & Merge command button (shown in the margin), which is the sole item in the Finish group on the Mailings tab. At long last, the ordeal nears an end. Several options are available, as discussed in this section.

Merging to a new set of documents

When you want to save merged documents and print them, follow these steps:

1. **Choose Finish & Merge ⇨ Edit Individual Documents.**

   The Merge to New Document dialog box appears.

2. **Ensure that the All option is selected.**

3. **Click OK.**

   Word creates a new document — a huge one that contains all merged documents, one after the other. Each document copy is separated by a Next Page section break. (See Chapter 14 for more information on section breaks.)

4. **Save the document.**

After saving, you can print the document, close it and edit it later, or do anything else you like.

Merging to the printer

The most common destination for merged documents is the printer. Here's how it works:

1. **Choose Finish & Merge ⇨ Print Documents.**

   A dialog box appears, from which you can choose records to print.

2. **Choose All from the Merge to Printer dialog box to print the entire document.**

   Or, specify which records to print.

3. **Click OK.**

   The traditional Print dialog box appears.

4. **Click the OK button to print your documents.**

5. **Save and close the main document.**

REMEMBER

When merging and printing envelopes, use the printer's envelope slot or its special feeding mechanism to supply it with envelopes. You may have to monitor the printer to insert the envelopes, which has to do with how your printer eats envelopes.

See Chapter 9 for more information on printing documents in Word.

Merging to email

To send out multiple email messages, abide by these steps:

1. **Choose Finish & Merge ⇨ Send Email Messages.**

   The Merge to E-Mail dialog box appears.

2. **Choose the email address field from the To drop-down list.**

   Your document's recipient list must include an email address field, though the field may not be part of the document. If the recipient list doesn't contain the email address field, go back and edit it to include the email address field.

3. **Type a message subject line.**

4. **Choose the Mail Format.**

   HTML is standard. The Plain Text option removes any formatting applied. Use the Attachment option to send the message as its own attachment, which is weird, though it's still an option.

5. **Click OK.**

   It looks like nothing has happened, but the messages have been placed in the Outlook outbox.

6. **Open Outlook.**

   After you open Outlook, the queued messages are sent, or they sit ready to be sent when you give the command. (Whether the messages are sent right away depends on how you configured Outlook.)

Yes, this trick works only with Outlook, not with any other email programs.

WARNING

Unsolicited email is considered spam. Sending spam may violate the terms of your Internet service provider's or email service agreement, and they can terminate your account. Send mass email only to people who have cheerfully agreed to receive such things from you.

Chapter **28**

Labels and Envelopes

S tretching the notion of what a word processor does, Word features commands to print labels and envelopes. After all, a sheet of labels is just a table, and an envelope is a squat document printed on a special type of paper. Rather than conjure a hack to perform the task, Word offers ready-made label- and envelope-creation and printing commands.

Labels Everywhere

Word's label powers include printing sheets of identical labels or creating individual labels for a mass mailing. This feat is possible because the labels are, at their core, merely cells in a table. The table's dimensions on the page match the label paper stock, where each cell in the document's table lines up perfectly with a sticky label. The printed result is a sheet of labels popping out of the printer.

Obviously, to print a sheet of labels requires that you have handy a blank sheet of sticky labels. These can be found wherever office supplies are sold. It's important to obtain these labels first, because to print on the labels requires that you inform Word of the label manufacturer name and paper stock number.

Printing sheets of identical labels

It might seem impractical to print a sheet of identical labels, yet I use such a sheet for my return address. This peel-and-stick trick is convenient for other types of labels as well. Follow these steps:

1. **Click the Mailings tab.**

2. **In the Create group, click the Labels button.**

The Envelopes and Labels dialog box appears, with the Labels tab ready for action, as shown in Figure 28-1.

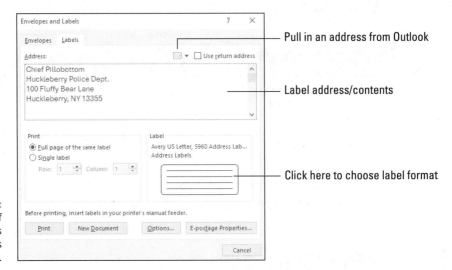

FIGURE 28-1:
The Labels side of
the Envelopes
and Labels
dialog box.

3. **In the Address box, type the text you want printed on the label.**

Press the Enter key at the end of each line. The paragraph format is single-spaced.

You can apply some simple formatting at this stage: Ctrl+B for bold, Ctrl+I for italic, or Ctrl+U for underline, for example. If you right-click in the Address box, you can choose Font or Paragraph from the pop-up menu to further format the label.

4. **Click the Full Page of the Same Label radio button.**

5. **To choose a new label type, click in the Label area (refer to Figure 28-1).**

The Label Options dialog box appears.

6. **Choose a label vendor.**

   For some reason, Microsoft is chosen as the default, which is weird because I've never seen Microsoft-branded labels in any office supply store. Instead, choose Avery, which is the category leader. Most other label manufacturers use Avery's numbering system anyway.

7. **Choose the proper stock number.**

   For example, Avery US Letter 5960 (refer to Figure 28-1) is the standard address sticky label most folks use.

8. **Click the New Document button.**

   By placing the labels in a new document, you can further edit them, if you like. Plus, you can save the document for use (and printing) later.

TIP

9. **Press Ctrl+P to print the labels.**

   Ensure that the sheet of label paper is loaded into the printer, proper side up.

On my computer, I have a folder full of label documents I reprint from time to time. For example, one document holds my return address, one is for the IRS, another has my lawyer's address, one for the bail bondsman, and so on. These all come in quite handy.

See Chapter 9 for details on printing in Word.

Printing an address list

To print a sheet of different labels, such as your club's mailing list, you encroach upon the terrifying territory of mail merge. This topic is covered in detail in Chapter 27, though this section deals with printing one or more sheets of different labels.

Before getting started, you must have available a recipient list file created or available. Refer to Chapter 27 for details. If you're fortunate enough to use the Outlook program as your digital address book, you can use it instead.

To print a list of names on a sheet of labels, follow these steps:

1. **Start a new document in Word.**

2. **Click the Mailings tab.**

   All commands and buttons mentioned in the remaining steps are found on the Mailings tab.

3. **Click the Start Mail Merge button and, from the menu, choose Labels.**

The Label Options dialog box appears.

4. **Choose the label vendor and product number representing the sheet of labels on which you're printing.**

For example, to print on a sheet of standard Avery address labels, use Avery catalog number 5160.

5. **Click OK.**

Word builds a table in the document, one with cells perfectly aligned to match the labels on the sheet you selected. (The gridlines may be hidden, but the table is still there.)

Do not edit or reformat the table! It's perfect.

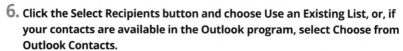

WARNING

6. **Click the Select Recipients button and choose Use an Existing List, or, if your contacts are available in the Outlook program, select Choose from Outlook Contacts.**

If you choose to use an existing list, use the Select Data Source dialog box to choose the list. For Outlook, select your contacts folder and use the Mail Merge Recipients dialog box to select the contacts you want to print as labels.

After choosing the contacts, Word fills all but the first cell in the table with Next Record fields. Your job is to create this first record, which sets the pattern for the rest of the labels.

The insertion pointer should be blinking in the first cell. If it isn't, click that cell.

7. **Click the Insert Merge Field button.**

8. **Choose a field to place into the document.**

For example, choose the First field to set the <<First>> placeholder for the label's first name into the table's first cell.

9. **Repeat Steps 7 and 8 to continue adding fields.**

Don't worry about the cell's contents looking messy; you can edit the layout later.

10. **Format the first label.**

Add spaces between the fields to separate them. Press Shift+Enter to create multiple lines. Add a comma between the city and state.

When you finish adding fields, the document looks kinda like the one shown in Figure 28-2.

«First» «Last» «Address» «City», «State» «ZipPostal_Code»	«Next Record»	«Next Record»
«Next Record»	«Next Record»	«Next Record»
«Next Record»	«Next Record»	«Next Record»

FIGURE 28-2:
The first label
dictates how
other labels are
formatted.

11. **In the Write & Insert Fields group, click the Update Labels button.**

Word populates the remaining cells in the table with the same fields and text placed into the first cell.

If you make a mistake, press Ctrl+Z to undo. Fix the first cell. Repeat Step 11.

12. **Click the Preview Results button to confirm that everything looks okey-doke.**

Confirm that the formatting looks good, and the spacing, and that all the text fits on the labels. If not, click the Preview Results button again (to disable the preview) and adjust the formatting for the first cell. When you've fixed the issue, continue with Step 11 again.

13. **Click the Finish & Merge button and choose Print Documents.**

14. **Ensure that the All radio button is chosen in the Merge to Printer dialog box.**

15. **Click the OK button.**

The traditional Print dialog box appears. Ensure that you have enough of the proper label paper in the printer and that the labels are correctly oriented.

16. **Click the OK button in the Print dialog box.**

The address labels print.

I recommend saving the document when you're done. This way, you can more easily perform the merge again or use the same document to print a fresh batch of labels.

Instant Envelope

Suddenly you need an envelope! Don't revert to using your fist to scribble text on that envelope, and please don't dust off that typewriter. Yeeks. Join the digital realm and let Word do the task for you. Obey these steps:

1. **Click the Mailings tab.**

2. **Click the Envelopes button.**

The Envelopes and Labels dialog box appears, with the Envelopes tab forward, as shown in Figure 28-3.

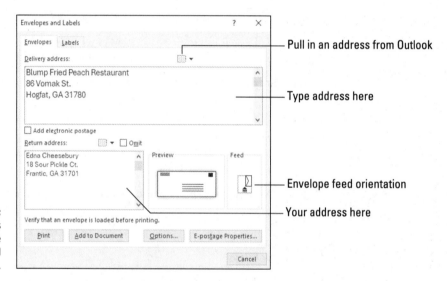

Pull in an address from Outlook

Type address here

Envelope feed orientation

Your address here

3. **Type the recipient's address in the Delivery Address box.**

Press Enter to separate the lines in the address. Word stacks each line atop the other, so don't fret over weird line spacing on the envelope.

TIP

If you use Outlook as your computer's address book, click the Address Book button to fetch the delivery address info for contacts where you have such info already provided.

4. **Ensure that an envelope is queued in the printer and ready to print.**

Most printers prompt you to manually enter envelopes. A guide on the printer's manual-feed mechanism describes how to orient and insert the envelope.

5. **Ensure that the way the envelope feeds into the printer matches the Feed item in the Envelopes and Labels dialog box.**

   Refer to Figure 28-3. Click the Feed button until the orientation matches how the printer eats the envelope. The envelope can be oriented in one of six ways, including face up and face down.

6. **Click the Print button.**

   You might need to press the printer's OK button or Ready button to print, though some printers may instantly consume the envelope.

If you want to print the envelope again, save it: Before Step 5, click the Add to Document button. Word inserts a new first page into the document that contains the formatted letter. (The page size is specific to the type of envelope.) When that's done, you can save the document so that you can reuse the envelope.

TIP

The Add to Document button's official purpose is to add an envelope to a letter. If you haven't written a letter in Word, you don't need the second (blank) page. To delete it, click that page and press the Backspace key. The page is removed, leaving only the envelope.

>> Any text appearing in the return address in the Envelopes and Labels dialog box is supplied by Word. If the field is blank, type the return address. Word asks whether you want to save it when the Envelopes and Letters dialog box closes. Click Yes.

TIP

>> If the delivery address is already typed in the document, select it before you summon the Envelopes and Labels dialog box. Word automatically grabs the selected text and sets it as the delivery address.

>> If you have trouble remembering which way the envelope feeds into the printer, draw a picture of the proper way and tape it to the top of the printer for reference.

>> In the United States, Size 10 is the common envelope paper size.

>> To change the envelope size, click the Envelope icon in the Preview area of the Envelopes and Labels dialog box (refer to Figure 28-3). Use the Envelope Options dialog box to choose the proper envelope size.

TECHNICAL
STUFF

>> The Envelopes button merely creates a special Word document (or a single page). The paper size is set to an envelope. A text box is placed in the center of the page, into which you type the delivery address. The return address is text typed at the start of the page. You can use various Word commands to create such a page, but the Envelopes command saves you the trouble.

IN THIS CHAPTER

» Configuring the status bar

» Customizing the Quick Access toolbar

» Finding special commands for
the toolbar

» Adding tabs and groups to the ribbon

» Expanding Word with add-Ins

Chapter **29**

A More Custom Word

Customization is available in many computer programs and mobile apps. It gives you the ability to change the way things look, alter program colors, add goobers, and make other fun modifications. Many people shy away from such customization, but it's *your* tool. If you can fine-tune Word to make your workflow more productive, go for it. This chapter offers many suggestions to give you a more custom Word.

A Better Status Bar

Clinging to the bottom of the Word window is the extremely useful status bar. Chapter 1 introduces this gizmo, but only hints at its potential. Now it's time to reveal all: Right-click the status bar to pop up the helpful Customize Status Bar menu, illustrated in Figure 29-1.

The Customize Status Bar menu controls the info you see on the status bar, showing you the various informational tidbits available as well as certain controls.

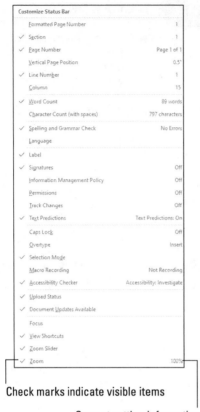

FIGURE 29-1:
The Customize
Status Bar menu.

Check marks indicate visible items

Current setting information

In Figure 29-1, you can see the status of many optional settings. A check mark indicates that an item is either visible or appears when necessary. To add a check mark, click an item; clicking a check-marked item removes the check.

» Choosing an item from the menu doesn't cause the menu to disappear, which is handy. To make the menu go away, click the mouse elsewhere in the document window.

» The topmost items on the menu display document information. To have this information displayed on the status bar, choose one or more of these items.

» The Selection Mode option directs Word to display the text *Extend Selection* on the status bar when you press the F8 key to select text. Refer to Chapter 6 for more information on selecting text.

» The Overtype item places the Insert/Overtype button on the status bar. You can click this button to easily switch between Insert and Overtype modes. However, most Word users prefer to use Insert mode all the time.

>> The last three items on the menu control whether the View buttons or Zoom shortcuts appear on the status bar.

The Quick Access Toolbar

Before the ribbon interface confused Word users back in 2007, command buttons were located on toolbars — many of them crowning the document window. You could add toolbars, remove toolbars, modify toolbars, create your own toolbars, and generally use the word *toolbars* over and over again until it loses its meaning.

Word isn't quite as flexible as it once was in the lotsa-toolbar days, but one toolbar remains that you can customize: the Quick Access toolbar. This toolbar is found in the upper left corner of the window and illustrated in Figure 29-2.

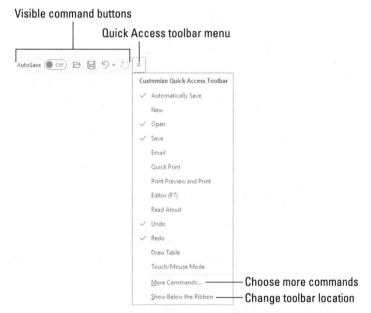

FIGURE 29-2:
The Quick
Access toolbar.

Click a wee icon on the Quick Access toolbar to activate a feature, such as Save or Undo. Customize the toolbar by adding icons you use and removing those you don't.

TIP

>> When the Quick Access toolbar grows too many custom buttons and begins to crowd into the document's title, place it below the ribbon: Choose the Show Below the Ribbon command from the toolbar menu (refer to Figure 29-2).

>> Word is configured to show several buttons on the Quick Access toolbar: AutoSave (for documents saved to OneDrive), Open, Save, Undo, and Redo. If the laptop or computer has a touchscreen monitor, another button appears: Touch/Mouse Mode.

Adding buttons to the Quick Access toolbar

When you adore a command so much that you must see its command button icon on the Quick Access toolbar, follow these steps:

1. Click the Quick Access Toolbar menu button.

Refer to Figure 29-2.

2. Choose a command from the menu to add it to the Quick Access toolbar.

A check mark indicates that the command is already present on the toolbar.

TIP

For commands that don't appear on the Quick Access Toolbar menu, locate the command's button on the ribbon. Right-click the button and choose Add to Quick Access Toolbar from the shortcut menu that pops up.

>> Word remembers the Quick Action toolbar's commands. They show up again the next time you start Word, in every document window.

>> Some commands place buttons on the toolbar, and others place drop-down menus or text boxes.

Editing the Quick Access toolbar

If your adoration of the Quick Access toolbar turns into an obsession, you can go hog wild modifying the thing: Choose More Commands from the Quick Access toolbar's menu. You see the Word Options dialog box with the Quick Access Toolbar area shown, as illustrated in Figure 29-3.

Use the list on the left to choose a new command to add to the Quick Access toolbar.

The list on the right shows those items currently on the toolbar. Use the up or down buttons (refer to Figure 29-3) to rearrange the order of items on the Quick Access toolbar.

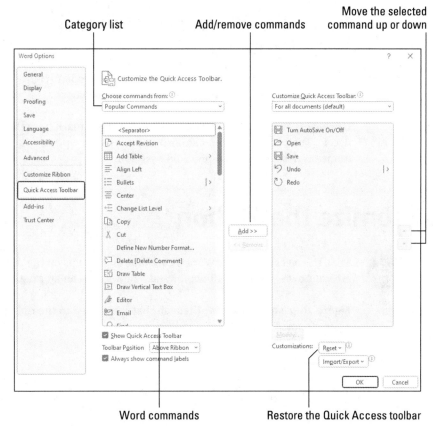

Category list

Add/remove commands

Move the selected
command up or down

Word commands

Restore the Quick Access toolbar

FIGURE 29-3:
Adjusting
the Quick
Access toolbar.

Click the OK button when you finish editing.

TIP

>> Choose the All Commands item from the Choose Commands From menu (refer to Figure 29-3) to view every possible command in Word. Sometimes, a missing command that you think could be elsewhere ends up being available on the All Commands list — for example, the once popular Save All command or the Tabs command to quickly show the Tabs dialog box.

>> When the command list grows long, consider organizing it. Use the <Separator> item to help group similar commands. This item appears as a vertical bar on the Quick Access toolbar.

>> Yes, some commands lack specific graphics on their buttons; they show up as large dots on the toolbar.

>> To return the Quick Access toolbar to the way Word originally had it, choose Reset ➪ Reset Only Quick Access Toolbar from the Word Options window (refer to the lower right corner in Figure 29-3).

Removing items from the Quick Access toolbar

To remove a command from the Quick Access toolbar, right-click its command button and choose Remove from Quick Access Toolbar.

Likewise, you can choose a command with a check mark from the Customize Quick Access Toolbar menu. You can also use the Word Options dialog box to remove items, as described in the preceding section.

Customize the Ribbon

TECHNICAL STUFF

Though you can't change Word's core tabs and groups on the ribbon, you can create your own tab on the ribbon or add a new group on an existing tab.

Figure 29-4 shows the Favorites tab that I've added to the ribbon, along with the groups named Home, Insert, and Macros.

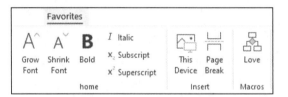

FIGURE 29-4:
A custom tab and groups on the ribbon.

I used the Word Options dialog box to create this custom tab. You can, too:

1. **Right-click a blank part of the ribbon.**

2. **Choose Customize the Ribbon.**

   In the Word Options window, tabs on the ribbon are listed on the right, and Word commands are shown on the left. The ribbon is your oyster.

The commands in the Word Options dialog box, in the Customize Ribbon area, let you craft your own, unique tab as well as mess with the ribbon in other ways.

TIP

If you mess around creating your own tab and goof things up horridly, click the Reset button, found in the lower right corner of the Word Options window, in the Customize Ribbon area. Choose the Reset All Customizations command.

Add More Features with Add-Ins

Microsoft Word is jealous of popular web browsers that have plug-ins, so to keep up, Word features add-ins. These are tiny programs, or *applets,* that expand what Word can do. In fact, some programs you install on your computer may add their features to Word, such as Adobe Acrobat. If you see an Adobe Acrobat tab on Word's ribbon interface, it's the Acrobat add-in in action, letting you do PDF things with your document in conjunction with the Acrobat program.

 To view, manage, or add the add-ins, click the ribbon's Home tab and, in the Add-ins group, click the Add-ins button, shown in the margin. You see the My Add-Ins menu, which lists any installed add-ins as well as a list of popular add-ins, as shown in Figure 29-5.

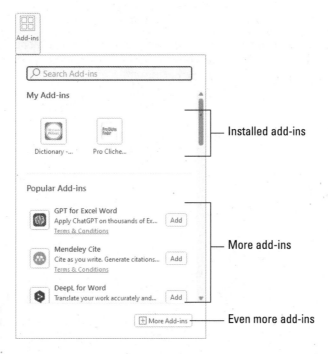

FIGURE 29-5:
Add-ins
to peruse.

Click the Add button to mix in the specific new add-in for Word. Follow the directions presented on the screen.

To use an add-in, choose it from the Add-Ins menu (refer to Figure 29-5). The add-in appears on a panel to the right of the document window.

To remove an add-in, click the Add-Ins button and choose More Add-Ins, as shown in Figure 29-5. In the Office Add-Ins window, choose My Add-Ins to view any installed add-ins. Click the one to remove and, from the Overflow menu (the three dots), choose the Remove command.

Not every add-in is available or installed from the Add-Ins button on the ribbon. Some are installed automatically and can be controlled only from the Word Options dialog box: From the File tab, choose Options. In the Word Options dialog box, choose the Add-Ins category to review application add-ins, such as Acrobat PDF Maker and others. The Type column categorizes the add-in; use the Manage menu to choose the add-in's type, and then click the Go button to further manage the specific add-in.

>> Add-ins appear in panels on the right side of the document window. To help you manage multiple panels, a tiny tab appears to the right of the panel. Click on the add-in's icon to switch between add-in panels.

>> I confess that many add-ins are unimpressive: Check the ratings in the Office Add-Ins window (choose More Add-Ins from the Add-Ins menu, as shown in Figure 29-5) to review the ratings.

Chapter **30**

Meet Your Copilot

t's true that robots — specifically, artificial intelligence (AI) — will eventually take over the world. For all I know, you're a robot right now reading this text, nodding assuredly as you stroke your aluminum chin. Until then, we humans can pretend that AI is a useful tool, helping to inspire or provide that wee bit of a nudge to get those creative juices flowing. To assist you with your word processing task in Word, Microsoft has introduced the Copilot AI tool.

REMEMBER

» Copilot does not come with Word or the Microsoft 365 subscription. It's a separate paid subscription service. After signing up, restart Word to install and activate Copilot.

» All AI-generated content should be taken with a grain of salt, which isn't meant to offend any robots reading this text. My point is that just because AI content looks good and was generated quickly doesn't guarantee that it's accurate.

» The public is leery of AI content, and many organizations as well as publishers require that you cite material as AI-generated.

Write Me Something

Where teachers and professors once warned against Wikipedia, they now warn against AI content — and for good reason! When it comes to word processing, Copilot can write for you, not just drafts but also full documents. But rather than cheat, I recommend you use Copilot to help you with that missing introductory paragraph, or just to complete a thought.

Finding your Copilot

 To ensure that Copilot is installed on your computer and available to Word, look on the Home tab for the Copilot command button, shown in the margin. When this button isn't present, you are either not a Copilot subscriber or you must restart Word for the button to appear.

Copilot also makes its presence known in the document itself. When you first open a document, a Copilot Summary box appears above the first page. Click this box to see an assessment of the document's text.

 When you start a new paragraph, you see the Draft with Copilot icon lurking in the left margin. You may also see the ghostly text "Select the icon or press Alt+I to draft with Copilot" appearing before you type any text. Using this icon and its keyboard shortcut is covered in the next section.

 If Copilot still fails to appear after you purchased a subscription and restarted Word, check for an Office update: Click the File tab and choose Account. Click the Update Options button and choose Update Now to ensure that Copilot is available in Word.

TIP

Drafting with Copilot

 To get those creative juices flowing, put Copilot to work: Click the Draft with Copilot button or press the Alt+I keyboard shortcut. You see a Draft with Copilot dialog box pop up, as shown on top in Figure 30-1.

Type a direction into the Draft with Copilot box. You can type up to 2,000 characters, though only with a brief prompt does Copilot generate a mountain of text, as shown at the bottom in Figure 30-1. This AI-generated text is highlighted, and a feedback prompt appears as illustrated in the figure.

You can choose to keep the text, regenerate it, or delete it. You can also edit your original prompt or direct Copilot to refine the output. For example, from Figure 30-1 you can direct Copilot to make the Evil Witch a slightly testy short-order cook.

 The AI-generated content is just to get you started. It's not meant as a substitute for you doing the work.

REMEMBER

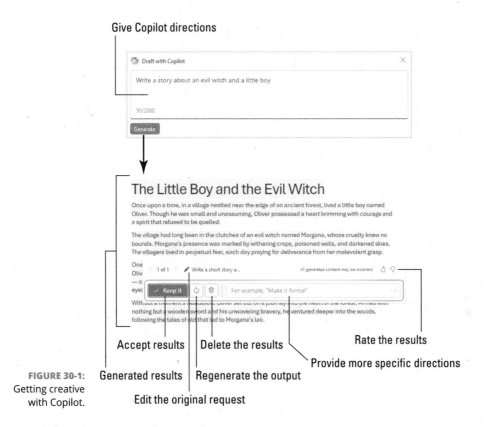

Give Copilot directions

The Little Boy and the Evil Witch

Accept results | Delete the results

Rate the results

Provide more specific directions

FIGURE 30-1: Generated results | Regenerate the output
Getting creative
with Copilot. Edit the original request

Help from That AI Brain

I rarely use Copilot to draft text, but I do use it often to help me make suggestions or create images. Summon the Copilot panel to best use this feature: On the Home tab, click the Copilot button. The Copilot panel appears to the right of the document, as illustrated in Figure 30-2.

The Copilot panel may show some prompts, such as the Ask prompt, illustrated in Figure 30-2. Another prompt is Understand, which you can click to perform an action such as summarizing the document.

The key to using the panel is to ask a question or direct Copilot to do something. In Figure 30-2, I asked for a list of alternative sayings. You could ask for a specific date — for example, "Why do space invaders like New York City so much?" Copilot can even draw images for you: Ask it to draw a picture of a cute puppy dog and it complies. Select the image and click the Insert button to set it into your document.

Question

Prompts

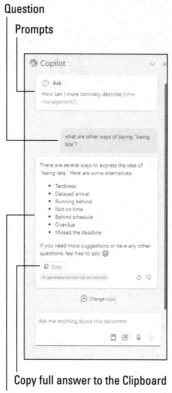

FIGURE 30-2:
The Copilot panel.

Copy full answer to the Clipboard

Answer

REMEMBER

Though all this Copilot business is fun and useful, keep in mind the admonition shown in various Copilot prompts: *AI-generated content may be incorrect*. It's up to you to verify that material is accurate. And for AI-generated images, ensure that you flag them as such in your documents.

6 The Part of Tens

Discover several handy and useful tricks.

Investigate some highly unusual Word features.

Deactivate features that truly bug you.

Chapter **31**

Ten Cool Tricks

've been using a word processor to write text for decades now, yet I still marvel at how word-wrap works and how you can change margins after a document is written and all the text quickly jiggles into place. Everything in this book can be considered a cool trick, but when it came down to the wire, I found ten cool tricks barely (or not) mentioned anywhere else and then listed them here.

Side-to-Side Page Movement

In Print Layout view, you can arrange the document window to display pages from side to side, as illustrated in Figure 31-1. Workflow moves down the left page and then hops up to the top of the right page. This arrangement takes full advantage of widescreen computer monitors.

Page Movement group

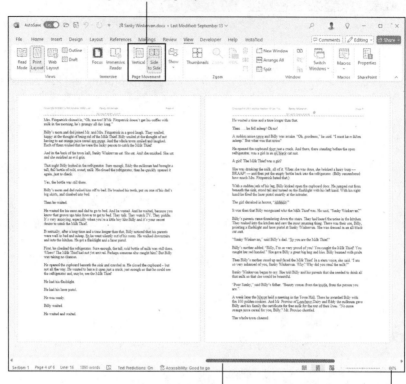

FIGURE 31-1:
Working on a
document from
side to side.

Use the horizontal scroll bar to page   Zoom is relative to window size

 To enter Side to Side view, click the View tab and, in the Page Movement group, choose Side to Side, shown in the margin. You may need to adjust the Word window to enlarge the document presentation; the Zoom command is disabled when Side to Side page movement is activated. Therefore, the wider you can make the document window, the better everything looks.

In the Side to Side presentation, the horizontal scroll bar becomes more useful. Use it to page through the document. The pages automatically flip as you edit and create text.

 To restore traditional document presentation, click the Vertical button.

 The Page Movement command you choose is sticky. The next time you open a document, it appears in Vertical or Side to Side presentation, whichever you last chose.

REMEMBER

Automatic Save with AutoRecover

Someday, you will sing the praises of Word's AutoRecover feature. It periodically saves your document, even when you neglect to do so. In the event of a computer crash or some other type of mishap, Word recovers your document from a super-secret safety copy it secretly made for you. How nice.

To ensure that AutoRecover is active, heed these directions:

1. **Click the File tab.**

2. **On the File screen, choose Options.**

    The Word Options dialog box appears.

3. **Choose Save.**

4. **On the right side of the dialog box, ensure that a check mark appears by the item Save AutoRecover Information Every 10 Minutes.**

    You can change the time, though 10 minutes seems good.

5. **Click OK to close the window.**

    Whew! You're safe.

Most of the time, you never notice AutoRecover. On that rare, terrifying occasion that something goes awry, you see the Document Recovery pane on the left side of the window when you restart Word. Information about unsaved documents appears in this pane, along with directions on how to recover a document.

>> Word documents saved to OneDrive are automatically saved — and recovered when the AutoSave feature is active. Refer to Chapter 8.

>> The best way to avoid accidentally losing stuff is to save now and save often!

REMEMBER

Accelerate the Ribbon

Word has always been a mouse-based program, even when it ran in Text mode on old DOS PCs. Still, the keyboard remains a fast and effective way to access commands, especially given that in a word processor your fingers hover over the keyboard most of the time. As such, you can use keyboard shortcuts, or *accelerators*, to access any command on the ribbon.

The secret is to use the Alt key: Tap Alt and you see letters in boxes appear on the ribbon, like tiny, square freckles. Within each box are one or two letters. These are the accelerator keys. Tap a letter, or the two letters in sequence, to "click" a specific part of the ribbon.

For example, to change the page orientation to Landscape mode, you press Alt, P, O to display the Orientation menu. Press the down-arrow key to choose Landscape. Press Enter to choose that menu item.

>> If you accidentally tap the Alt key, press it again to exit Accelerator mode.

>> You can also press the F10 key to access the ribbon accelerators.

TECHNICAL STUFF

>> The original Microsoft Word command to save a document was Esc, T, S for Transfer Save.

Ancient Word Keyboard Shortcuts

Before the ribbon rode into town and freaked out all the townsfolk, Word relied upon keyboard commands. These ancient Word keyboard shortcuts still work in Word today. They're handy, though not too memorable.

F4: The F4 key is the Repeat key, identical to Ctrl+Y, the Repeat key.

Shift+F4: It's another Repeat key, but this one is the Repeat Find command. It works even when the Find dialog box (or Navigation pane) isn't visible.

Shift+F5: This key combo is the Go Back command, which returns to the spot you last edited. See Chapter 3 for details.

Shift+F8: The Shrink Selection key is the opposite of the Selection key, F8. For example, when the entire document is selected, press Shift+F8 to select only the current paragraph. Press Shift+F8 again to select only the current sentence. Press it again to select only the current word. Press Shift+F8 one more time to deselect the word. Refer to Chapter 6 for more text selection tricks.

F12: Tap this key to quickly summon the traditional Save As dialog box. I use this key a lot because it's quicker than wading through the Backstage to summon the Save As dialog box.

Ctrl+F12: This key pops up the traditional Open dialog box, which I enjoy using more than the hideous Backstage.

Build Your Own Fractions

Word's AutoCorrect feature builds common fractions for you, replacing your clumsy text with beautiful fraction characters. Sadly, Word has only a few of these fraction characters. When you need your own, custom fraction, such as $^3/_{64}$, create it this way:

1. **Press Ctrl+Shift+= (the equal sign), the keyboard shortcut for the superscript command.**

2. **Type the numerator — the top part of the fraction.**

   For example, type **3** for $^3/_{64}$.

3. **Press Ctrl+Shift+= again to disable superscript.**

4. **Type the slash character (/).**

5. **Press Ctrl+= to activate subscript.**

6. **Type the denominator — the bottom part of the fraction.**

   For example, type **64** for $^3/_{64}$.

7. **Press Ctrl+= to turn off subscript.**

Behold the fraction.

Electronic Bookmarks

When you must find your place in a document, you can write text like *WORK HERE*, or you can take advantage of Word's Bookmark command. The bookmark is invisible, but Word knows where it is. You can use the bookmark to return to a page for editing, to add a cross-reference, or to perform a bunch of other handy tricks that I don't have space here to gush about. Instead, follow these steps to set a bookmark:

1. **Place the insertion pointer where you want to insert the bookmark.**

   For example, place it in that spot in a long document where you need to continue working on character development because Sheila would never say something like that.

2. **Click the Insert tab.**

3. **In the Links group, click the Bookmark button.**

   The Bookmark dialog box appears.

4. **Type a name for the bookmark in the Bookmark dialog box.**

   Try to keep the bookmark name to one word, letters only.

5. **Click the Add button.**

   The bookmark is created.

To hop to bookmarks in the document, use the Go To command: Press Ctrl+G to summon the Find and Replace dialog box, with the Go To tab forward. Choose Bookmark from the Go to What list.

You can also click the Bookmark button again (refer to Step 3). Select the book-mark name from the list and click the Go To button to visit the bookmark's location.

Lock Your Document

When you really, *really* don't want anyone messing with your sweet text, you can lock the document. Several levels of protection are available, but you start the journey by following these steps:

1. **Click the File tab.**

2. **Choose Info.**

3. **Click the Protect Document button.**

   Of the several choices, I recommend these options:

   Mark as Final: The document is flagged as final, which means that further editing is disabled. Still, you can easily override it by clicking the Edit Anyway button that appears.

   Encrypt with Password: The document is encrypted and a password applied. To open the document in Word, you must enter the password. You cannot remove a password after it's applied.

   Restrict Editing: You can limit whether a user can edit a document or whether all changes are tracked or restrict that person to making only comments.

4. **Choose an option and answer the questions in the dialog boxes that appear.**

5. **Click OK.**

   The document protection you've chosen is applied.

WARNING

Locking a document is a serious decision! No one can help you if you forget a password or are otherwise unable to remove the restrictions you've applied to the document.

File permissions are also set when sharing a document for collaboration. Refer to Chapter 26.

The Drop Cap

A *drop cap* is the first letter of a report, an article, a chapter, or a story that appears in a larger and more interesting font than the other characters. Figure 31-2 shows an example.

nce upon a crime

FIGURE 31-2:
A drop cap.

To add a drop cap to a document, follow these steps:

1. **Set the insertion pointer in the paragraph, such as the first paragraph in a document.**

You need not select only the first letter or first word.

2. **Click the Insert tab.**

3. **In the Text group, click the Add a Drop Cap button.**

4. **Choose a drop cap style.**

The drop cap appears.

It helps if the drop cap's paragraph is left justified and not indented with a tab or any of the tricky formatting operations discussed in Part 3 of this book.

TIP

To remove the drop cap, choose None in Step 4.

Map Your Document

Whenever I'm writing, I show the Navigation pane on the left side of the document window. This pane shows the Big Picture, an overview of my document based on the heading styles. I can use it to quickly hop to a specific header. As a bonus, it also shows the handy Search Document text box, as illustrated in Figure 31-3.

Collapsed heading

Search box

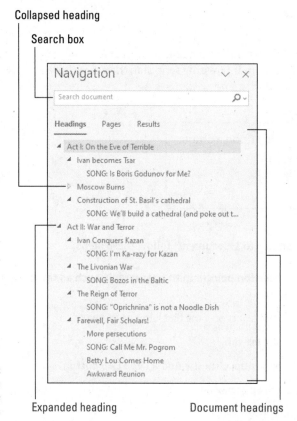

FIGURE 31-3:
The Navigation
pane
document map.

Expanded heading   Document headings

To summon the Navigation pane, follow these steps:

1. **Click the View tab.**

2. **In the Show group, click to put a check mark by the Navigation Pane item.**

To close the Navigation pane, click its Close (X) button.

TECHNICAL STUFF

The Navigation pane replaces a popular but long-gone Word feature called the document map.

Sort Your Text

Sorting is one of Word's better tricks, though it's surprising how few people know about it. You can use the Sort command to arrange text alphabetically or numerically. You can sort paragraphs, table rows and columns, and more.

Save your document before sorting. It's just a good idea.

REMEMBER Sorting isn't difficult. First, arrange whatever needs to be sorted into several lines of text, such as

```
Lemon
Banana cream
Apple
Cherry
Rhubarb
Tortilla
```

After you know what you're sorting, obey these steps:

1. **Select the lines of text (paragraphs or parts of a table) as a block.**

2. **Click the Home tab.**

3. **In the Paragraph group, click the Sort button.**

    The Sort Text dialog box appears. It's most useful when sorting multicolumn items, which is where the Then By parts of the dialog box are most useful.

4. **Choose Ascending or Descending to sort the text from A to Z or from Z to A, respectively.**

5. **Click the OK button.**

As if by magic, the selected text is sorted.

IN THIS CHAPTER

» **Inserting pretty equations**

» **Inserting video**

» **Hiding text**

» **Beholding the Developer tab**

» **Hyphenating text**

» **Setting document properties (or not)**

» **Reviewing document versions**

» **Using collect-and-paste**

» **Disabling click-and-type**

» **Translating text**

Chapter **32**

Ten Bizarre Things

f Word were only about word processing, this book would end at Chapter 17. Fully half the text references features more relevant to the topics of desktop publishing or graphics. These tasks are done far better by using other software, but Word doesn't stop there with its unique and weird features. Welcome to the *Twilight Zone*, Word edition.

Equations

If you dabble in rocket science or brain surgery, you'll appreciate Word's Equation tools. These tools sate your desire to place a polynomial equation or quantum calculation in your document without having to endure the tedium of building the thing yourself.

To place a premade equation into your third doctoral thesis from MIT, click the Insert tab. In the Symbols group, click the Equation button menu and choose a preset mathematical monster from the list. Or you can choose the Insert New Equation command to share your own brilliance by crafting the equation yourself.

» An equation *content control* is inserted in a document at the insertion pointer's location. When selected, the Equation Tools Design tab appears on the ribbon.

» Word cannot solve the equation.

Video in Your Document

Seriously? I'm guessing that Word's capability to stick a video into a document doesn't translate well when the page is printed. That's just a guess — I haven't tried it, though I think I'm probably correct.

When you've stayed up late and the alcohol in your bloodstream is flirting with every neuron in your brain, why not follow these steps to shove a video into your document:

1. **Click the Insert tab.**

2. **In the Media group, click the Online Videos button, shown in the margin.**

3. **Type the URL (web page address) for the video you want to shove into your text.**

   It can be a YouTube video or a movie from another service.

After way too much time passes, the video appears as a large graphical goober in the document. You can play it right there on the screen. Amazing.

Videos are best viewed when a Word document is presented in Read mode — which in and of itself is yet another bizarre thing. To enter Read mode, click the Read Mode button (shown in the margin) on the status bar; or, on the View tab, choose Read Mode from the Views group.

Hidden Text

One text format not covered in Chapter 10 is hidden text. I mean, why bother? Hidden text doesn't appear in a document. It doesn't print. It's just not there!

If you desire to write hidden text so that you can put it on your résumé for application to the CIA, select the text and press Ctrl+Shift+H. The same keyboard shortcut deactivates this format. The following text is hidden:

TIP

Hidden text can be useful — for example, to remove part of a document you may want to revive later. To find this text, on the Home tab, and in the Paragraph group, click the Show/Hide button, which looks like the Paragraph symbol. The hidden text appears in the document with a dotted underline.

The Developer Tab

Computer users love secrets, especially when no one else knows about them. One such secret in Word is the Developer tab. Shhh!

The Developer tab plays host to some of Word's advanced and cryptic features. These commands don't make creating a document any easier, and they open a can of worms that I don't want to cover in this book. Still, you're reading this text, so follow these steps to summon the mysterious Developer tab:

1. **Right-click a blank part of the ribbon.**

2. **Choose Customize the Ribbon from the pop-up shortcut menu.**

   The Word Options dialog box appears, with the Customize Ribbon area active.

3. **On the right side of the window, below the Customize Ribbon list, place a check mark by the Developer item.**

4. **Click OK.**

The Developer tab is best suited for people who use Word to develop applications, create special documents for online forms, and use macros to customize Word. Scary stuff.

Hyphenation

Hyphenation is an automatic feature that splits a long word at the end of a line to make the text fit better on the page. Most people leave this feature disabled because hyphenated words tend to slow down the pace at which people read. To control hyphenation, on the Layout tab, in the Page Setup group, choose the

Hyphenation command (shown in the margin) and select an option from the menu. None is my favorite option.

REMEMBER

Automatic hyphenation works only on paragraphs formatted with full-justification alignment. If the paragraph is otherwise formatted, the Hyphenation command button is dimmed. Refer to Chapter 11 for information on paragraph alignment.

Document Properties

Word merrily tracks lots of details about the documents you craft, stuff you normally wouldn't pay attention to if you didn't know about the Document Properties feature.

To view a document's properties, click the File tab and choose the Info item. The properties appear on the right, showing document size, pages, word count, and other trivia. To view or set other options, click the Properties button and choose Advanced Properties.

Document Version History

You write, you save, you write, you save. These different document versions can be recovered, providing that you've saved the document to OneDrive.

To check out previous editions of a document, click the document name, top and center of the window. From the menu, choose Version History to view the Version History pane. If no menu appears, the document was saved locally or to cloud storage other than OneDrive.

The Version History pane lists all major document revisions by date, time, and author. To see a revision, click the Open Version link. The selected revision appears in a new window.

Collect-and-Paste

Word's Collect-and-Paste feature takes the understandable concept of copy-and-paste and adds a hallucinogenic that allows you to copy multiple chunks of text and paste them in any order or all at once. The secret is found on the Home tab:

Click the dialog box launcher in the lower right corner of the Clipboard group. The Clipboard pane appears.

With the Clipboard pane visible, you can use the Copy command multiple times in a row to collect text. To paste the text, click the mouse on a chunk of text in the Clipboard pane. Or you can use the Paste All button to paste into the document every item you've collected.

You can amp up this feature by selecting multiple separate chunks of text at one time: Select the first chunk, and then, while holding down the Ctrl key, drag over additional text. As long as the Ctrl key is held down, you can drag to select multiple chunks of text in different locations. The various selected chunks work as a block, which you can manipulate for fun and profit.

Click-and-Type

A feature introduced in Word 2002 that few users have bothered with since then is click-and-type. In a blank document, you can use *click-and-type* to stab the mouse pointer anywhere on the page and type text at that spot. *Bam!*

I fail to see any value in click-and-type, especially when it's a more positive aspect of your Word education to learn basic formatting. But click-and-type's oddball mouse pointers may bother you when you see them displayed; thus:

These weird mouse pointers indicate the click-and-type feature in action. The mouse pointer itself tries to indicate the paragraph format to be applied when you click the mouse.

See Chapter 33 for information on disabling this feature.

Translations

Allora, hai il desiderio di scrivere il tuo testo l'italiano? Rather than get bored trying to learn Italian in school or waste precious time vacationing in Italy, you can use Word's Translate feature to magically create Italian or any other foreign language text. The secret lies on the Review tab, in the Language group.

To translate a chunk of text in a document, follow these steps:

1. **Write the text you want to translate.**

   I came. I saw. I ate pasta.

2. **Select the text.**

3. **On the Review tab, in the Language group, click the Translate button and choose Translate Selection.**

   The Translate command button is shown in the margin.

4. **Click the Turn On button if prompted to activate Intelligent Services.**

   The Translator pane appears on the right side of the document window. The pane automatically detects the language selected, which I assume is English for this book.

5. **Choose a target language from the To menu.**

   Alas, Latin isn't one of them, but Italian is!

6. **Review the translation.**

   If you know a smattering of the selected language, consider fixing it up. For example, the Italian sentence at the start of this section was originally translated with the second person plural instead of second person singular.

7. **Click the Insert button to set the translated text into the document.**

   Ho venuto. Ho visto. Ho mangiato la pasta.

8. **Close the Translate pane.**

   Click the X button to close.

TIP

If you have a Copilot subscription, you can use its AI to translate text and insert it into your document. Refer to Chapter 30.

As with all computer translations, what you get is more of an approximation of what a native speaker would say. The text is generally understandable, but nothing truly substitutes for a knowledge of the language — or a month in Italy.

Chapter **33**

Ten Automatic Features Worthy of Deactivation

Y ou need not put up with them. You know what I'm referring to: those annoying things that Word does — those features you might dislike but tolerate simply because no one has told you how to turn them off. Until now.

Bye-Bye, Start Screen

I prefer to see a blank page when I start Word, not a screen full of options. The Word Start screen can easily be disabled. Follow these blessed steps:

1. **Click the File tab.**

2. **Choose Options.**

   The Word Options dialog box appears, with the General category chosen for you.

3. **In the Start-Up Options section, remove the check mark by the item Show the Start Screen When This Application Starts.**

After completing these steps, Word starts with a blank document, or whichever document you've opened.

Restore the Traditional Open and Save Dialog Boxes

When you use the Ctrl+O or Ctrl+S commands, you see the Backstage, which is Microsoft Office's way of prompting you to open or save. If you prefer instead to use the traditional Open and Save dialog boxes, follow these steps:

1. **Click the File tab and choose Options to bring up the Word Options dialog box.**

2. **Choose the Save category on the left side of the dialog box.**

3. **In the Save Documents section, place a check by the item Don't Show the Backstage When Opening or Saving Files with Keyboard Shortcuts.**

4. **Click OK.**

The *Backstage* refers to the Open and Save As screens on the File tab.

REMEMBER

One benefit of the Backstage is that it shows recent files. It also lets you pin popular files so that they're easy to find. Refer to Chapter 8.

Disable the Mini Toolbar

When you use the mouse to select text, Word displays the Mini toolbar, which looks like Figure 33-1.

This item appears only when Copilot is installed

You may find its assortment of commands useful, or you may just want to set the floaty thing on fire. If it's the latter, you can disable the Mini toolbar by following these steps:

1. **Click the File tab and choose Options.**

    The General category is automatically chosen for you.

2. **Under the heading User Interface Options, remove the check mark by the item Show Mini Toolbar on Selection.**

3. **Click OK.**

If you would rather not eternally banish the Mini toolbar, note that it hides itself whenever you move the mouse pointer beyond the selected chunk of text.

TIP

Select Text by Letter

When you're selecting more than a single word, the mouse grabs text a full word at a time. If you want Word to select text by characters rather than by entire words (which is what I prefer), follow these steps:

1. **Click the File tab and choose Options to display the Word Options dialog box.**

2. **Choose the Advanced category on the left side of the dialog box.**

3. **Remove the check mark by the item labeled When Selecting, Automatically Select Entire Word.**

    This item is located below the Editing Options heading.

4. **Click OK.**

TIP

You can still select text a word at a time: Double-click to select a word, but keep the mouse button down. As you drag, text is selected one word at a time.

Disable Click-and-Type

Click-and-type is that feature where you can click anywhere on a blank part of the page and start typing. The feature is made evident by an odd-looking mouse pointer and strange lines around the insertion pointer in the text (refer to Chapter 32). To mercifully disable click-and-type, follow these steps:

1. **Click the File tab menu and choose Options.**

The Word Options dialog box appears.

2. **Choose Advanced.**

3. **Remove the check mark by Enable Click and Type.**

4. **Click the OK button.**

Seriously: Who uses this feature? For the past few editions of this book, I've asked readers to send me an email if they use click-and-type. So far, nothing.

Set Paste Options

When you copy-and-paste text from one part of a document to another, the format is retained. Similarly, the format is kept when you copy-and-paste text from another Word document. If you like, you can direct Word to paste only plain text or attempt to paste formatted text. Heed these directions:

1. **Click the File tab and choose Options.**

2. **In the Word Options dialog box, choose Advanced.**

Below the Cut, Copy, And Paste setting, you find four text-pasting options. These options describe how text is pasted based on its source.

3. **Change the paste settings according to how you prefer text to be pasted.**

In most cases, keeping the source formatting is what you want. I prefer to choose the Keep Text Only option when pasting from other programs because it doesn't mess up my document's formatting.

4. **Click OK.**

REMEMBER

You can use the Paste Special command at any time to override your decision: Click the Home tab and, in the Clipboard group, click the Paste button to choose whether to keep the formats. Refer to Chapter 6 for details.

Disable AutoFormat Features (×4)

The final four items worthy of deactivation fall under the domain of the AutoCorrect dialog box. Specifically, the overeager AutoFormat feature, which aggressively interrupts your writing with jarring suggestions you probably neither want nor need.

Start your disabling binge by summoning the AutoCorrect dialog box. Follow these steps:

1. **Click the File tab and choose Options.**

2. **In the Word Options dialog box, select the Proofing category.**

3. **Click the AutoCorrect Options button.**

   The AutoCorrect dialog box shows up.

4. **Click the AutoFormat as You Type tab.**

   You've arrived.

Here are four annoying features you can disable:

Automatic Bulleted Lists: This feature assumes that whenever you start a paragraph with an asterisk (*), you really want a bulleted list, so it changes the format to an indented, bulleted list.

Automatic Numbered Lists: This feature works like Automatic Bulleted Lists, but does the same annoying thing for any paragraph you start with a number and a period.

Border Lines: Type three dashes in a row and you see this feature activated. Use the Borders paragraph format instead. See Chapter 18.

Format Beginning of List Item Like the One Before It: This feature assumes that just because the first word of the preceding paragraph is in bold or italics that you desire all other paragraphs to start that way as well.

Deselect each of these items. Oh, and while you're at it, look for other items to disable in the AutoCorrect dialog box. Some of those features may bother you more than they bother me.

Index

word underlining format, 114
word wrap feature, 27
WordArt, 257–258
words
  choosing best, 297
  deleting, 44–45
  frequently misspelled, 76

selecting with mouse, 65
variations, finding, 55
wrapped image layout, 258, 259
writers, features for. *See also*
  Outline view
  chapter documents for large
    documents, 295–297

overview, 287
tips from author, 297–298

Z

Zoom command, 17–18, 37

About the Author

Dan Gookin has been writing about computers since the reign of Charles II. He combines his love of writing with his gizmo fascination to create books that are informative, entertaining, and not boring. Having written over 170 titles with 12 million copies in print translated into over 30 languages on several planets, Dan can attest that his method of crafting technology tomes seems to work.

Perhaps his most famous title is the original *DOS For Dummies*, published in 1991. It became the world's fastest-selling computer book, at one time moving more copies per week than *The New York Times* number-one bestseller (though, as a reference, it could not be listed on the Times' Best Sellers list). That book spawned the entire line of *For Dummies* books, which remains a publishing phenomenon to this day.

Dan's least famous title is *Compute's Problem Solving with Sidekick Plus* (Compute! Books, 1989).

Dan's most popular titles include *PCs and Laptops For Dummies*, *Troubleshooting and Maintaining PCs All-In-One For Dummies*, and *C Programming For Dummies*. His website is www.wambooli.com, which was once ranked 104,578,296th most popular website on the Internet.

Dan holds a degree in Communications/Visual Arts from the University of California, San Diego. He lives in the Pacific Northwest with his wife, children, animals, and various robots. He enjoys being sesquipedalian and inaniloquent.

Publisher's Acknowledgments

Executive Editor: Steven Hayes

Development Editor: Nicole Sholly

Copy Editor: Becky Whitney

Managing Editor: Ajith Kumar

Production Editor: Tamilmani Varadharaj

Cover Image: © Art Wager/Getty Images